The Beauty Pageant's Greenroom

Rita Gangwani nicknamed GURU-COOL by her students is an inspiring Indian motivational speaker, author, pageant coach, etiquette consultant, actress, healer and entrepreneur of international repute. Ranked very high amongst Indian motivational speakers, her seminars and workshops are well known for their high quality content backed by her unique and entertaining style of delivery. Her energizing sessions are insightful and stimulate participants to unleash their innate energies, fulfill their potential and create an intense desire for success and personal excellence.

She has been an expert as well as a jury for many prestigious national and international beauty pageants and contests. She has trained many aspiring models, beauty pageant contestants, some of whom have gone on to represent India at various prestigious pageants and contests all over the world.

For her exemplary work and commitment, she has been honoured by prestigious decorations year after year. To name a few, Rajiv Gandhi Lifetime Achievement Award, Lord Baden Powell National Award, National Award by Journalists Association of India, Aadhi Abadi Award, Indian Icon, Woman Role Model Award, Apar Sewa Samman, Rashtriya Sanskar Bhushan, Jewel of India, Kesari Woman, Indian Shakseeyat Award, PHD Premia Award and many more. She is also designated as one of the top ten thinkers of India by MTC Global.

The Beauty Pageant's Greenroom

THE ULTIMATE GROOMING BIBLE BY THE LEADING INDUSTRY EXPERT

RITA GANGWANI

ACADEMIC FOUNDATION
NEW DELHI

www.academicfoundation.org

First published in 2016
by

ACADEMIC FOUNDATION

Delhi Sales Office:
4772-73 / 23 Bharat Ram Road,
(23 Ansari Road), Darya Ganj,
New Delhi - 110 002 (India).
Phones : 23245001 / 02 / 03 / 04.
Fax : +91-11-23245005.

Corporate Office:
No. 35, Sector 7,
IMT Manesar,
Gurgaon - 122050.
Haryana (India).
Tel: +91-124-4215070 / 71.

E-mail : books@academicfoundation.com
www.academicfoundation.org

Disclaimer:
The findings/views/opinions expressed in this book are solely those of the author and do not necessarily reflect the views of the publisher.

All photographs appearing in the book are from the author's personal collection. The copyright of the photographs used in the book rests with the author.

Cataloging in Publication Data--DK
Courtesy: D.K. Agencies (P) Ltd. <docinfo@dkagencies.com>

Gangwani, Rita, author.
The beauty pageant's greenroom : the ultimate grooming bible by the leading industry expert / Rita Gangwani.
pages cm
ISBN 9789332703803

1. Beauty contestants--Handbooks, manuals, etc. 2. Beauty contestants--India--Handbooks, manuals, etc. I. Title.

HQ1219.G36 2016 DDC 791.62 23

Diary number: 7546/2016/CO/2
Date of registration : 27/6/16

Printed and bound by The Book Mint, New Delhi.
www.thebookmint.in

To

Kuldeep Gangwani—Pillar of my strength
who taught me the meaning of "Never Give Up" come what may!

Divya Sahgal, Shiv Sahgal & Sasha Sahgal
for letting me believe I was the best, even if I wasn't

Prashant Gangwani
for teaching me how to laugh and giving me his patient ear

All my canine kids
Angel, Snoop, Sultan, Louie, Chip & Mia for their unconditional love!

Contents

Foreword 11
Message 15
Preface 16
Introduction 19

SECTION 1: PRE-CONTEST

1. What is beauty pageant 22
2. Advantages of entering a pageant 23
3. Self preparation for pageant 24
4. Building an attractive persona 25
5. Overcoming stage fear 27
6. Confidence building 29
7. Working on self esteem. 31
8. Working on diction 33
9. Voice modulation 34
10. Pageant questions for practice 36
11. Personal hygiene 52
12. What skin tone are you? 63
13. Check your skin type 65
14. Daily skin care 67
15. Care for different types of skin 68
16. Skin care for winter. 70
17. Skin care for men 71
18. Tricks for glowing skin 72
19. Flash your pearly whites 74
20. Your crowning glory 76
21. Different hair, different care 77
22. Lets nail it. 78
23. Be fit physically. 80

24. Eat consciously 81
25. What to eat 83
26. Understanding your facial shape 89
27. Oval face 91
28. Round face 92
29. Oblong face 94
30. Diamond face 95
31. Heart face 96
32. Triangular face 97
33. Square face 98
34. Know your body shape 98
35. Clothing and personality 101
36. The colors you wear 103
37. Wardrobe management 106
38. Picking the right gown 107
39. Pageant shoes 110
40. Basic make up tips 112
41. How to make down. 114
42. Image builders and image destroyers 115

Section 2: During the Contest

43. History of beauty pageants. 118
44. Types of beauty pageants. 119
45. Major international pageants 120
46. Major men's international and Indian pageants 126
47. Major women's international pageants and Indian pageants 130
48. Miss India auditions 138
49. Kids contests 140
50. Major kids contests. 142
51. First time contestant 143

52. Filling up the form 144
53. Pre-contest audition 146
54. Checklist of things 147
55. Orientation before the contest 149
56. Practice sessions 150
57. Understand your audience 152
58. Body language. 153
59. Practicing introductions 156
60. Practicing ramp walks 158
61. Practicing for the gown round 160
62. Practicing pageant hair styles 161
63. Creating the first impression. 162
64. Pre-final round 164
65. Final day. 173
66. Last minute beauty fixes 175
67. Talent round 178
68. Swimming costume round 179
69. Question-answer round 180
70. Final judgment 182
71. On winning the title 185

Section 3: Post Contest

72. Right conduct for a winner. 188
73. Responsibilities after winning 189
74. Dealing with media. 190
75. How to be camera ready 194
76. Dressing to look slimmer. 197
77. Social introduction etiquette. 199
78. Party etiquette 200
79. Meal time etiquette. 202
80. Courtesy title etiquette. 209
81. Gym etiquette. 211
82. Networking etiquette. 213

83. Cultural etiquette 214
84. Small talk etiquette 223
85. Business card etiquette 226
86. Greeting etiquette 228
87. Punctuality etiquette 229
88. Traveling etiquette 231
89. Social media etiquette 233
90. Social etiquette 235
91. Gifting for all occasions 236
92. Safety precaution for women 245
93. Garment care 247
94. Sportsmanship 248
95. Stress management 250
96. Giving and accepting compliments 251
97. Writing thank you notes 253

Section 4: Confidence Boosters

98. Are you on a negative diet 256
99. Happify yourself 257
100. Swinging bridge 258
101. The rolling pin of life 259
102. From moments to minutes 260
103. Tearing down life 261
104. Share to care 262
105. Geometrical shapes of life 264
106. Did you attend your life university 265
107. Turning green 266
108. God's gift to you 267
109. Be your own mentor 268
110. There's no emergency stop button in life 269
111. Misfits! 270

Foreword

"The Beauty Pageant's Greenroom"—is how the writer of this book has chosen to name it. Those of us who have known the experience of being a contestant at a pageant can very well understand how much of hard work goes behind the scene and upfront into competing for a Tiara. The journey doesn't end there; the crown comes packed with a lot of responsibility and commitment. Being humble, good mannered and projecting the right image can take you a long way as a cultural citizen of the word.

Rita Gangwani has intended that the reader of this book comes out well prepared and ends up being a winner. Winning is no rocket science. It's just the question of understanding, practicing and mastering the inside secrets. Unfortunately, most of the pageant contestants come to the auditions without any preparation or prior knowledge to what lays in store for them. Each chapter of this book is a step forward and moulds you into a better YOU. The book prepares you not only to look beautiful outside, but also helps you feel beautiful inside. It's a self-help book written with personal anecdotes and innovative teaching techniques by one of the most sought after pageant coach of India, who herself won a prestigious beauty pageant in her younger years.

From country to country, border to border, the boundaries that separate our cultures are slowly fading, crafting the need for a discipline that binds cultural dissimilarities into a union that is an adaptation of global multi-cultural social learning. Beauty contest is one such platform which merges the world together. That is why we needed one Rita Gangwani to put in all her treasured experience as a Pageant coach and jury into a book—hopefully the first of many to follow and making all behind the scene experience available to a contest aspirant, at the turn of a page. She did not stop there; but also added a few chapters to motivate the contestants to look at life with coloured glasses.

As Former Miss Universe, I cannot but delight in the fact that the book is a mini encyclopedia of the pageant world covering information on filling the form to having that beautiful Tiara rest on your crown, it has it all. You'll find valuable information to help you succeed and to get the most life-enhancing and positive experience from a contest. It's a "total package" of what is assessed. a book that can help turn your dreams to reality! Must have for every person who aspires to enter and win a beauty contest.

Your journey awaits you........

With love,

Sushmita Sen

Comments...

Her warmth, wisdom and teaching techniques have made Rita Gangwani a trusted voice to millions of students worldwide. Now Rita invites you on the journey to find your dreams, the search for...the Tiara.

In this evocative book, Rita Gangwani encourages you to work on various aspects of becoming a winner. She prepares you right from the scratch and guides you through your tenure as a winner....creating and maintaining the right image and keeping your feet firmly planted on the ground. From abandoned dreams of making it to the crown, to 'excavating' the authentic winner buried inside you. Uncovering and mastering your beautiful self will be challenging, but exhilarating. Dare to find your dreams. Within these pages lie powerful behind the curtain requirements that can help you to stand out...and inspire you to settle for nothing less than being the Best!

—Ratan Kaul, *Advisor, Delhi Literature Festival*

At a time when everything seems unreal, yet so deliciously welcomed what really would bring me back to reality were all the grooming sessions that we were made to go through at the time of our pageant at Miss India Contest. It was at that time that I got to meet Rita Gangwani whose talks really got me thinking and smiling at the same time... she not only took some of our grooming sessions, but also made us realize our self worth at the time when it was very easy to have doubted it. In such stiff competition it was important to have understood and nurtured our individual selves because that's what kept all of us going till the very last minute of our pageant. I am sure this book will be a great help to all those who want to make it in this industry.

—Aishwarya Sakhuja, *Renowned Television Actress and Miss India finalist 2006*

I have been in the industry of Pageantry for a long time now and have been associated with Rita Gangwani as a coach for various International pageants. "The Beauty Pageants Greenroom" authored by Rita Gangwani is a practical, hands-on and user-friendly book to enable a pageant contestant or a model to learn how to navigate the road map straight to the crown. She has made it easy for the reader by dividing the chapter in various sections. In fact it has all the ingredients of self development. One can pick up the book as a beginner to understand the milestones or as a winner to build the image. From A to Zee...it has it all. I highly recommend it to all ladies, gentleman and kids who are eyeing the crown.

—Pawee Ventura, *CEO, Missosology*

Message

"The Beauty Pageant's Greenroom" is a veritable treasure trove of invaluable information on the "ins and outs" of world's four most prestigious beauty pageants. Things are never easy when achieving a goal is concerned. When the goal is as high and significant as winning the diamond tiara in a world beauty pageant such a book can work as mantra for success. Intense and informed preparations are required, constant course-correction and focused energy, stamina of a marathon runner, agility of a deer and killer instinct of a tigress are some of the ingredients which have brought laurels to the winner and her country. Yes, and I would assume that winsome manners imbued with humility and an inquiring intelligent mind would also play significant role in the process of final rounds of selection. Perhaps more than ever contestants are expected to be well informed about current affairs of their country and the world with special attention to social issues where philanthropic ideas would give rich dividends in winning strategy. Many contestants have announced donating entire or part of prize money to well known charities and have been applauded globally, sometimes even being invited to become Brand Ambassadors for UN agencies and other such organizations.

Ms. Rita Gangwani (Retired Lieutenant) has taken great pains to chart out the course to success, an effort almost like planning to climb Mt. Everest! One can only hope that the book will become Bible for all beauty pageant aspirants as also for those whose aspirations go beyond regular visits to a beauty salon! Ms. Gangwani must be congratulated for putting together this beautiful and informative book, a compendium which will serve as beacon light in the world of beauty for many years to come.

सत्यम शिवम् सुंदरम!

That which is auspicious and beautiful is the eternal truth.

— Dr. Sonal Mansingh

Padma Vibhushan

Preface

Beauty contests and winning one is a dream for everyone, be a boy or a girl. Many youngsters grow up watching these beauty contests on television, imagining themselves on that stage, with the eyes of the entire globe admiring them. Yes, I am no different. I had stars in my eyes too. When I was still a teenager, my brother looked at me in shorts and remarked with awe, "hey you bulky teddy bear, you have legs just like a piano! And yeah...you certainly look like a mini road roller!" Not surprisingly, things remained the same for many years as I was busy completing my education till I decided to experience what it's like to enter a beauty contest whose hoardings were floating all over the town.

The prize was big and the advertisement was tempting to the eyes, so, I went ahead to fill the application, which asked for my name, address, and color of my eyes and hair blah...blah. Days after I filled out the form, the director of the pageant called and excitedly welcomed me to the competition. "Don't you want to interview me and see if I'm contest material?", I asked. "Relax…it's not all about winning", she reassured me. "It's about building your knowledge and confidence." It will be a great learning experience for you!

When the pageant director opened the door to the audition room and saw me on the stairs, I suddenly knew that she was under shock. Her eyes popped, and she let out a deep breath trying to cover her reaction with a smile.

Not that I'm fat. My grey area is that I am 4 feet 10 inches tall. Most of you are probably rolling your eyes and thinking, "Well, this ought to be interesting...4 feet 10 inches? And crowned a beauty queen? How did she make it?" (I did that contest.) That's exactly what I want you to think—because it proves my point that pageants are not just about looks, it's a combination of lot of things. Of course over the years, height has become one of the major criteria for entering a contest.

Well, I am talking of the time way back in 1982 where only five participants landed up for a local pageant named "Himachal Queen". Two super tall ladies, two mid height, and one petite, me. The organizers had to make do the best they can with five of us and carried the pageant forward.

We were directed to groom ourselves for the final day and were suggested some groomers. On contacting one of them, she suggested we meet immediately to start my preparations.

When I met her, she looked and sounded unconvinced. We sat, and she gave me a thorough looking over. She suggested I lose weight and learn to walk with heels, get my hair styled, get a pair of green contact lens....The list was endless. She asked me to plump up my lips. I looked quizzical, and was starting to worry that all this cosmetic improvement would leave me looking like a Barbie doll.

She made me feel like a looser and that's why I took the decision to prepare for the contest on my own.

I started working on myself, and yes, I did all the necessary cosmetic requirements to a certain limit where I looked as good as natural, but also worked on my other skills.

I was intimidated by the height of the other contestants and was really nervous. There's always one contestant in any beauty pageant who gives great pleasure by allowing the audience to wonder how this bow-wow ever got in. That contestant was about to be me.

The contest began...with not just one or two, but three rounds and voila; this little short girl was crowned the winner. How? No guesses on that! It's not just the height, but your poise, confidence, communication skills, presence of mind and a lot more that makes a winner.

I will never forget how the contest coach made me feel and how it had affected my self esteem. There may be plenty of beauty contest aspirants out there who need someone to help and guide them in the right direction. My passion for the contest and desire to help the contestants eventually landed me into a finishing school and turned me into a pageant coach. However, after judging for 15 years and talking with other judges and directors, and being a former contestant myself, I went deeper into the nitty gritties of preparing for a pageant and hence decided to pen them into this book. It's a kind of self help book with some information and requirements of the major pageants which happen around the world.

Writing a book is always a team work. It would not have been possible without the help of many people who worked hand in hand with me.

I would like to thank Mehar Ahluwalia for the beautiful cover picture, and Anil Kumar and Sandeep Kumar for all the related pictures to go with the chapters.

Thank you to my models Shefali Sood (Miss India Elite 2013 and Volvo Miss Indian Diva 2016) Sandy Singh Chhikara (Mr India Global 2013) and super model Barkha Sharma. You all did a tremendous job. Thank you for bearing with my tantrums.

Thank you, Nidhi Gaurav Gupta and Ajeet Bacchas (Aashmeen Munjal Academy) for experimenting with the models with various hairstyles and make up looks.

Thank you Ashma Khanna Sachdeva, Ratan Kaul, Tamanna Singh, Shahana Mookerjea for your unconditional support.

Thank you Sudhir Behrani and Rekha Behrani for always being there!

Thank you Dr Ramesh Mirchandani, Ashok Mirchandani and Manoj Michandani—your encouragement has turned my dream to reality.

Heart felt thank you to Ms Sushmita Sen (Miss Universe 1994 and Bollywood star), for touching millions across the world through her Foreword for the book. We can't forget even for a second that she continues to be the most beautiful woman in the Universe!

Last but not the least, humble thanks to Padamshree Sonal Mansingh ji for her showers of blessing.

— Rita Gangwani

Introduction

"The Beauty Pageant's Greenroom" is a guide which reveals the ins and outs of the pageant. Right from filling the form to winning the beautiful Tiara, it has it all. There is valuable information to help one succeed and to get the most life-enhancing, and positive experiences in pageantry. It's a "total package" of what is assessed. Books that can help turn dreams to reality! Must have for every person who aspires to enter and win a beauty contest.

In the process of my training's, I found a lot of kids wanting to get into glamour industry and majority of them wanting to win a beauty contest. Nowadays, there are contests for all age groups and also for married people. Parents push even little kids to enter such contests. The sad part is that sometimes they get into wrong hands or lose a lot of money as they are not prepared and have no idea what will happen during the contest. The reason I came up with this book is to give some basic guidelines to aspiring women, men and kids who wish to enter a beauty contest about how to prepare and win the crown.

For the convenience of the reader, the book is divided into four sections. Each section is complete in itself.

- Section one (Pre Contest) - has all the nitty gritties required to enter a contest. It covers grooming to diction, voice modulation to question and answers. Every aspect of personality which will be judged as a contestant.
- Section two (During contest) - covers the history of beauty pageant, information on some important pageants, audition, training, choosing garments and takes you through various rounds till the grand finale and selection of winner.
- Section three (Post contest) - is the most important part. After you win a pageant you are in the public eye and become a role model for many. You need to be responsible for your actions and to project the right image. It's important to know how to conduct yourself on various occasions like party, travel, wed-

dings, sad situations like funerals and even daily texting. Human brain is like cement; whatever falls on it makes an impression. Unfortunately impressions are often permanent. No one likes people who walk around with their nose in the air and no manners. The section deals with etiquette in various situations of life.

- Section four (Confidence boosters) - we all have a bad day....a day we feel deflated. These motivational nuggets will help you face life with confidence and help you to put your best foot forward.

My best wishes to all those who are holding this book. The fact that you have taken this book indicates that you have a dream....a dream to be a winner! A dream to stand out in the crowd.... someone who knows the "P's and Q's well and is well versed with social and life skills. May you all find your rainbow!

Section 1

Pre-Contest

Chapter 1

What is beauty pageant

Beauty contests have now a lot more to do then just look beautiful. It's not about walking the ramp in pretty clothes, perfect hair do and flashing a smile; it's also about cracking the tough round of questions and answers with confidence. It's about the balance between the beauty and the brain. It can be an extremely nerve wrecking experience if you are not quite prepared for the tough competition. Contestants have to prepare for the competition involving the three aspects of their personality—body, mind and soul. They have to work on the five major pillars of personality—physical (looks, fitness etc.), mental (stress, anger, ego management etc.), social (personal and professional etiquette), cultural (understanding cultural diversity, respecting it) and spiritual (belief in self, meditation etc).

What is Beauty ?

The word is confusing – Is it your fair skin, height, manners? Nature of beauty has been one of the most fascinating riddles since eternity. The secret of beauty has constantly been explored by humans for as long as we have been civilized. In bookish terms, beauty is the combination of qualities which please the mind as well as the senses. Beauty has different meaning and perception for different people. For some beauty is only about fair skin and for others it could be a nice proportionate body, thus justifying the saying that "Beauty lies in the eyes of the beholder. I believe Beauty means not only appealling to the eyes of others but also having a compassionate heart.

What is Pageant ?

A beauty pageant or in other words, a beauty contest is a competition that focuses on the visible or physical beauty of the contestants. However over the years as the mind set of people have changed regarding beauty, these contests have evolved, and their focus have shifted. They are now more comprehensive, judging the overall personality, intelligence, presence of mind and talent of the contestants (not only women, but also men and even children) along with the physical beauty and body proportions.

Beauty pageants happen all over the world and at different levels—at city level, state level, national and then at international level. However, there are some prestigious contests which have evolved over the years like Miss Universe, Miss World, Miss Earth, Miss Super Model, Miss Tourism, Eco Queen and closer home—Femina Miss India, Campus Princess, Indian Princess, Rubaru Miss India, Miss Teen India, Mr and Miss Junior India, Mrs India, Mr India, Rubaru Mr Global and so forth.

Chapter 2

Advantages of entering a pageant

Beauty pageants are not only competitions focused on beauty; they are also life universities where the participants learn various skills, meet people, share their interests and work on their strengths and weaknesses. Beauty pageants is an effective and important platform for those who want to be in limelight or get into show biz. Let's focus on some of the advantages of entering a beauty contest.

Pageant is a huge opportunity to the world of media and entertainment. It's connected to modeling, acting, performing arts, radio, theatre, T.V. and much more. The skills learned during the training sessions of the pageants can help one enter these industries with ease.

During the pageant, the coaches and experts guide and provide tools that helps one to open up ones persona. They provide the ability to face fears and develops self confidence Speaking in front of a large crowd is the biggest fear of most people. By practicing on one's speech, pitch, timbre, modulation, one is able to face the audience with confidence. Daily practice, rehearsals, reflections, watching others perform and constant interactions and sharing of thoughts are a great confidence booster exercises which helps in overcoming shyness and makes you more confident.

The more the person recognizes and understands their strengths, weakness, fears, mental blocks, values, likes, dislikes, beliefs and personality, the greater fulfillment and satisfaction they experience from their life.

The main reason why people participate in games is for building a good support system, sharing, caring and to learn sportsmanship. Since pageant is a competition and has a spirit of either winning or losing, it helps the participant to accept the decisions gracefully.

Pageants are a good way of showcasing ones talent in front of important people and experts. It provides a good opportunity and help build a great network and meet various industry professionals. Performing in front of large audience helps ones talent to be noticed and recognized by the right people at the right time.

To be unique, one needs excellent communication skills. With the rigorous training during the pageants, one learns to pick up the right words, diction, pronunciation, accent, rate, timbre and is able to improve the quality of one's speech. The practice sessions help one to speak extempore no matter how nervous one may be feeling.

Pageant teaches one to have fixed goals and helps in taking steps to achieve the same.

Chapter 3

Self preparation for pageant

Every contestant who gets selected during the auditions is normally given a grooming session by the organizers where industry experts from various fields train them in various aspects of pageantry. These training sessions can be a month long, fortnight, weekly, couple of days to few hours. However, the contestant should not solely depend on these. The responsibility of the contestant starts right from the time the form is filled.

Remember, the more prepared and groomed you are, the more the chances of getting noticed. Try and find a pageant coach in your area, get some guide books or simply look up the Internet. Some key areas the contestant must focus on are: polishing the personality; improving posture; communication skills, vocabulary, voice modulation and diction; creating first impression; perfecting physical appearance; stage presence and public speaking; fitness levels; building self confidence; personal style; introductions and small talk; perfecting question and answers; body language and still pose; walking in heels and ramp walk; facing the camera; hair and skin care; hair styles; makeup techniques; dental care; nail care; personal hygiene; social etiquette; wardrobe management; swimwear comfort; carriage of traditional attire; understanding your body shape, structure and tone; self SWOT analysis; everyday essentials; picking the accessories; footwear as per dresses; wearing of pageant gown; positive attitude; business etiquette;

confidence building; current affairs and general awareness; time management; handling wardrobe malfunctions; fitness; sportsmanship; and coping up with stress.

Also start looking for the right dresses, gowns and shoes. Be on high alert as you walk the streets. Sometimes you get the unique dress just off the sheet. Getting the perfect gown, accessories etc. requires lot of time and attention. Practice self makeup and some hairstyles.

Just getting coached and mastering these techniques is not enough. It's important to practice them also. The more you walk in heels the more comfortable you will feel. Ask a friend or family member to help you. Make a video of yourself. Record your voice. Look into the mirror and practice your pose, your smile etc. Working on all the above mentioned techniques will surely give you a lot of confidence and will make you stand out amongst your fellow contestants.

Chapter 4

Building an attractive persona

Personality/Persona is a word used almost every day in our conversation. Without understanding what exactly a personality is or what goes behind it, a lot of people have made it a blind benchmark for judging people. It's a very dangerous word as one gets labeled as good personality if they like a person or bad personality if they don't.

Before we think of a building a good personality, its utmost necessary to understand the real meaning of this word. Unfortunately, this word lies clouded in our mind due to a whole lot of conditioning we've picked up right from our childhood via our family, friends and teachers.

Let me tell you a story. There was an old lady who lost a bunch of very important keys outside her home when she had stepped out for some work. By the time she returned home it was dark, and as she searched her purse for the keys to open her cabinet, she realized the keys were missing. She desperately started searching them all over the house. A neighbor walked in and asked her what she was up to? To which she replied that she is searching for keys which she lost outside when

she went shopping. But you lost them outside…the neighbor said, to which she replied, Yes I did! But it's too dark outside to look for them, at least I have light inside the house, that's why I am looking for them here.

What's the learning behind this story? It's just that we are looking for personality at a wrong place...searching everywhere, without realizing that personality is not something outside but it's something which is within you. You can discover it and polish it like a diamond and the brilliance is sure to reflect from within.

When we are born, we are like a blank sheet of paper. We have no idea of good and bad, but as we grow, we get influenced by the thinking of people who are around us and form perceptions and start reflecting these thoughts and labels unconsciously. Let's understand what a personality is. A good personality is made of five elements: physical (neat and clean, grooming etc), mental (control on anger, ego, stress etc), social (etiquette in various situations), cultural (understanding diversity, rituals etc.), and spiritual (belief in self, divine etc.).

I have dissected the word personality to highlight various qualities one needs to build a good persona. Each alphabet of the word 'personality' highlights some important quality that we need to polish.

- P: Presentable (knowledge of what colors suit you, right grooming, hairstyle, make up, body language, accessories etc.).
- E: Etiquette (manners required in various situations in life like in professional, social, and personal life).
- R: Responsible (accepting mistakes, taking charge, leadership qualities etc.).
- S: Speaking (a person who knows how to interact in an effective way using the right words, modulation etc. and has the tact of what to say when).
- O: Optimistic (someone who sees good in every situation and has the right attitude).
- L: Listener (a person who not just hears but makes an effort to understand).
- T: Tolerant (someone who is flexible and adjustable in nature and understands the uniqueness of others).
- Y: Ying and yang (accepting the balance of both the positive and negatives and thus accepting self).

Personality is like a packet of various qualities. Not only the cover of the package is attractive, but even the contents are. So, go ahead....find a paper and pen and jot down all the qualities you wish you had and start working on them. Read more, explore the internet, attend seminars and constantly try to improve yourself one step at a time.

We all have the best of us hidden somewhere...you just need to find yourself. As the saying goes "we are not human beings on a spiritual journey, but we are spiritual beings on a human journey".

Chapter 5

Overcoming stage fear

Research says that there are two major fears dominant in human's—fear of death and fear of public speaking. Most people experience nervousness on stage. The fear of public speaking or stage fright is one of the most common fear which robs one's self-confidence. Many experienced professionals too sometimes get jittery before going on stage.

What is Stage Fear? It's kind of a mind block also known as Topophobia. Before going on stage a lot of people start having (ANTS) in their brain, automatic negative thoughts, e.g., the size of the audience is too large for me to handle; what will happen if I cannot even utter a word; they all seem so intelligent and well read than me; will people laugh at me if I can't answer a question, what will people say! All these thoughts lead to anxiety, sweating, increasing heartbeat, heavy breathing; drying up of the mouth; wonky knees, and the mind going blank.

Anxious thoughts generate extra amounts of adrenaline resulting in fogging of brain. In order to look good, we start compromising on feel good factor. In this state, one starts to wring hands; drum fingers on the podium, tap a pencil, constantly press the click button of pen, tap foot, remove and put glasses on and off, lean on the podium; grab the mike tightly, touch the face and so forth, indicating lack of confidence. To ease these symptoms:

- Accept the feeling of fear like any other normal emotion. Instead of visualizing negative situations, focus on thoughts and images that help you feel safe and in charge of ourself.

- Breathe deeply and slowly through the diaphragm. Try to release and relax any tension that you are holding in your body and focus on the present moment.
- Control your body language. Smile and create an open, relaxed, confident stance. Positive body actions will automatically generate confidence in you. The saying goes 'fake it till you make it'.
- Flow with the situation and try not to control it. Don't look and sound desperate for attention. Go with the flow, believe in yourself and the things will turn out to be okay.
- Concentrate on the audience rather than yourself. It's not just about you! Sometime, people in the crowd are also as nervous as you. Relax it's ok!
- Eat something before you step up on the stage. Hunger pangs along with nervousness will give you a headache and that can be a big disaster.
- Another way to relax your jaw muscle and face tightness is to chew gum before the performance.
- Avoid caffeine. People feel it's a great way to relax the nerves, but it always has an opposite effect making you jittery.
- Don't just sit silently. Talk to people around you, crack a joke and divert your attention.
- Sometimes it pays to imagine that your favorite person is sitting in the audience. Imagine a clone of that person. Imagine this person loves you, supports you and will listen to everything you say with full attention.
- However nervous you may be, just act like the coolest person on the earth with head high and a big smile on your face.
- Never tell anyone how nervous you are. Repeating it to people and thinking about it all the time can intensify your nerves.
- Nothing can be as great as a practice. The more you practice on the stage, the better you will become.
- Personally, I start reciting a mantra focusing my mind on something. This really helps. Let me explain with the help of a story. Once a genie was gifted to man saying, he will do everything for you, but you need to be careful that if he has nothing to do, he will eat you! The receiver gave various tasks to genie and they were done in seconds. Everything the man could think of was done and his list exhausted. Now, the genie was all ready to eat him. That's when a friend suggested that you can keep the genie

busy very easily. Just give him a pole and tell him to keep going up & down till your next order. The trick worked and genie never bothered the man again. Mind is just like the genie. It keeps wondering if there is nothing to focus upon. Mantra is like climbing up & down the pole with concentration. It helps relax you before your important tasks.

Chapter 6

Confidence building

Confidence comes with positivity and having the right attitude. As contestant, you will face a tough competition and at many steps you will feel inadequate, unsure and may want to give up. To have confidence in oneself, you need to accept yourself as you are. No one is perfect in this world. Everyone is born with their unique strengths and weaknesses and you are no different.

Things that hold you back from pursuing your dreams are fear of failure and lack of self-confidence. Whenever you face low self esteem or lack of confidence, remember the following!

- Do not compare yourself to anyone one. You are unique with your own set of qualities and fears like everyone else. There is no one like you.
- Be comfortable with your strengths and weaknesses. Focus on your positives rather than negatives. Remember, there is no one like you on this earth. In fact you are a designer piece which god has created. So, instead of comparing yourself to others, find your uniqueness and create your own designer life.
- Pat your back for all the good you do. Accept compliments with grace and compliment yourself regularly.
- Don't take things to heart. Use criticism as a learning experience and improve yourself.
- Everyone makes mistakes. Do not punish yourself. If you fall, get up and start again.
- Stand up for what you believe in and stick to your principles.

- Read well and empower yourself with knowledge
- Always be humble. Avoid feeling or acting superior to others
- Stay away from negative friends, situations, and influences.
- Change your body language, be more confident.
- Love yourself, take care of yourself and groom yourself well.
- Dress nicely all the time. Understand your body and accept its flaws.
- Work on your posture. Walk with your head high.
  Do not stoop.
- Try to set small goals and achieve it.
- Show gratitude.
- Don't sweat about the small stuff.
- Identify your talents and work on developing them.
- Develop patience in whatever you do.
- Keep yourself fit and exercise regularly.
- Sleep well and follow time management.

Besides the above mentioned tips, you need to be in control of yourself during the pageant to feel confident enough to win. As a contestant, when you are centre stage, you can project confidence by–

- Smile.
- Don't miss your exercise routine.
- Hold your head high wherever you go and pretend that the crown is already on your head.
- Don't lie on your paperwork or in the interview.
- Come up with some unique talent
- Have someone proofread your paperwork for any mistakes before you submit them.
- Keep yourself up-to-date with the current events and important issues in news.
- Cover tattoos and remove all piercing other than the your ears.
- Never portray yourself in a negative light in any part of the competition.
- Keep your clothes and things organized.
- Make sure your clothes and gown fits perfectly.
- Never get yourself down because you think the other girls are better.

- Keep your answers short and concise.
- Wear heels everywhere. It'll help your walk immensely.
- Your talent costume should be comfortable but also a little flashy.
- Be nice to everyone during the pageant and if someone is not nice to you, don't seek revenge.
- If at first you don't succeed, try again. Most pageant winners have competed before.
- Practice, practice, practice. The more you practice, the more confident you are, and the better you'll do.

Chapter 7

Working on self esteem

These is a beautiful story which says that usually a baby elephant is tied up with chain. He tries his best to set himself free but is unable to do so. Hence his mind gets conditioned that he cannot set himself free. As the elephant grows old, the chains get replaced by rope. It's a seconds job for the huge elephant to break the rope and set himself free, but he does not even try as he is conditioned right from his childhood that nothing can set him free from the rope. Similarly, as kids we get conditioned by the remarks of family, friends and teachers. We feel we will not be able to do well in life etc. But remember, you can always reprogram yourself! This is how you can do it and raise your esteem.

- Make conversation easy by practising small talk with friends and relatives and staying in the present, listening, and becoming curious about the other person(s).
- Believe in yourself by removing negative influences from your life. Negative thoughts and people pull you down. Don't let that happen! If your friends' comments, thoughts, or actions are dragging you down, find new "positive" friends.
- Train your mind to think and visualize the life you want. If, in your mind you want to contribute to a worthwhile cause, make it happen. Be selfish and spend time on yourself and take control of your mind. Only let positive thinking drive you to your destiny. Carry this saying by Napoleon Hill

around with you: "Whatever the mind can conceive and believe, it can achieve." Believe in yourself, take control of your life, and be who you want to be. Take control of your mind and don't let your mind control you.

- Feel good about yourself. Create your own happy place with feel good memories of good times, music, a holiday, souvenir or remebering a happy face. When you're feeling low, think about the good things in life.
- Learn how to keep attention off yourself. We are too critical of ourselves. By practicing this form of self-criticism, we focus too much on what's wrong versus what's right. Practice "positive" self-criticism.
- Focus on your purpose; where you are and whom you're with. Learn what you can about others and focus on positives.
- Don't take undue criticism, even from yourself. That should be rule #1. Next time you tell yourself something negative, add 2 or more positives to it.
- Don't let yourself make sweeping statements about yourself as it damages your self-image. Extreme statements are heavy and weigh you down fast. Take it easy on yourself. Focus on the positive.
- Have patience and don't expect everything at once. Change takes time. If you're still having problems after a few days or a few weeks, keep practising until it comes naturally to you.
- Talk to yourself. Talk positive to yourself. Find something new everyday to say that will raise your spirits. Ask friends to give feedback constructively. Work on areas where you have problems and decide up front that you will "conquer the negatives" and develop more positives.
- Use positive affirmations like "I am a very nice person" and practice saying them daily. Say "I accept myself as I am". Or "I am Unique". Or "I am not a failure". Stand in front of the mirror, smile and say positive affirmations out loud to yourself.
- Visualize how you want to be. Focus only on the positives, be the best you can be, do what's right for you and for the others. Believe in yourself. Have fun!
- Do something you've always wanted to do but were always afraid to do. What better way to build your confidence than to experience life the way it's meant to be. Take a class in learning music, join a runner's club, take golf lessons. If you don't try

something, you won't know if it's for you or not. If it's not, try something else until you find your niche.

Chapter 8

Working on diction

Our mother tongue, upbringing etc. forms the base of our speech we tend to pick up words from here and there and replicate their pronunciation. Sometimes the way we speak is not understood by others. Having good articulation is must. Its an important aspect of projecting a polished personality.

Diction is a term that includes enunciation and the choice of words. In other words, diction is basically sound play. Sound, is produced by vibration. The vibrations in the human voice occur in the larynx (made up of cartilage and muscle and situated at the windpipe). Speech is the result of three distinct combinations of sound production, tone production, and actual word formation.

Diction refers to speaking more clearly. Good communication is a must for a contestant as they have to introduce themselves, answer questions, appear for interviews and handle the media. If the accent is not right, not clear, or the speech is not perfect, they may not be able to impress others. Record yourself during regular conversations. If you have more than three or four jumbled up words in a short conversation, you've got a problem. Take feedback from friends. Do work on your sound so that its clear.

There are many tools used for language development and tongue twisters are one of them. Tongue twisters are used by people who are perfecting their English to improve their accent and speech. One has to recite a rhyme which has a repetition of a sound starting with a similar letter or a phrase that can slip the tongue very easily. Reciting a tricky tongue twister as fast as possible without tripping over can be very challenging. Tongue twisters help to improve constant and vowel sounds and help to articulate the syllables and not slur the sounds together. Some people have difficulty differentiating between the sound of 'p' and 'b'; in such cases tongue twisters help loosen the tongue.

You may have written a wonderful speech with great content but unless your audience can understand what you're saying, your message is lost.

To improve one's articulation, select tongue twisters which have phonemes and are difficult to recite. The trick to mastering the tongue twister is not to rush. Start by reciting the tongue twisters at a slow pace and try to be as clear as you can. Try to learn the twister by heart. Keep reciting till you have mastered it and are able to recite it three times in a row without stumbling. When one tongue twister is mastered, try another.

Once you feel confident of your speech, stand and give your speech in front of a mirror. Notice how your mouth moves while speaking and if you don't like it, try and consult an expert who can correct your mistakes, if there are any. Slow down while practicing your diction. If you go too fast you may mumble and muddle the words.

There are plenty of exercises to improve your diction. Run your tongue around the walls of the mouth and stretch the jaws to relax them. Filling balloons, chewing gum and sucking through straws are good exercise for facial muscles. Practising tongue twisters are a must and should be done as frequently as possible. Talk as much as possible in order to overcome the obstacles you are facing regarding your speech.

Few examples of tongue twisters are: Peter Piper; Pheasant plucker; Betty Botter; Seventy seven; Skunk stunk; Swan Swam; Good blood, bad blood; A big black bug bit a big black bear and made the big black bear bleed blood; Susan Simpson strolled sedately, stifling sobs, suppressing sighs; She sells sea shells on the sea shore.

Chapter 9

Voice modulation

Have you ever heard a Robot talk? There are no feelings in his speech. You can never make out any difference between happy and unhapply statements. Speaking without proper expression or emotions puts people off.

The saying goes, it's not what you say, but how you say that matters. Without voice, we would not be able to deliver a single word because we will never be heard. For a contestant, it's most important to have control over the voice. Shaky, inaudible, monotonous tones will put off the judges and the audience. Your voice should be pleasing to the ears of the others and only than would they be interested in listening to what you have to say. A 2-3 minute self introduction in an unpleasant boring voice will never impress anyone.

Voice is a God's Gift, but delivery of the same can be learnt. People may have a nice, melodious voice by birth but it still needs to be trained to modulate, and have more bases, rhythm and some control on throat to produce variation and modulation

Voice modulation exercises

- To have that great quality in your voice, speak aloud 'Om' or simple 'Aaaah' in an earthen pot which has a close mouth. Holding of breath on these sounds works wonders. You can practice your introduction speech the same way.
- Alternatively, cup your ears like a cup with one hand and cover your mouth with another. Make sure the hand which covers the mouth and the one which covers the ear cup join together like a tunnel. Speak inside this tunnel. You will clearly hear how you sound on the mike and adjust your speech accordingly.
- Avoid very cold beverages, aerated waters, oily fried food, chocolates, pickles, fiery spices and anything very sour few days before your performance.
- Try to gargle a few times a day with warm water. It helps to keep infection at bay.
- Practice or do "riyaaz" every morning. Take a really long and deep breath from mouth, from nose, and start reciting "Sa" with your full base voice with continuous long pitch without any breaks, variations or modulations of your voice, till the end of breath. This helps in improving base voice and improves voice stamina.
- Try to breath from the diaphragm instead of chest with controlled exhales.
- Talking loudly and shouting make the vocal chords vibrate so harshly that they can be damaged.
- Yoga can keep the throat and voice healthy. Chanting of "OM" for 3-4 minutes every day give positive results. Practising Asanas for throat such as "Singasana" and "Bharamri Pranayam" clears the throat.

- Try singing a song at various pitches. It helps to control the voice.
- Check your speed and try to bring it within this range of about 125 to 150 words per minute.
- Avoid using vocalized pauses such as 'er', 'ah', 'unh', 'umm', etc.
- Change your tone based on what you're saying and feeling. "Lean" on important words and phrases. Put emphasis at the ends of statements and questions. Raise the pitch of your voice during the last few words whether you're asking a question or making a powerful statement. Practice modulating your pitch, volume and base. Keep your back and neck straight
- Some people are in a habit of repeatedly using phrases as 'you see', 'I mean', 'What I meant,' 'Understand? 'Have you understood,' 'Clear?', 'Is it clear?', 'Was it clear?', etc. These can kill the impact of your speech. Check if you use them and consciously avoid them.
- Lazy lip movements, a stiff jaw and an inactive tongue strangle the voice. So, always try to modulate and balance your voice whenever you speak. If you have enough practice, you should be able to control your voice easily.

Chapter 10

Pageant questions for practice

(collected from various sources: Google)

1. What is the most important event in our nation's history?
2. If you could be beautiful and not so smart, or brilliant and not so beautiful, what would you be and why?
3. If you could be either water or fire, which would you be and why?
4. One fine day you get up and realize that you have turned into a man/woman. What will be your reaction?
5. Is God a man or a woman?
6. What has been the most significant accomplishment in your life? At what point does a girl become a woman?
7. Do you consider yourself to be a giver or a taker? Why?
8. If women were to rule the world by 2050, how different would the world be?

9. Which quality of women gives them an edge over men?
10. What is the essence of being a woman?
11. How would you change the world if you were to play God for a day?
12. Do you think that the youth of today faces more pressure of performance than the previous generation?
13. Which role of a man compliments a woman better: father, son, or a partner?
14. Do you prefer a love marriage or an arranged marriage?
15. Tell me something about yourself.
16. What would you say is the biggest problem facing our education system today? Why?
17. In terms of being a woman in India, what is your opinion on the treatment of women in business and otherwise?
18. Tell me about a recent goal you accomplished.
19. What is your definition of success?
20. If you could be on the cover of any magazine, which would you choose and why?
21. Who is your role model?
22. What do you expect to gain by participating in pageants? Why?
23. What has been the biggest disappointment in your life to date?
24. Why should we select you as our title holder?
25. Tell us about the recreational activities in your city.
26. Tell us about the cultural activities in your city.
27. What is important to you now that was not important to you when you were younger? Why?
28. What has been the biggest disappointment in your life? Why?
29. What is your message to young women today?
30. What song best describes your outlook on life? Why?
31. If you had one message to the world, what would it be?
32. There is a group of people who does not support the concept of beauty contests. What will you tell them?
33. Which all countries would you like to visit in your entire life and why?
34. What made you decide to enter this pageant?
35. How important is it to look your good at all times?
36. If you could go anywhere in the world, where would you go and why?

37. What is your greatest obstacle? Why? How will you overcome that?
38. Would you like to be born as a man or a woman in your next life? Why?
39. What do you think about gay marriages?
40. How can we make this world a better place to live in?
41. Do you think euthanasia should be made legal across the world? Why?
42. What do you think about juvenile crimes and life imprisonment?
43. What is the most ideal punishment for a rapist?
44. What is your opinion on sex change?
45. Imagine that you have been selected as the President of the country for a week. What do you plan to do for the country in just a week?
46. What is the importance of beauty pageants in today's world?
47. If God granted you one wish, what would you wish for?
48. Who do you feel is the most popular person in the world. Why?
49. What would you like to see done to improve the public's understanding of the importance of organ donation? Why?
50. What do you want to do in life?
51. What are the best qualities a parent could share with their children? Why?
52. If you showed me around your state (county, city, etc.), where would you take me? Why?
53. What do you expect to gain by participating in pageants? Why?
54. What do you think makes India special?
55. If you could interview anyone in the world, whom would you choose to interview? Why? What would you talk to them about? Why?
56. Women have been elected to many high-level government posts. If you could choose a government position for your future, what job would you choose? Why?
57. As a possible Miss/Mrs/Mr__________, you would travel around speaking to a lot of people. What will be your message?
58. If you were invited to be a special guest on one of the talk shows, what would you want the host to discuss with you? Why?
59. Is it important for the husband to help do chores, such as cooking and cleaning? Why or why not?
60. How important is winning to you?
61. What are the names of your governor, mayor, council members, senators and representatives?

62. What types of people seem to rub you the wrong way?
63. How can the education of our children be enhanced by parental involvement?
64. Give me an example from your life where you turned a negative into a positive.
65. Do you think it is important for women to have equal opportunities as men ? Why?
66. Would you marry a man who wants to stay home and care for the children while you support the family?
67. How do you feel about trials for juveniles who commit adult crimes?
68. If you found yourself in a situation where you were being discriminated against because of race, what would you do? Why?
69. Do you want your children to experience the same childhood as you?
70. Do you think that the future is as bright for your generation as it was for your parents? Why or why not?
71. What has been your most meaningful achievement in life? Why?
72. What element of today's (tonight's) competition do you like the least? Why?
73. Tell me about your self-confidence.
74. How would you define a family unit?
75. Who do you feel possesses more confidence: Men or women? Why?
76. Who is your favorite actor (actress)? Why?
77. What have you learned not to take for granted? Why?
78. Is there anything in your life that is important now that was not important before?
79. Who do you consider being the most influential political figure in the world today? Why?
80. If you had one hour to spend with your great-grandmother (great-grandfather, etc.), what would you want to do or talk about? Why?
81. Of all the aspects of your life, which do you like least? Why?
82. Are celebrities appropriate role models for your generation? Why or why not?
83. What is the best advice you could give your friend? Why?
84. How do you define pride?
85. How do you feel about animal testing?

86. How important is the weight of a person in making a first impression?
87. Would you say that we live in a racist society? Why or why not?
88. Is there any job that a woman cannot do? If so, what?
89. If you were stranded on an island with only one book, which book would you like to have? Why?
90. If you won 100 crore in the lottery and could not spend it on yourself or your family, how would you spend it?
91. If you become Miss/Mrs/Mr, and you have a press conference in the morning, what question do you hope the reporters will not ask?
92. If it comes down to you and one other contestant for the title today (tonight), how will you react if they win?
93. What is the most important advice you could give to a young couple about to be married?
94. Besides "fine", how are you really doing?
95. If you had the chance to go back and change one event or occurrence in your life, what would it be? How would you do it differently?
96. Tell me about a recent purchase.
97. What is the key to success? Why?
98. If you found yourself in a situation were you were being discriminated against because of religion, what would you do? Why?
99. Experts claim that preventive medicine is the way for the future. What do you think?
100. There is controversy about eliminating the swimsuit competition from the pageants. What do you think about this?
101. How do you feel about the way women are portrayed in contemporary songs and music videos?
102. If you were to have a son and/or daughter someday, what is the most important lesson you would want to teach them?
103. Do you think the world would be a better place if we just had one world government and no separate countries?
104. If you knew there would be no tomorrow, how would you spend the rest of this day?
105. If you could bring someone from history into this year, whom would you bring? Why?
106. If you had the power to do anything you wished to improve the status of women in this country, what would you do? Why?
107. From where did your parents get your name?
108. What is the key to your success? Why?

109. If you had 30 minutes a day to do anything you wanted, what would you do? Why?
110. Do you feel that the government has the right to restrict the size of families? Why or why not?
111. If you were a judge, what question would you ask the contestants? Why?
112. Do you believe in love at first sight? Why or why not?
113. If you could receive one gift, what would it be? Who would give it to you?
114. How do you handle rejection?
115. Other than physical appearance, what do you like most about yourself? Why?
116. Tell me about peer pressure in your age group.
117. What is the nicest thing someone has ever said to you? Who said that?
118. With what social issue do you feel strong enough to get involved?
119. Tell me about your favorite television show.
120. If you could change one thing about someone in your family, who and what would it be? Why?
121. What is the biggest challenge facing the working woman today? Why?
122. What impresses you most about your city (town, community)? Why?
123. If you could take me to your house, what would you first want to show me? What would you not want me to see? Why?
124. Which has been your better teacher: life's experiences or formal schooling? Why?
125. What do you most value in your friends? Why?
126. What living person do you most admire? Why?
127. If you had to live outside India, where would you live? Why?
128. If you were given a free vacation in another country, where would you go?
129. Tell me about the last book (magazine, poem, etc.) you read.
130. What are your beauty secrets?
131. Tell me about your favorite sports team.
132. If you were to win this title, what one thing would you like to accomplish? Why?
133. How do you feel about teenage suicide during exams? How does this affect you?

134. Describe to me a stressful and unpleasant situation in your past, and tell me how you dealt with it.
135. Apart from your parents, who is (has been) your greatest influence? Why?
136. How do you think your family (friends) would respond if they were asked to identify your strengths?
137. Tell me about your funniest pageant experience.
138. What is a typical day like in your hometown?
139. What is your message to teachers today?
140. What bothers you most about what is happening in families today?
141. What is the most important element in a marriage? Why? Do you possess this element?
142. More than all else, I want...
143. How do you feel about euthanasia?
144. What bothers you most about what is happening in the world today? Why?
145. Which is more important: those who are in the news, those who report the news or those who interpret the news? Why?
146. What can you learn from children?
147. What feeling is most difficult for you to express? Why?
148. What is it that you do that drives your parents crazy? Why do you do it? Is there a substitute for this?
149. Is regular exercise important to you? Why or why not?
150. What do you want to do for the rest of your life? Why?
151. What is your favorite month of the year? Why?
152. What makes you hopeful? Why?
153. Is there any age that you would like to repeat? Why or why not? If so, which one and why?
154. What do you hope the judges notice about you? Why?
155. What question do you hope the judges will ask you? Why?
156. What is the greatest responsibility of a friend? Why?
157. All of your life, your parents have taught you. What have you taught your parents?
158. What would it take for someone to get to where you are?
159. Who is your role model? Why?
160. If you had to choose between intelligence and common sense, which would you choose? Why?
161. How do you feel about capital punishment?
162. What is something that you once had that you wish you could have again? Why?

163. If you could change one thing about this pageant, what would it be? Why?
164. What do you do in your spare time? Why?
165. What three words describe you best? Why?
166. What do you want people to see in you when they have their "first impression"? Why?
167. How would you describe yourself to a stranger on the telephone?
168. What is your most treasured possession? Why?
169. What is your greatest fear? Why?
170. If you had the time and money to embark on a great adventure, what would it be? Why?
171. Which is more important: money or power? Why?
172. Is there anything that I did not ask you that you would like to tell me about yourself?
173. What do people say about you?
174. What advice could you give today's parents to help them understand their children?
175. Besides your friends and family, what one thing can you not live without? Why?
176. What is your next goal? Why?
177. Who do you think is the greatest woman in history? Why?
178. Tell me about the last time you were sad.
179. Who is your favorite celebrity? Why?
180. What kinds of people do you surround yourself with? Why?
181. What would you do if you noticed a self-destructive behavior pattern in a friend?
182. If you could be any part of a car, which part would you choose to be? Why?
183. On what occasion do you lie? Why?
184. Let's say that your Principal is seeking consultation about changing her image. What would you suggest?
185. What is your favorite day of the week? Why?
186. Tell me about your feelings concerning air and water pollution.
187. What makes you laugh? Why?
188. If you could ask only one question in determining who your friends would be, what would you ask? Why?
189. Tell me about something you dream of doing. Why? When will you do that?

190. What do you do to keep up your good health?
191. Do you consider it more important to be liked or respected? Why?
192. How would you like to be remembered?
193. Quick, the local newspaper has just called, and they need you to write an article about this pageant for the morning paper. What will it say?
194. If you could star in any television show (movie, music video, etc.), which would you choose? Why?
195. What is the most pressing problem facing young people today? Why? How does this problem affect you?
196. What makes you happy? Why?
197. What is the most important element in a friendship? Why? Do you possess this element?
198. Other than marriage and career, what special things would you like to accomplish in your lifetime? Why?
199. What is your favorite quote? Why? Who wrote it?
200. What is the biggest challenge facing you today? Why?
201. Who (What) influenced you to enter this pageant?
202. Tell me a good story.
203. If you could choose only one, which would you choose: to be smart, rich or beautiful? Why?
204. Are you pleased with the quality of your education? Why or why not?
205. Tell me about some of your short-term goals.
206. The youth of today are preoccupied with...
207. If you went to a foreign country for a year, what (who) do you think you would miss the most? Why?
208. Tell me about your favorite book. Who wrote that book?
209. What are the disadvantages of being from a small town (large city)?
210. At what point are you in your life?
211. If you had the chance to start your life over again, would you choose to be a boy or a girl? Why?
212. Which is more important: AIDS education or AIDS research? Why?
213. If you were a finalist and you learned that another finalist had the final question in their possession, what would you do? Why?
214. If you could live any time in the past, present or future, when would you live? Why?

215. What has been the most difficult thing for you in growing older? Why?
216. What are you self-conscious about? Why?
217. What is funny about you? Why?
218. Are today's women becoming more aggressive and less romantic? Why or why not?
219. What is the most important advice that you could give to someone entering a Miss/Mrs/Mr pageant? Why?
220. What makes you sad? Why?
221. Tell me about your favorite author.
222. Which do you feel offers a better education, public schools or private schools? Why?
223. Are you a sensitive person? Why or why not?
224. If you were to paint me a picture that included your favorite things, what would you paint?
225. What do you think the judges see in you that brought you to the finals today (tonight)?
226. As times change, what contemporary woman is the best role model for your generation? Why?
227. Can you get too used to being in pageants, or do you find each one to be new and exciting? Why?
228. Do you take more after your mother or father? Why?
229. What is your nickname? Why?
230. What is the biggest problem facing the elderly today? Why? What is the solution?
231. If you had only one year (day, hour, etc.) left to live, what would you do? Why?
232. Other than your family, who has played an important role in your life?
233. What will you be doing ten (five, one, etc.) years from now?
234. If you had three (two, one, etc.) wishes, what would they (it) be? Why?
235. What person in history do you admire the most? Why?
236. How do you define poise?
237. How do you define beauty?
238. You have 15 minutes on prime-time television. What will you do or say? Why?
239. How would the dictionary define you?

240. What is the biggest challenge facing women today? Why?
241. If you could be any animal, which would you choose to be? Why?
242. Describe a typical day in your life.
243. If you saw another contestant doing something that would disqualify her, what would you do?
244. What makes you most uncomfortable.
245. What is your take on pre-marital sex?
246. Do you have a boyfriend? Is he ok with the idea of you taking part in this pageant?
247. What makes you uncomfortable?
248. What all can you sacrifice for this pageant?
249. Are your parents ok with the swimsuit round?
250. Do you think the swimsuit round is derogatory?
251. How do you feel about people being judged on their looks?
252. What one thing about men do you not understand?
253. How old is "over-the-hill"?
254. Tell me about a time when you lied to your parents (best friend, boyfriend, etc.).
255. In judging a pageant, what is the most important quality a contestant should possess? Why? Do you possess this quality?
256. Why do you want to win this pageant?
257. Where would you rather be right now?
258. What kind of kid were you?
259. Should material on the Internet be censored? Why or why not?
260. What can women learn from men?
261. What is the best way to teach a child responsibility?
262. Who is your favorite unsung hero?
263. What is your current state of mind?
264. Which word do you not like to hear?
265. How can teachers more effectively encourage their students to complete their education?
266. What do you consider to be your greatest achievement?
267. How do you feel about who you are?
268. Can you combine a career and a family? If so, how?
269. What do you regret?
270. What is the best advice you have ever been given? Why?
271. What kind of person turns you off? Why?
272. What is the most important thing you did to prepare for this pageant? Why did you do that?

273. How would you describe your ideal wedding? If you could give any gift to your parents, what would you give to them? Why?
274. Some people have cosmetic surgery to change their appearance. Would you? Why or why not?
275. When did you first realize that you were beautiful?
276. What living woman is the best role model for your generation? Why?
277. People will follow only someone who they can trust. Can you be trusted? Why?
278. What is your dream? How long has that been your dream?
279. How do you relax?
280. What would you name your autobiography?
281. When do you feel most tired?
282. How far are you willing to push yourself?
283. Would you resort to unethical practices in order to win this pageant?
284. Where do you go when you want to "get away"? Why do you go there?
285. How do you respond to the criticism that young women are more materialistic and worried with their appearance than with their inner self?
286. If you could give away one of your possessions to an under-privileged young woman (man), what would you give?
287. Everyone has a mission in life. What do you think your mission is?
288. If you married, would you agree to your husband doing the housework while you worked a job?
289. Should music lyrics be censored? Why or why not?
290. What is your weakest point? What are you doing about it?
291. What is your favorite word?
292. What is your favorite sound?
293. What color best describes your outlook on life? Why?
294. On a scale from 1 to 10, how would you rank the importance of the grades that you make (made) in school? Why?
295. What should be the punishment for someone who commits murder?
296. If you could be famous, in what way would you choose?
297. What have you learned most in your preparations for this pageant? Why?

298. What would you say are the top news stories today? How do they affect you?
299. What is your greatest obstacle? Why? How will you overcome that?
300. Who is your best friend? Why?
301. What do you think money can buy?
302. What do you think money can't buy
303. What makes you most proud of your generation? Why?
304. Tell me about your favorite things.
305. What have you learned today?
306. How would you describe the 90s (80s, 70s, 60s, etc.)?
307. When you see photographs of yourself, what is your reaction?
308. What is the closest you have ever been to death?
309. What is enthusiasm? Do you have it?
310. How can we encourage healthy living?
311. What is your philosophy in life?
312. Does pageant competition help you develop as a person? Why or why not?
313. What do you want to be when you grow up? Why?
314. If you could wake up tomorrow having gained any one ability or quality, what would it be?
315. What is your message to young people today?
316. What is the most important element in a relationship?
317. What is the role of today's teachers?
318. What advice could you give to someone about to enter pageants for the first time?
319. Why is it that people who are attractive tend to be more successful?
320. What was the greatest discovery of the 20th century?
321. Are you a public or private person? Why?
322. What is/was your favorite school subject? Why?
323. What can be done to wipe out breast cancer?
324. Tell me something that will make me remember you. Tell me something else.
325. If you could be any age, what age would you be? Why?
326. What makes you more qualified than the other contestants to win this title?
327. Should women in the armed forces be allowed to serve in combat? Why or why not?
328. Tell me about your earliest childhood memory.

329. Where would you pinpoint the cause for violence in youth today?
330. What is your favorite song? Why?
331. How do you describe sex appeal?
332. What are some of the games people play?
333. Comment: "I am OK, you're OK"
334. What is the one thing that sets a woman apart from a man?
335. If you were not here where would you be?
336. Do you read? Tell us about one book you read recently?
337. What is the role of today's religious leaders?
338. What do you see as the difference in a woman and a lady?
339. What do you dislike most about yourself?
340. Is life fair? Why or why not?
341. What is your definition of a winner?
342. What do you like to do on a rainy day? Why?
343. What motivates you? Why?
344. What is the best thing that you have ever received that was free?
345. What do you take most pride in? Why?
346. What is the best advice that you have ever been given?
347. Should sex education be taught in public schools? Why or why not? If so, at what age?
348. If you had to write your autobiography, what would it say?
349. What is your favorite article of clothing that you own? Why?
350. How do you feel about organ/tissue donation?
351. Tell me about your favorite childhood toy.
352. What is your favorite pageant question?
353. Do you find it easy or hard to say, "No"?
354. When was the last time you cried? Why?
355. Tell me about your favorite sport.
356. What is it that makes your parents proud of you?
357. Do your comments and suggestions influence other people much? Why or why not?
358. How would you describe your perfect evening?
359. If you could be any fictional, film or literary character, which character would you choose to be? Why?
360. What is your best habit? Why?
361. Are you superstitious?
362. Would you give dowry?

363. Do you believe in horoscope matching?
364. Do you believe in blood group matching before marriage?
365. If you were to have fever on the final day what would you do?
366. Looks can be deceptive do you agree?
367. The thing that scares me the most is...
368. Would you say that people all over the world are the same or different?
369. Rate yourself on a scale from 1 to 10: personality, achievement, appearance.
370. Do you take chances? Why or why not? Please, give an example.
371. What are the qualities of the ideal man?
372. What makes you different from other people? Why?
373. What are your strengths?
374. If you could be someone else for a day, who would you be? Why?
375. What is your philosophy in life?
376. Is there any job that a woman cannot do that a man can? If so, what?
377. Who is your favorite musician or musical group?
378. If you could change one thing in the judicial system, what would it be?
379. What is the role of today's woman?
380. What do you think is the most important invention of this century? Why?
381. Tell me about something you would like to invent.
382. What is your good luck charm?
383. What is your greatest responsibility as a friend?
384. What is your favorite vacation destination? Why?
385. How important is it to look your best at all times?
386. When you look into a mirror, what do you like most about what you see? Why?
387. From whom would you most like to receive a great, big hug? Why?
388. What is your idea of perfect happiness?
389. What does freedom mean to you? Why?
390. Tell me about something you would like to forget.
391. Do you consider yourself a woman or a girl?
392. What is your favorite season of the year? Why?
393. Tell me about your pets.
394. What measures do you take to safeguard yourself?

395. Where have you traveled? When?
396. Some people say, "It's a man's world". What do you say?
397. Who will be (Who is) in the audience supporting you tonight?
398. If you had to serve to the judges your favorite dessert, what would you serve?
399. In your opinion, what is the best age for marriage?
400. Do you believe that everyone is a winner? Why or why not?
401. How have you been active in protecting the environment?
402. Tell me about the last time you laughed hard.
403. What is your greatest extravagance?
404. What is your greatest regret?
405. Will you compete again if you do not win this time? Why or why not?
406. Are you afraid of losing? Why or why not?
407. If you knew there would be no tomorrow, how would you spend the rest of today?
408. Does it make a difference what you look like? Why or why not?
409. Are you a traditional person or a modern person?
410. Why will enthusiasm sell when nothing else will?
411. Can a convicted criminal turn their life around? Why or why not?
412. What would you do with a red crayon?
413. When you look into the mirror, what do you see?
414. What is the name of the contestant that stands in front/behind you in the line up? How do you feel about her?
415. The ideal Indian woman is...
416. Do you think contestants with cosmetic surgery should be permitted to compete in pageants? What if the contestant was in a severe accident?
417. You have been granted a miraculous healing power that could terminate any single disease, which one disease would you choose?
418. Every few seconds another Indian becomes infected with HIV. What do you know about HIV and AIDS?
419. It is okay for women to wear pants, but why are people so uncomfortable with men in skirts?
420. How do you plan to celebrate after winning the title?
421. What is the role of the Internet or social networking sites on the youth?

422. What is the biggest mistake you have ever made in your life? What have you done to overcome it
423. What problems you had to face before entering the field of modeling/participating in the contest?
424. Would you have been still a part of the show if your parents did not allow you?
425. Describe what motherhood means to you
426. What would life after rape be like?
427. What is your take on one night-stands?
428. Do you believe in karma? Why?

Chapter 11

Personal hygiene

Have you ever interacted with someone who appears to be just out of bed. Hair messy, mouth stinking & emitting bad body odour. No one likes to talk to them as they put people off.

Personal hygiene is a routine of personal care and rituals that keeps you clean, fit and healthy. It is an important part of confidence building and displays ones positive self esteem. Everyone loves to be around people who are neat and clean but sometimes we are lazy and neglect our body leading to illness and disease.

Poor hygiene can lead to more chance of disease, infections, loss of teeth, loss of friends, Poor self-image and loss of confidence. On the other hand, good hygiene helps you keep free of dirt and germs, helping you look and feel your best, raises your self esteem, confidence level and makes you attractive to others along with keeping your body in top condition

Skin hygiene

The skin is the outer layer of the body that protect internal organs, regulates body temperature and eliminates wastes by sweating. For keeping the skin clean and healthy, one should take a bath everyday even if you feel you are clean. Daily bath helps in keeping you clean,

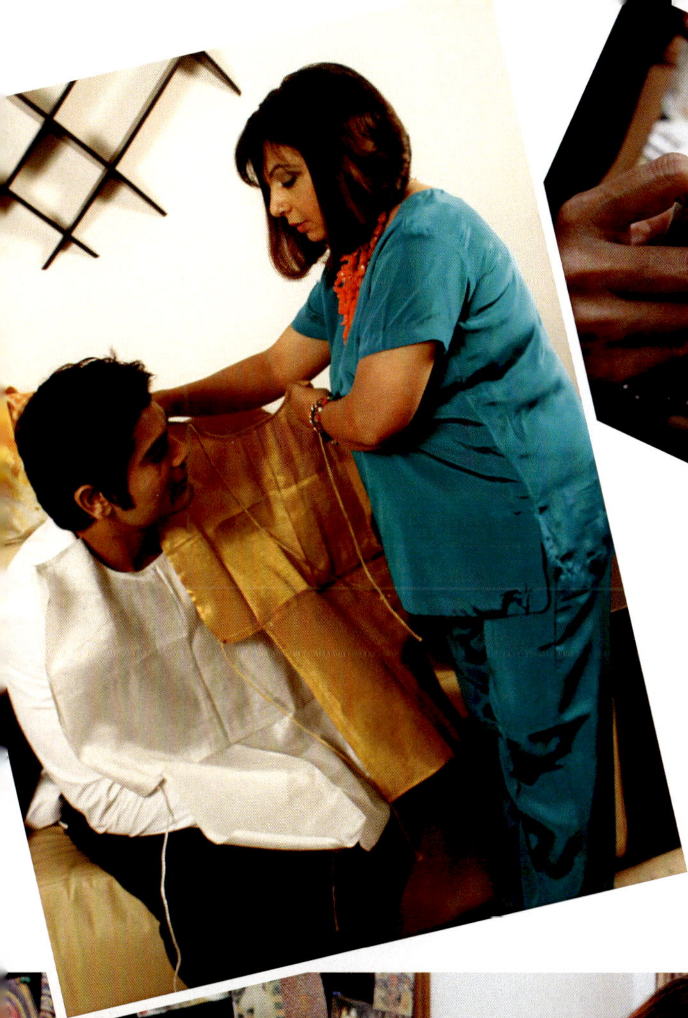

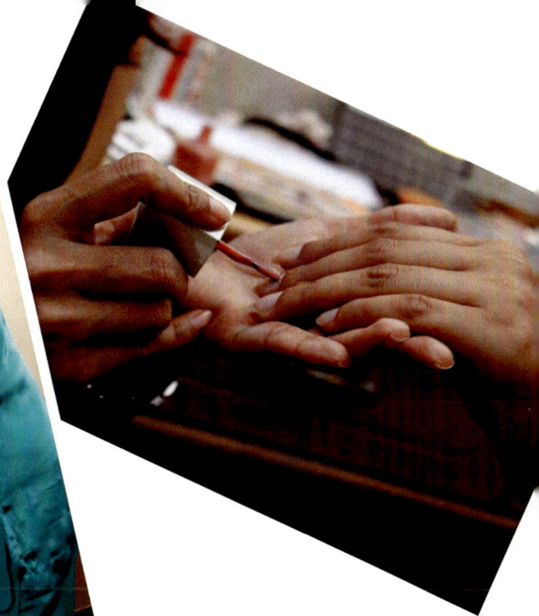

DIESELBOY
THE UPBEATS
TRUTH

RU-BA-RU
MISS INDIA
ELITE

RU-BA-RU
MISS INDIA
ELITE 2013
GROOMING

GROOMING PARTNERS
Lets Make Female Foeticide A History
RU-BA-RU MISS INDIA ELITE 2013
INDIA ELITE 2013
GROOMING PARTNERS

MISS INDIA
MISS INDIA
MISS INDIA
MISS INDIA

ELITE 2013
S INDIA EL
DIA ELITE

fresh and smelling nice. Scrubbing of your body will remove dead, dry skin and help your skin stay healthy and refreshed, and will prevent acne, blemishes and other skin eruptions. Special attention is needed in skin areas with folds and creases. Dirt and germs collect in areas such as behind the ears, under arms and between fingers and toes. Never share your towel with anyone and wash it on a regular basis Rinse well to remove all dirt and soap. Use deodorants or antiperspirants after you bathe. Change under garments daily and keep them clean.

Body odor hygiene

Keep your underarms and groin area clean and dry to discourage bacteria growth. Change out of sweaty clothes fast. Trim or shave your underarm and pubic hair so there is less surface area allowing for the accumulation of sweat and bacteria. Cut back on fatty foods that may contribute to body odor and also some strong flavored vegetable like onion and garlic. Wear a fresh set of clothes as dirty clothes are a source of contamination and smell if worn over and over without washing them. Also, try wearing a clean pair of socks every day as this keeps your feet dry and not smelly.

Nail hygiene

Keeping your fingernails and toenails trimmed and in good shape is a must. Trim them weekly and while washing hands check that no dirt or residue remains beneath the nail. Moisturize nails and cuticles regularly. Girls should avoid walking around with chipped nail polish. Regularly get manicure and pedicure done. You can do so at home too and change your nail polish if it's chipping off.

Hair hygiene

Shampoo your hair almost every alternate day to keep your hair and scalp healthy and in good shape. If you suffer from lice or dandruff, then take necessary action at the earliest. For dry hair, less often is usually enough. Oily hair needs to be shampooed more often, every day. Brush hair daily to remove snarls, knots, and surface dirt. This cleans and stimulates the scalp. Brush from the roots to the tips to spread natural oils throughout the hair. Wash your brushes and combs each time you wash your hair.

Dental hygiene

Brush your teeth after every meal and use dental floss to clean the plaque from between the teeth where the toothbrush cannot reach. Cut down on the amount of sugar and sweets. Choose a toothbrush with soft bristles. Invest in a tongue cleaner which will help freshen your breath, and remove bacteria. Rinse your toothbrush well after use. Toothbrushes should be replaced every three months. Go to the dentist regularly for check-ups

Foot hygiene

Wash your feet every day, and dry they well, especially between the toes to avoid any kind of infection. Using a little powder can help keep them dry. Never try to remove corns yourself. See your doctor. Shoes, which fit properly help, prevent problems. Cut toenails straight across, and do not cut down into the corners. Push back cuticles after you have washed your feet. Wear the right socks. Switch shoes on and off and also wash shoes or insoles of your shoes.

Shaving hygiene

Shave with a sharp blade. Avoid using a dull one to lessen the risk of cutting yourself. Rinse well. Shave your under arms and legs if you desire, but with care. Use shaving cream/gel. Be patient as you shave to avoid nicks and cuts. Pubic skin can get very sensitive after shaving. Instead of shaving, use Brazilian wax to clean the pubic area. This should be done at a clean parlor under the supervision of an expert.

Hand hygiene

Hands should be washed with soap often during the day, before and after meals, handling food, touching pets, dusting, mopping, after using the toilet, and before bed. Keep an alcohol based sanitizer handy in case you don't have water and soap around... always. Go for a sanitizer, which has a good amount of moisturizer in it.

Ear hygiene

Wash your ears every day, especially from behind. Never clean the inside of ear with any sharp object. You can clean your ears with a soft ear bud. Keep your earrings clean. Hair products may stick to the ears and should be washed often to avoid irritation to the skin of the ear

Genital hygiene

Genital hygiene is of upmost importance. Keep that area dry and clean. Shower daily and rinse out all the soap. Make sure your inner wear is not very tight. Wear cotton instead of synthetic inner wear. Use a panty liner to avoid odor and keep the area dry. Try to keep this area hair free. For any kind of vaginal itch see the doctor and use prescribed antibiotics and antifungal creams. Man should retract foreskin and rinse in water, wipe with clean towel and keep the area dry.

Toilet hygiene

Try not to hold back your urine. Use toilet at regular intervals. Stay hydrated. Men should lift the toilet seat always and women should use the seat cover whenever they can in public toilets. Wipe and wash from front to back after passing stool and urine. This will help avoid germs entering the vagina. Remember to flush and wash your hands.

Makeup hygiene

Wash your makeup brush and powder puffs on a weekly basis with a mild baby shampoo for best and safe usage. Dry the washed makeup product by using a clean towel. Never use your fingers to apply makeup, but, if you must use your fingers, then make sure they're clean.

Chapter 12

What skin tone are you?

The most important thing to keep in mind before you pick up dresses or makeup is to understand your skin's undertone. Don't get this confused with your skin tone. Lot of people uses the word complexion when they describe skin tone, but the undertone is different. Your undertone isn't visible, hence it's called under tone. It's the inner factor that shows how well certain colors will pop up your skin. The undertone is determined by the amount of melanin, size and number of blood vessels that lie closest to the skin surface. Skin tone normally never changes and so it's best to identify it before picking up your cosmetics, hair color, clothing etc.

There are many ways to tell what undertone you are, but the easiest way is trial by error. Below, you will find few easy ways to check your skin tone. Pick up whichever method suits you. If you end up confused with one method, try another. If still not clear, ask an opinion from someone and seek help. Nowadays you can visit an image consultant who use various tools to identify your color tone.

There are basically two types of skin undertones—warm and cool. People sometimes use different terms to describe them like summer or gold for warm and winter or silver for cold.

Test 1: The vein test

This is the quickest and the easiest method. Stand in the natural day-light and look at your wrist. Notice, what color do the superficial veins appear?? If they appear blue than you have cold undertone and if they seem green you have a warm undertone. If your veins look like the mixture of green and blue, you are neutral toned. You will be able to understand warm, cold and neutral undertones when I will explain the genetics test.

Test 2: The genetics test

Your hair, skin and eye color also help in identifying your skin undertone. Warm undertones tend to have a hint of yellow, orange, red, copper or goldish hair color. The eyes are dark brown, amber, hazel or green. The skin undertone for them is gold, yellow or apricot. Cool undertones have a hint of violet, blue, silver or ash hair color with eyes being light blue, blue green, grey blue, grey green or black. The basic skin undertone is pink, rose or blue. Neutral toned people have reflections of both undertones and look nice in all colors.

Test 3: The metal test

Get hold of a large piece of gold and silver jewellery. Stand in natural light holding a mirror in one hand. Hold each piece against your face one at a time and examine your face. If silver makes your face look brighter and alive, you are cool toned, and if gold looks nice on you, you are warm toned.

Test 4: The fabric test

Get hold of a large table cloth size of a blue fabric and a brick colored fabric. In natural light stand in front of a mirror. Wrap the cloth like a shawl below the chin level one at a time. If the blue cloth looks more vibrant on you, you are cold undertone and similarly if the brick one looks good, you are warm undertone.

Test 5: The paper test

Hold a piece of white paper next to your face. Notice your skin tone in contrast to the white paper. If it looks yellow or gold, you have a warm undertone and if it's pinkish blue, you have a cold undertone.

Test 6: The ear test

Clean behind your ears nicely. Take help from someone to pull your ear forward and look behind the ear in natural light. The skin behind the ears reflect the tone very well. Yellow hue indicates a warm undertone and the pink hue indicates a cold undertone.

Things to keep in mind before you do a test:

- Wash your face well and pat dry.
- Do not rub your face with towel. Friction will bring out the red flush which will make it tough to detect the undertone.
- Avoid using any toner or moisturizer.
- Wait for 15 minutes for face to recover normal mode.
- Make sure you are in natural light without any shadows.
- Avoid the test on a cloudy day.
- Have a mirror handy.

You are now ready to test.

Chapter 13

Check your skin type

Skin is body's biggest organ. It covers and protects the inside of one's body and holds everything together, or else our organs will be floating around. Skin also protects our body from outside injuries and helps in maintaining right temperature and is also an important sense organ which depicts touch.

Skin has three layers. The outermost is called Epidermis and this is what we can see. Epidermis is always making new cells which rise up to the top to replace the old ones. 95 percent of the cells in the epidermis work to produce new cells, the rest 5 percent make a substance called Melanin which gives skin its color.

The second layer of the skin is called Dermis. This dermis contains the nerve endings, blood vessels, oil glands, sweat glands. collagen and elastin.

The third layer is subcutaneous fat. It's mostly made up of fats and helps keep our body warm and also helps in absorbing shocks.

Just like hair is not of the same quality for everyone, similarly we all have different types of skin. There are basically five types of skin: normal, oily, combination, dry, and sensitive.

Skin types depend upon a lot of factors like water content, lipid (oil), level of sensitivity, genetic predisposition, diet, medications, stress, pollution, climate, smoking and general skin care routine

Once you can identify the type of skin you have, it becomes easy to take its care. There are many ways to check your skin type, but the easiest is The Tissue Test.

How to check your skin type

Take a clean piece of tissue. As soon as you wake up in the morning, immediately cover the face with a tissue to blot your entire face and then take a closer look.

If the tissue has lots of transparent spots, then you probably have oily skin prone to blackheads, blemishes and breakouts. If the tissue is clean and your face feels tight, then you have dry skin which is prone to premature signs of aging. If the tissue picks up only a tiny amount of oil in the T-Zone, then you have normal skin. If the tissue has oil spots just on forehead, nose and chin, then you have a combination skin.

There is another method to check your skin type is called The Visual Test.

- Normal skin: No or few visible imperfection; no severe sensitivity; barely visible pours; a radiant complexion.
- Combination skin: Overly dilated pours; black heads; shiny skin on T-Zone (nose, forehead or skin area).

- Dry skin: Almost invisible pores; dull and rough complexion; red patches; dry skin; less elasticity; more visible lines.
- Sensitive skin: Red blotches on exposure to certain products and weather.

Chapter 14

Daily skin care

A lot of people think that washing your face is the only thing they need to do to have a good skin. But along with the wash, cleansing, toning and moisturizing (CTM) routine is a must for a healthy skin.

Why cleansing your skin is important

Washing your face with soap only cleans the skin superficially. All throughout the day, your face gets exposed to pollution, dust, dirt, germs and bad climatic conditions. To remove dirt and other harmful particles from your skin, cleansing it is a very important step. Cleansing your skin means getting collected oil, dirt and makeup from your skin, without removing its natural moisture. It also improving blood circulation, opens the pores and removes the left over makeup from the skin, making it clean and glowing.

Step 1: Cleaning the face

Never use dirty hands. Wash your hands before cleaning your face. When cleansing the face avoid using water that is too hot or too cold; lukewarm is the ideal temperature. Apply cleanser on your face and rub gently on the entire face with your fingertips or squeeze some of the cleanser onto a cotton ball and then apply. Cleanse from the neck up to the hairline in a circular motion concentrating on forehead and T-Zone. These areas are more prone to holding oil and dirt. Spend about 3 minutes massaging the cleanser into your skin. Rinse the skin with lukewarm water. Repeat this until you remove all cleanser. Do not rub towel vigorously on your face…pat dry gently to avoid stretching the skin which may lead to premature wrinkles. Cleanse your face twice a day, once in the morning and once in the evening . Never sleep with your makeup on.

Step 2: Toning

Toner removes any residue left behind by your cleanser and it also tightens the pores which were left exposed due to cleanser. It helps to even out the skin tone and cools the face. Left over traces of makeup and dirt also get lifted off. A toner must be used before putting on the makeup and before going to sleep/removing makeup. Using toner before bedtime helps your skin to feel fresh and free and lets it breathe through the night.

Step 3: Moisturizing

After you have toned your face, it may feel stretchy or extra tight which means that it is lacking in moisture. By using a good moisturizer, you help your skin to feel soft and dewy, it repair itself faster and regain its elasticity and glow again! People with dry skin should always use a good moisturizer matching their skin type whereas those with combination and oily skin should use a good water-based moisturizer. If you have normal skin, then you can use either a heavy moisturizer or a water based one as per your liking!

Chapter 15
Care for different types of skin

Care for dry skin

- Try and take shorter showers in lukewarm water rather than hot water not more than once daily.
- Use very mild and gentle soaps and washes.
- Avoid any soap which contain deodorants.
- Don't scrub vigorously while bathing and drying.
- Apply moisturizers immediately after bath when your skin is still damp.

- Use hydrating masks at least twice a week.
- Drink plenty of water. Have plenty of proteins and vitamin A, C and E.
- Keep a humidifier in the room to keep your skin hydrated.
- Avoid moving in and out from too much of temperature difference.

Care for oily skin

- Wash your skin no more than twice a day.
- Don't pinch, pop or squeeze the pimples.
- Avoid very sugary and oily foods.
- Use non-greasy moisturizers.
- Reduce sugar and other carbohydrates from your diet.
- It is important to moisturize. Most oily skin types think they should keep their skin dry; in fact, it is the opposite.

Care for sensitive skin

- Watch what you eat and make sure to consume a fair amount of essential fatty acids, fermented fruits and vegetables, organic protein, seasonal fruits, and yogurt.
- Protect your skin from sun by using sun protecting factor cream of at least 30 potency.

Care for combination skin

- Use hydrating face masks.
- Use a toner on T-Zone.
- Use bloating paper to soak oil from T-Zone throughout the day to keep skin looking even.
- Use a good quality make-up, but do not overindulge.

Chapter 16

Skin care for winter

Winter season is very damaging to the skin. It becomes chapped and dry due to cold air. It thus needs special care during this season.

- Apply moisturizer to damp skin within 2-3 minutes of getting out of the bath or shower. Use your moisturizer at least two times a day—morning and night. You can also apply baby oil all over your body immediately after you step out of the shower, while your skin is still wet. The old grand ma recipe is to pot a few drops of oil in your umbilicus as it keeps the skin moist and soft.
- Reduce bathing time and shower to only 5 minutes and once a day. Turn the temperature of the water down so that you are not using very hot water, this will prevent natural oils from being stripped from your skin. Use glycerin/cream based soap or a moisturizing body wash to keep your skin healthy. Pat yourself dry, don't rub. Leave your skin a bit damp.
- Protect your skin from the cold and the wind by using scarves and hats to cover your head and gloves for hands. Avoid wearing wool and other rough materials right next to the skin. Have a cotton layer at the bottom. Clothing helps to protect the skin from the cold dry air, which can take away all moisture from the skin.
- Cold weather and wind can crack your lips in winter. Do not lick your chapped lips. You can exfoliate dry skin with a soft toothbrush. As well as this, before you step outside do not forget to apply some vaseline/petroleum jelly to your lips, creating a protective barrier between the cold air and your lips.
- We tend to drink less water as we turn to hot drinks like coffee and tea, but don't forget that skin needs hydration. A little warm water with lemon or warm jasmine tea can be very refreshing.
- To keep the air moist, invest in a humidifier or place plants around the room. Another solution is to place water steamers around the house. The water will evaporate and add moisture to the air.
- Seasonal and natural plants, fruits and vegetables can seriously aid your skin, especially when temperatures drop. Vegetable mar-

ket is full of seasonal healthy food like green leafy vegetables. So remember to eat your seasonal veggies.

- Don't forget to use sunscreen. Winter sun combined with dry air can damage your skin. Apply a broad-spectrum sunscreen to your face and your hands about half an hour before going out. Reapply frequently if you stay outside a long time. The weather outside may be unsightly, but that doesn't mean you go that way too.

Chapter 17

Skin care for men

Men also need to take special care of their skin. They tend to have not only thicker skin but also oiler skin due to larger sebaceous glands and because they shave daily and there are more chances of nicks and cuts.

- We have heard upteen times that drinking 8 glasses of water every day is a must for a glowing skin. Water helps to flush out toxins from the body and keeps the skin soft and elastic. Drinking water especially with two sliced lemons really starts to change skin for the better. Having healthy skin is amazing but having healthy, moist skin is even better.
- Eat wisely. Many of us indulge a lot in junk and fried food. Practice portion control whenever you have this kind of food. Instead of eating fatty foods high in sodium every day, why not just eat them once a week, or eat in a small plate to control the potions. Greasy fried food and junk food with lots of added flavors etc., can ruin your skin leading to pimples, acne etc. Eating wisely will help your digestive system. Most cases of bad skin come from the things we eat, so pay close attention.
- Removing dead skin is a must. Keeping your skin exfoliated is something we all know we should be doing. One can either buy a good exfoliater or make one at home. Take few grains of sugar on your palm and add few drops of lemon. Rub the grains in between your hands to smooth out the pointy edges. Now,

rub your face gently with this scrub. Another nice trick can be to rinse your face with warm water and than take a tablespoon of salt into the palm of one hand and place it on the bar of soap. Make sure the soap is wet. Massage your face with the solution in an upward motion to avoid any wrinkles and sagging. Rinse your face clean with warm water. Do not rub for a long time as this will generate heat, causing skin burn.

- Keeping safe from sun rays should be a part of your life. This will not only lower your chances of being diagnosed with skin cancer but it will also help you to keep your skin healthy. Use sun block when outdoors. Cover your head and carry an umbrella.
- Its best to shave during your shower time preferably with warm water. Make sure that your face is nicely wet. Invest in a good quality shaving brush and cream. Shave in the direction of the beard growth. Rinse with warm water and soothe the face with an after shave lotion.

Chapter 18

Tricks for glowing skin

- Always use the cleansing, toning and moisturizing (CTM) method to keep your skin glowing.
- Never sleep with your makeup on. Use some baby oil to wipe the face clean, rinse and apply moisturizer
- Moisturize, make sure to apply a face moisturizer every morning and night.
- Keep a humidifier in the bedroom to keep skin soft and supple.
- Exfoliate at night three times a week to slough off dead skin cells and reveal brighter skin. Do not rub for a long time, or you will land up with internal skin burn making you look darker. For acne-prone skin, try using baking soda as an exfoliator.
- Cover your head or carry umbrella for protecting your skin when going outdoors
- Give yourself a facial massage a couple times a week. It will help increase circulation so skin looks its best.

- Never compromise on the quality of makeup. Buy the best you can and also keep an eye on the expiry date.
- To help boost circulation, splash cold water on your face first thing in the morning.
- Don't keep touching your face and hair with dirty hands all the time.
- Do not lean your face on things which collect sebum or skin residue like phone receivers, metro and train walls.
- Use sun protecting factor (SPF) every day to prevent future dulling of the skin. Tthe number next to SPF indicates the time for protection. Such as SPF 15 means, protection for 150 minutes and SPF 30 means 300 minutes and so on.
- Go make up free sometimes to let your skin breathe
- Wash your hands before you wash your face. This keeps bacteria away from getting onto your face.
- If you wear shades or reading glasses, then clean them regularly to avoid residue oil to rub and create bacteria.
- Drink at least 8 glasses of water every day to flush out your system.
- Include plenty of salads and fruits in your diet.
- Don't stay up late. Try and get at least 5 hours of sleep.
- Dry your face with a soft towel. A regular one can be too rough for the delicate skin of the face.
- Mix mashed papaya pulp, honey, two tablespoons of milk powder for a home mask to restore glowing skin.
- Mix few berries and some plain yogurt. Apply for 15 minutes and then rinse off.
- Mix one egg white with one tablespoon of honey for instant brightening and glow. Apply for 10 minutes and rinse off.
- Blend half a banana, half sweet potato, 2 teaspoons olive oil, and add 1 teaspoon sugar. Apply the mask for 15 minutes then rinse.
- Mix little aloe vera gel, two tablespoons coconut oil, one teaspoon vitamin E oil, and two tablespoons almond oil and use as moisturizer.

- Mix one teaspoon sugar, half a teaspoon honey and a squeeze of lemon juice to use as a scrub.
- Make your legs glow by mixing one cup water, three tablespoons almond oil, and one teaspoon of vitamin e oil into a spray bottle.
- Cut few strawberries, kiwi, mint leaves and cucumber slices. Blend them with water, and freeze ice cube trays. Rub the frozen ice cube over your face for pore shrinking. It works excellently before make up.
- Take some grapefruit juice, carrot juice and plain yogurt. Apply to your face for 15 minutes, and then rinse off.
- Cook food with olive oil. It's full of antioxidant-rich vitamins that moisturize the skin from within.
- Cut back on the carbohydrates. These will make your insulin levels rise, which can keep skin from looking its best.
- Drink warm water with lemon first thing each morning. The lemon will help draw toxins from your body and restore a nice glow to the skin.

Chapter 19
Flash your pearly whites

Dental hygiene and a dazzling smile are both very important for a contestant. Bad breath also known as Halitosis can be very embarrassing and tough on those around you. This is something no one will dare to tell you on your face for fear of hurting you, but they will consciously start avoiding you. So, the entire responsibility of having a fresh breath is in your hands only.

No one is ever an exception. Everybody has nasty breath at some point like when you get out of bed in morning. If you are not sure whether your mouth stinks, ask a trusted friend or maybe small your dental floss after you've used it.

Breath stinks due to many reasons. It could be plague deposits, wrong brushing technique, digestive problems, smelly food, smoking etc. The following points will help you in dealing with bad breath and keep your mouth smelling fresh all the time:

- Brush and clean in between each tooth to remove plague. Place your brush at 45 degree angle and brush with up and down strokes gently.
- Use tongue cleaner or your brush to clean your tongue after every brushing routine. Tongue is where the most bacteria thrive. Deposits on the tongue can cause foul smell. Brush twice daily and floss every alternate day.
- A mouth rinse in addition to daily brushing and flossing cleans and keeps the mouth smelling fresh longer.
- Change your tooth brush every 3-4 months even if it looks as good as new.
- If you have an important pageant interview or would be meeting a lot of people, avoid having smelly and spicy food like raw onions, and garlicky dishes. Avoid smoking before you go in for the meeting. Also, keep a mouth spray or a mouth freshener handy.
- Most of the people who skip breakfast land up with bad breath. I suggest, do have something for breakfast even if it's just a cookie.
- Cough, cold, constipation must be kept in check and if you suffer from any of these ailments, be conscious that your mouth will definitely have bad smell so keep freshening it with a spray.
- Never avoid breakfast after a sound sleep at night.

Not only fresh breath, but a beautiful smile is also an extremely important quality in creating a winning pageant image. The smile needs to be the best it can be, especially with close-up head shots, and one-on-one interview situations

The most common dental problems that stop you from having a winning smile are yellow, poorly shaped, crooked, chipped or spaced teeth. Thankfully, yellow teeth can easily be whitened with dental bleaching techniques. There are plenty of home tooth-whitening systems available which can be used at home with a custom mouthpiece that holds a bleaching agent. One has to put it in and wear it every night while sleeping for about two weeks.

Uneven and crooked teeth with wide spaces can be corrected with cosmetic dental procedures. If you're worried about the crooked

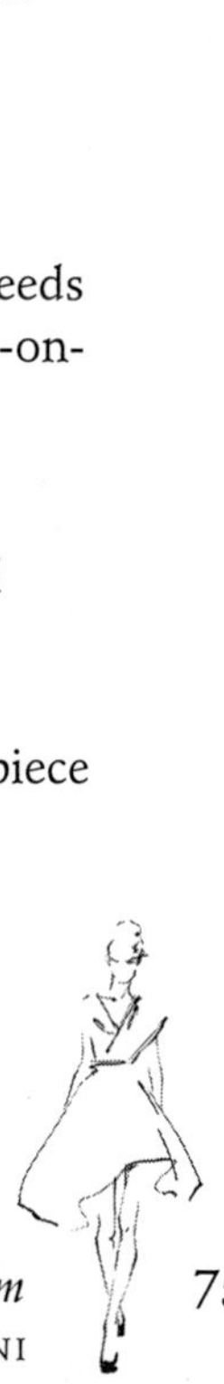

or uneven teeth, consult an orthodontist. Nowadays you even get transparent braces. Make it a habit to visit your dentist every six months for scaling and for check up.

Chapter 20

Your crowning glory

What is hair? Its made up of dead cells. We have thousands of hair follicles on our head that produce hair. Each follicle produces hair continuously throughout life. It keeps falling and regenerating. Live hair cells are generated inside the follicle by the papilla. As the new cells grow, the old cells die and are forced out of follicle towards the scalp. The dead cells are compressed to form a protein called keratin. The hair shaft we see is keratin emerging out from inside the scalp. Small amount of water or moisture along with the binding agent holds the hair firmly.

There are different textures of hair such as straight hair, which will not hold any curl. Wavy hair, which is very fizzy and resists any styling, Curly hair, which appears straight when wet, but curls on drying and kinky hair, which is very kinky, tightly curled and very wiry. Along with being of different textures, the hair is also of many types. Mainly being normal, oily, dry or a combination of all.

It's difficult to care for your hair unless you know the type of hair you possess as the care is entirely different for all. So, how can you find out what is the type of hair you have?

Let's do a simple test. Take a tissue paper and press it at the center of the head, and on the sides behind the ears. Remember to just press the tissue paper and not rub it. A careful look at the tissue now will tell you about your hair type. If the paper looks dry after this test, your hair is of dry type, if there are oily traces, then it's oily. Combination and normal is difficult to identify. But if you check carefully and find that your scalp is oily and the ends are dry, then you have combination hair. If your hair is not dry, greasy, and feels the same from shaft to ends and is shiny, you have normal hair.

Chapter 21

Different hair, different care

Care for dry hair

- People with dry hair should use shampoo with low PH. Look carefully at the label and avoid shampoo which has lemon or your hair will get even more rough and dry. Just like the shampoo, use conditioner with low PH. Apply it immediately after the shampoo and let it rest on your hair for at least five minutes.
- Avoid washing you hair everyday as it will strip away even a bit of sebum the scalp is generating.
- Massage a little bit of butter from scalp to ends. Butter is heavy and sticky. It makes the hair softer and smooth. Now, cover your hair and keep it for at least 30 minutes. Take a normal shampoo and you will be surprised to see super soft silky hair.
- Never apply cold oil. Always heat it or make it lukewarm.
- Avoid using too many styling products and coloring products. If you do so, then go for a fortnightly hair spa to retain the health of your hair.
- Reduce the use of heat appliances like hair dryers, hair rollers, hair irons etc. Air dry your hair when wet. Use heat resistant sprays and low intensifying temperature if you cant avoid using heat appliances.
- Drink plenty of water and always cover your hair when you go outdoors.

Care for oily hair

- Select shampoo with high sodium lauryl sulfate and low lanolin. Even anti-dandruff shampoos works well for oily hair.
- While shampooing, leave it on for few minutes for the lather to work. One round of shampooing is not enough, repeat it at least twice to remove the oil completely.
- Squeeze a lemon in a cup of water. After shampoo, towel dry your hair. Now apply this lemon water and leave it for five minutes, then rinse again with cold water

- Vinegar, which is also acidic in nature, can also help a lot in keeping oil in control. Mix one cup vinegar with one cup of water and pour it over your hair after the final rinse. Don't worry about the smell, will disappear in a while.
- You can even try using mouthwash if your hair is extremely oily, to reduce production of sebum in the scalp. Take half a cup of witch hazel and half a cup of mouth wash. They are both astringents. Dip a cotton wool swab in the mixture and dab it all over your scalp (not hair) after the shampoo and rinse.
- Don't keep touching your hair the whole day and also wash your comb everyday to avoid slow oil secretion.
- Its also very important to rinse your hair properly so that no shampoo residue is left. If so, your hair will appear oily and heavy. People with oily hair should avoid using conditioner. If you still want to do so, use it only at the hair ends.

Care for combination hair

- Apply shampoo only on the scalp and give a gentle rub so that the excess sebum is removed. Applying shampoo till the hair ends will dry out the hair. Your ends do not need too much rubbing with shampoo. Just give them a gentle squeeze. Reverse the process with the conditioner. Apply it only at the ends and not at the scalp.
- Use olive oil or jojoba oil to massage the hair strands as they are good moisturizers.
- Use wet and hot towel treatment on and off to keep sebum in control.
- Trim dry ends once in a while for good growth. Combination hair, just like dry hair is prone to split ends.

Chapter 22

Lets nail it

Manicure/pedicure

While communicating three things are noticed very prominently: your hands as they gesture, your face and your eyes. Many a times, a good image gets ruined when people notice unkempt hands and nails with scum trapped in them, chopped nail polish, broken nails.

In spite of our best efforts to keep hands protected, the everyday chores often wreaks havoc on the nails and cuticles of our hands and feet. A person's hands and feet are the most used and abused part of the body and they certainly require some pampering. Please do not ignore them. If you do not have time to go to a parlor, you can use the following tips at home to give your hands and feet a wow effect.

The first thing you need is to gather all the supplies. Tools required for at-home manicure are: non-alcoholic nail polish remover; nail file; cuticle cream; orange stick; nail polish of your choice; top coat; hand lotion; two bowls with warm water and soap to dip hands; soft towel.

Manicure steps

- Remove old polish. Non-acetone nail remover acts much slower than acetone, therefore if you are trying to remove dark color, use acetone based remover. Nails turn slightly yellow due to dark nail shades and may need buffing before you repolish them.
- File and shape nails preferably with a soft sandpaper file. File the sides inward for a flatter, edge to avoid any splits.
- Buff using gentle strokes. Buffing helps the polish to stick and smoothens the surface of the nail. Avoid overdoing as you will weaken your nails.
- Soak your hands in warm water and scrub gently. Remove and dry with a soft towel
- Massage cuticle oil into cuticles, pushing them back gently with a cuticle pusher. Avoid cutting your cuticles to prevent infection.
- Remove any oil residue before polishing. Base coat will also help polish to stick better. Don't apply polish too close to the skin.
- Going by the latest trends, the classic French manicure is most popular. Some people like to tip the nail with fun colors or with gold and silver instead of white. You can even try nail art using some ready made stick on designs and covering with base coat. Self-stick nail art jewels, crystals are also very popular.
- Paint nails using two coats of polish. Brush the polish down the nail using soft strokes. Cover with the top coat and be sure to cap the edge to let the polish stay longer. Clean up around the nails for neat look.

Pedicure steps

- Remove old polish from toes with acetone polish remover.
- Soak feet in warm water using soap and a capful of hydrogen peroxide to remove yellow stains from toenails. You can also add some rose water or rose petals.
- On the wet foot, use a foot file to smooth out the skin and remove the dead one.
- Next, apply cuticle remover and trim your nails into shape.
- Use an orange stick to push back the cuticle, and then clean the nail.
- Buff the nails to remove any stains, and then massage the feet with moisturizing lotion.
- Clean and dry the nails.
- Use toe separator or wind some cotton between toes to separate. Apply a base coat, two coats of polish, and finish with a top coat.

Chapter 23
Be fit physically

Exercising daily is an important routine which a beauty contestant should follow. If it is done improperly it may actually worsen your health. Start with as little as 5-10 minutes of exercise a day, and work your way up. As your energy and health improve, you will be able to do larger amounts of exercise, which will lead to weight loss and increased energy.

You need to exercise for one hour, five days a week to see some changes happening in body weight. This level of exercise is only required if you are overweight.

Cardio exercise that increases your breathing and heart rate is best for your daily fitness routine. If you enjoy aerobics, you could do two half hour sessions of fast-paced aerobics on nonconsecutive days, along with 10-15 minutes of cycling session.

Another alternative could be walking. The more vigorous your walking pace, the more dramatic the results. Walk at a steady pace that is fast enough to cause your heart rate to go up. Once you become comfortable with a routine, it is important to increase the time and also intensity in order to continue benefiting from it. Once you get in shape, you'll need to walk for more than two hours, do jogging, sprinting, or strength training, instead of merely walking.

Strength-training builds and tone muscles. Remember not to work the same muscle groups back to back. Alternate your muscle groups, with up to three sets of 8 to 12 repetitions for each exercise. Some common strength-training exercises are pushups, pull-ups, crunches and squats.

If you are going to use exercise for weight loss, remember that weight bearing exercise like swimming and bicycling, are not effective for weight loss.

At the beginning of each workout, warm up your body with five minutes of light activity, like walking or jogging in place, and gentle stretches. Do the same after you finish exercising. Stretch each major muscle group starting with your neck and working your way down your body. Hold the stretch as long as you can. Swimming is one of the best exercises, working all your major muscles

Keep an eye on your pace. If you can comfortably talk you aren't working hard enough. However, if you are breathing so heavily that you cannot carry on a conversation at all, then you are exercising too hard and need to cut back a bit. Creating a concrete daily workout schedules is an important first step toward creating the fitness you desire.

Chapter 24

Eat consciously

Many a times in spite of having healthy and balanced food, clean and healthy cooking, we still land up with upset stomach and many such digestive problems. One needs to check on the way we eat and what we drink with meals. These simple changes in our everyday meals will make us feel much healthier and disease free.

The manner in which the food is prepared can affect the meal. When prepared with love, food tends to taste better and promotes stimulating of the flow of gastric juices, encouraging good digestion and assimilation of food.

In today's fast paced world, we are on the run all the time. Sitting together as a family on the table and eating dinner seems to be out of fashion. Eating dinner in front of the TV is now becoming a way of life. No wonder that so many people are suffering from digestion problems such as gas, bloating, stomach pain, constipation, heartburn, and fatigue.

One needs a calm atmosphere in order to process and absorb nutrients from a good meal. It's important to be in a relaxed posture with awareness about the taste, texture, and smell of the food. Avoid standing, walking, or driving your way through a meal.

Ayurveda recommends that having an inch piece of fresh ginger with a few drops of lemon juice dipped in salt before meals activates the salivary glands, producing the necessary enzymes for easy digestion

Avoid cold drinks and ice-cold foods in general. This is like putting off a fuming fire. Very cold water extinguishes the digestive fire. Anything straight out of the refrigerator is too cold for the digestion. Juices should be taken at room temperature without any added ice. Cold mixed with warm can cause stomach cramps, bloating and general discomfort in the stomach area.

Dinner should be lighter ideally to be eaten before 8:00 p.m. Late night meals interfere with effective working of the digestive system.

Practice good eating habits

Just as important as a what you eat is the manner in which you eat. Poor digestion may simply be due to bad habits.

One of the biggest digestive crimes is overeating. Body can produce only a certain volume of digestive juices. Large meals put a lot of pressure on digestion. Moderate portions, on the other hand, are digested more comfortably. Overeating can also lead to obesity.

Follow a regular time for breakfast, lunch and dinner. Skipping meals can lead to excessive hunger, which often results in overeating. After disposing of one meal, the digestive organs need rest. At least five or six hours should intervene between meals.

Eat slowly and in a relaxed pace. When you're relaxed, you tend to chew your food more completely; gastric and intestinal juices flow more freely. When you eat too fast, you don't chew food thoroughly and often swallow more air, causing heartburn, belching, and bloating or excess gas.

Too much water or liquids taken with the meals will dilute the digestive juices, and slow digestion. If anything is needed to quench the thirst, drink some lukewarm water before or after the meal. Avoid cold drinks, tea, coffee, beer, wine, or any spirited liquids with meals.

Bathing or exercising vigorously, running etc., before or after eating draws the blood to the surface of the body or to the brain, thus diverting it from the digestive organs, and slow down the digestion.

Never forget to wash your hands before eating even if they appear clean, as you may be carrying harmful invisible bacteria. Also, wash your fruits and vegetables well to remove and chemicals sticking on them.

Chapter 25

What to eat*

A healthy eating plan gives your body the nutrients it needs every day while staying within your daily calorie goal for weight loss. A healthy eating plan will also lower your risk for heart disease and other health conditions.

What you must have

Green vegetables and fruits

In order to maintain good health it is not only important to look after your body by doing exercises but it is also important to have a well-balanced diet complete with green vegetables as they contain all important nutrients required for growth and maintenance of health. A diet consisting of insufficient amount of vegetables leads to deficiencies in the body which is great detriment to our health. Green vegetables provide sufficient quantity of fibre, vitamins, calcium, iron, and beta-carotene and vitamin C, riboflavin and folic acid. Hence, they must be consumed by children, pregnant and nursing women in generous quantities. Vegetables have various advantages. Due to their high

*: *Source: http://www.sethmaximustristan.com/#!healthy-eating*

fiber content they aid in digestion. Most importantly, the consumption of leafy green vegetables helps prevent the onset of diabetes, cardiovascular diseases and stroke. It is recommended to consume a minimum of three cups of green vegetables, specially the dark ones, every week. Some green vegetables that a person may include in his/her diet include spinach, cabbage, lettuce,spring onion, broccoli etc

Green vegetables retards age-related cellular degeneration and are helpful for skin, hair and nails. Green veggies also act as great detoxifying foods. They aid in the removal of toxins from the body and they also play a great role in strengthening the immune system. Fruits and vegetables are the foundation of a healthy diet. They are low in calories and are nutrient dense, which means they are packed with vitamins, minerals, antioxidants, and fiber.

Try to eat a rainbow of fruits and vegetables every day and with every meal—the brighter the better. Deeply colored fruits and vegetables contain higher concentrations of vitamins, minerals, and antioxidants—and different colors provide different benefits, so eat a variety. Aim for a minimum of five portions each day. Some great choices include:

- Greens. Branch out beyond bright and dark green lettuce. Mustard greens, broccoli, and Chinese cabbage are just a few of the options—all packed with calcium, magnesium, iron, potassium, zinc, and vitamins A, C, E, and K.
- Sweet vegetables. Naturally sweet vegetables—such as corn, carrots, beets, sweet potatoes, yams, onions—add healthy sweetness to your meals and reduce your cravings for other sweets.
- Fruit. Fruit is a tasty, satisfying way to fill up on fiber, vitamins, and antioxidants. Berries are cancer-fighting, apples provide fiber, oranges and mangos offer vitamin C, and so on.

A daily regimen of nutritional supplements is not going to have the same impact of eating right. That's because the benefits of fruits and vegetables don't come from a single vitamin or an isolated antioxidant.

Spices

They are an extremely important element in our food and any dish can be made tasty and nutritious at the same time by adding a few of the following spices. Turmeric or "haldi", is a spice used in almost every Indian dish. A compound in "haldi", curcumin, is responsible for decreasing bad cholesterol and chances of high blood pressure, increases blood circulation and prevents blood clotting which is essential in preventing heart attacks. Cardamom or "elaichi" promotes metabolism and helps burn body fat along with promoting digestion. So does cinnamon and cloves. Chillies contain a compound known as capsaicin which not only helps to increase metabolism but it also encourages the body to burn calories for 20 minutes after you eat it. Curry leaves are also good for weight loss and a popular weight loss remedy is to include 8 to 10 leaves in your daily diet. They reduce the fat deposits in the body and lower cholesterol levels. Garlic is another widely used spice which helps to reduce fat deposits thanks to the sulphur compound allicin in it.

Water

Water helps flush our systems of waste products and toxins, yet many people go through life dehydrated—causing tiredness, low energy, and headaches. It's common to mistake thirst for hunger, so staying well hydrated will also help you make healthier food choices.

Carbs

Choose healthy carbohydrates and fiber sources, especially whole grains, for long lasting energy. In addition to being delicious and satisfying, whole grains are rich in phytochemicals and antioxidants, which help to protect against coronary heart disease, certain cancers, and diabetes. Studies have shown people who eat more whole grains tend to have a healthier heart. Healthy carbs (sometimes known as good carbs) include whole grains, beans, fruits, and vegetables. Healthy carbs are digested slowly, helping you feel full longer and keeping blood sugar and insulin levels stable.

Unhealthy carbs (or bad carbs) are foods such as white flour, refined sugar, and white rice that have been stripped of all bran, fiber, and nutrients. Unhealthy carbs digest quickly and cause spikes in blood sugar levels and energy.

Whole grains

Include a variety of whole grains in your healthy diet, including whole wheat, brown rice, millet, quinoa, and barley. Experiment with different grains to find your favorites.

Make sure you're really getting whole grains. Be aware that the words stone-ground, multi-grain, 100% wheat, or bran can be deceptive. Look for the words "whole grain" or "100% whole wheat" at the beginning of the ingredient list. In the US, Canada, and some other countries, there are Whole Grain Stamps that distinguish between partial whole grain and 100% whole grain.

Try mixing grains as a first step to switching to whole grains. If whole grains like brown rice and whole wheat pasta don't sound good at first, start by mixing what you normally use with the whole grains. You can gradually increase the whole grain to 100%.

Avoid refined foods such as breads, pastas, and breakfast cereals that are not whole grain.

Eat healthy fats & avoid unhealthy fats

Good sources of healthy fat are needed to nourish your brain, heart, and cells, as well as your hair, skin, and nails. Foods rich in certain Omega-3 fats called EPA and DHA are particularly important and can reduce cardiovascular disease, improve your mood, and help prevent dementia.

Monounsaturated fats, from plant oils like canola oil, peanut oil, and olive oil, as well as avocados, nuts (like almonds, hazelnuts, and pecans), and seeds (such as pumpkin, sesame) are also healthy.

Polyunsaturated fats, including Omega-3 and Omega-6 fatty acids, are found in fatty fish such as salmon, herring, mackerel, anchovies, sardines, and some cold water fish oil supplements. Other sources of polyunsaturated fats are unheated sunflower, corn, soybean, flaxseed oils, and walnuts.

Reduce or eliminate from your diet saturated fats, found primarily in animal sources including red meat and whole milk dairy products and trans fats found in vegetable shortenings, some margarines, crackers, candies, cookies, snack foods, baked goods, and other processed foods made with partially hydrogenated vegetable oils. Avoid fried foods

Protein

Protein gives us the energy to get up and go—and keep going. Protein in food is broken down into the 20 amino acids that are the body's basic building blocks for growth and energy, and essential for maintaining cells, tissues, and organs. A lack of protein in our diet can slow growth, reduce muscle mass, lower immunity, and weaken the heart and respiratory system. Protein is particularly important for children, whose bodies are growing and changing daily.

Try different types of protein. Whether or not you are a vegetarian, trying different protein sources—such as beans, nuts, seeds, peas, tofu, and soy products—will open up new options for healthy mealtimes. Black beans, navy beans, garbanzos, and lentils are good options. Almonds, walnuts, pistachios, and pecans are great choices. Try tofu, soy milk, tempeh, and veggie burgers for a change.

Avoid salted or sugary nuts and refried beans. Focus on quality sources of protein like fresh fish, chicken or turkey, tofu, eggs, beans, or nuts. When you are having meat, chicken, or turkey, buy meat that is free of hormones and antibiotics.

Calcium

Calcium is one of the key nutrients that your body needs in order to stay strong and healthy. It is an essential building block for lifelong bone health in both men and women, as well as many other important functions. You and your bones will benefit from eating plenty of calcium-rich foods, limiting foods that deplete your body's calcium stores, and getting your daily dose of magnesium and vitamins D and K—nutrients that help calcium do its job.

Recommended calcium levels are 1000 mg per day; 1200 mg if you are over 50. Try to get as much of your daily calcium needs from food as possible and use only low-dose calcium supplements to make up any shortfall. Good sources of calcium include:

- Dairy: Dairy products are rich in calcium in a form that is easily digested and absorbed by the body. Sources include milk, yogurt, and cheese.
- Vegetables and greens: Many vegetables, especially leafy green ones, are rich sources of calcium. Try turnip greens, mustard greens, collard greens, kale, romaine lettuce, celery, broccoli, fennel, cabbage, summer squash, green beans, brussels sprouts, asparagus, and crimini mushrooms.
- Beans: For another rich source of calcium, try black beans, pinto beans, kidney beans, white beans, black-eyed peas, or baked beans.

Limit sugar and salt

Sugar causes energy ups and downs and can add to health and weight problems. Unfortunately, reducing the amount of candy, cakes, and desserts we eat is only part of the solution. Often you may not even be aware of the amount of sugar you're consuming each day. Large amounts of added sugar can be hidden in foods such as bread, canned soups and vegetables, pasta sauce, margarine, instant mashed potatoes, frozen dinners, fast food, soy sauce, and ketchup. Here are some tips:

- Avoid sugary drinks. One 12-oz soda has about 10 teaspoons of sugar in it, more than the daily recommended limit! Try sparkling water with lemon or a splash of fruit juice.
- Sweeten foods yourself. Buy unsweetened iced tea, plain yogurt, or unflavored oatmeal, for example, and add sweetener (or fruit) yourself. You're likely to add far less sweetener than the manufacturer would have.
- Eat naturally sweet food such as fruit, peppers, or natural peanut butter to satisfy your sweet tooth. Keep these foods handy instead of candy or cookies.

Most of us consume too much salt in our diets. Eating too much salt can cause high blood pressure and lead to other health problems. Try to limit sodium intake to 1,500 to 2,300 mg per day, the equivalent of one teaspoon of salt.

- Avoid processed or pre-packaged foods. Processed foods like canned soups or frozen dinners contain hidden sodium that quickly surpasses the recommended limit.
- Be careful when eating out. Most restaurant and fast food meals are loaded with sodium. Some offer lower-sodium choices or you can ask for your meal to be made without salt. Most gravy and sauces are loaded with salt, so ask for it to be served on the side.
- Opt for fresh or frozen vegetables instead of canned vegetables.
- Cut back on salty snacks such as potato chips, nuts, and pretzels.
- Check labels and choose low-salt or reduced-sodium products, including breakfast cereals.
- Slowly reduce the salt in your diet to give your taste buds time to adjust.

Chapter 26

Understanding your facial shape

Once I had picked up a beautiful pair of round chunky earrings similar to what I had seen a prominent film star wear at the red carpet. I worked my entire outfit around it and was sure that I will be loaded with compliments. I landed up at the party brimming with confidence and yes, all heads turned. I knew I have achieved what I wanted till a close friend came and said " Hey, you seem to have gained a lot of weight…Any good news"? Nooooooo….I said, what made her think that? She said that my face was looking fat and filled up, that's why. The shocking statement made me realize that something on or around my face is not right. Of course it's the round earrings…but why? Why did they make me look fat? Later when I sat through a session on determining face shape did I realize that my face shape is round and the round earrings made me look rounder and plumper.

As the face is the first thing we notice about a person, the wrong styling for your face shape can easily backfire. Understanding your face shape is very important as it helps you select the best accessory, hair and clothes. All people have one of 6 face shapes: round, square, long (or "oblong"), heart, diamond or oval.

When determining your facial shape we you will need to take a look of your front profile. You'll need:

- Mirror. Big enough to see your whole face and the area from your chest.
- Hair clips to pull hair from your face and expose your ears.
- A top that shows the full length of your neck and chest.

Tape method

Sit in front of the mirror. Avoid tilting your head as side profiles can alter your perception of your own face shape and won't always show the true shape of your jaw line and cheekbones. Keep a relaxed face—do not smile as this can make your lower face pointier and longer. Now look at your face in the mirror and measure yourself:

- How wide is the widest point of your forehead compared to your jaw line?
- How prominent are your cheekbones compared to your jaw line and forehead?
- Is the widest point of your jaw line wider than my forehead?
- How long is your face? Finally, measure the length of your face by using the "cross shape method." Put the ruler just under the eyes and measure from ear to ear. Then place the ruler at the top of your forehead at your hairline and measure to your chin. Your ratio will either be 1 (your width) to 1 1/2 (your length) or 1 to 1 or 1 to 2.

Write down the measured details as this can help you decide on your face shape. This is how the shapes will be!

- Oblong faces are longer than they are wide.
- Heart faces have an upside-down triangle shaped face, with pointy chin and medium-to-wide forehead and cheeks.
- Square faces are about as long as they are wide—their cheek and length measurements are within about an inch or two of each other.
- Oval faces are like an upside-down egg. They are longer than they are wide, with a forehead that is slightly wider than the jaw line and a gently rounded chin.
- Round faces, are about as wide as they are long. However, they have a relatively small forehead and a small, curved jaw line.
- Triangular faces are widest at the bottom and skinniest at the top.
- Diamond faces are widest at the cheekbones, with a tapering forehead and a pointed chin. They are longer than they are wide

Drawing method

- Stand in front of a mirror looking directly forward with your back straight, head high, and shoulders back. If you have fringes or bangs, pull them away from the face. Make sure the lighting is over head and not pointing towards you.
- Trace the outline of your face. Using lipstick, eye brow pencil, lip liner, or a marker, carefully draw the outline of your face in the mirror. Starting from the bottom of your chin, proceed up to the edge of your face on one side past your cheek bones, follow the curve of your hairline, go down the other side of your face, and end up back at your chin. Try to stay as still as possible while

you do this. Don't include your ears—just the edges of your face.

Now, determine which category (or categories) you fit into!

- Oblong: the drawing should resemble a tall rectangle with rounded corners.
- Round: If the drawing resembles a circle, you might have a round face.
- Square: Your drawing will not be rectangular or round but will have an angular jaw.
- Oval: The drawing will resemble an egg.
- Heart-shaped: The drawing will be almost oblong with a pointed chin.
- Triangular: Your outline will look like a triangle.
- Diamond: Your outline will look like a diamond with angular cheeks.

Knowing your face shape guides you to your best hairstyles; haircuts; sunglasses and eye wear; earrings and necklaces; necklines and print tops; hats; makeup techniques.

Chapter 27

Oval face

An oval face shape is considered to be the most desirable and an ideal face shape as it's easy to style compared to the other face shapes. An oval can carry any haircut and jewelry style due to its balanced proportions.

Features and styling of oral face

- Slightly wider cheekbone area, right below eye level and at the mid-points of the sides.
- Jaw line is neither narrow nor too wide, but softly rounded, with narrower at the temples.
- Hairline is slightly wider than lower face just like an inverted egg.

- The best hair cuts for this shape are side part bob, pixie cut and tousled shoulder-length. These styles help enhance the oval shape.
- Avoid bangs and dangling hair in front of the face as they will hide the face shape. If you still want have bangs than sweep them to one side, or part it in the middle and sweep it to both sides.
- The best eye frames for oval shape are square with gently rounded edges. High temple shades will also look good showing off the cheekbones.
- They look good in any kind of necklines. However if you have a short neck, go for slimming necklines like low v and scoop.
- Head scarves and headbands will draw a lot of attention to oval face.

Chapter 28

Round face

Characteristics of a round face shape

- In one visual look it appears like a circle.
- It is approximately as wide as it is long.
- The shape has gradual curving lines rather than hard angles
- Jaw line is full and round.

To sum up a round face—it's almost the same in width as it is in length with no sharp corners at the jaw.

I have a round face and often been complimented for my hair style. My hairstyle gives the illusion of an oval face. The visual effect of certain styles will either enhance or look sloppy based on the proportions of your face. It's tough to plan a hairstyle if you don't know what shape your face is!

- Keep a little hair out in front of the ear and do not tuck all of it back. Doing so will change the width of your face, cuts off the circle and tricks the eye to believe that the width of the face is narrow and stops there. Lot of people who have round faces try to hide behind lot of hair, framing the cheeks and making one look fat. Avoid the hair curtain and let your perfect features show by the simple trick of some loose hair in front.

- A straight or a zig-zag side part is great for a round face as it changes the focal point of the face's length. People won't be able to clearly make out if your face has the same length and width. Try to add some height on top of the crown. Very straight or very curly hair should be avoided as it can accentuate the roundness either by sticking to the face or framing it. Never let the ends of the hair fall directly onto your jaw line as it emphasizes your round face. If you have bangs or step cut, it should flow past your cheekbones.
- The best way to change the shape of a round face is contouring. One needs to bring out the cheek bones and cut away the extra width. A round face requires darker foundation to contour the temples, cheekbones and the sides of your jaws. This technique will make a round face appear more oval. Create angles with high lighter (two shades lighter than your natural skin tone) in the middle of your forehead and on your chin. This will help bring these areas forward to create a more angular look.

Round face is unable to project features well so highlight the eyes and lips. Use a darker shade of eye shadow toward the outer portion of your eyelid to raise the ends of the eyes. Use a dark lip color and add a dab of lip gloss.

Eye wear is a great way which can confuse the onlooker about the face shape. Sun glasses should reflect the scale of your face; so if you have a wide round face, look for oversized glasses and opposite for small round faces.

Long, chandelier and slimming angular style of jewelry is best for round faces. Go for oval and pointy earrings and pendants. Super chunky chokers and horizontal neckwear is a no. Earrings should flow past your chin as it elongates the neck.

Chapter 29

Oblong face

The oblong face is very close to the oval but it has more length and less width.

Characteristics of an oblong face

- Oblong face is like an egg.
- Your face is noticeably longer than it is wide
- You may have unnoticeable and flattish cheekbones.
- You may have a narrow mid-face.
- Oblong faces have a long chin or long forehead.

Features and styles for oblongs

- Any hairstyle that is flat and blunt will look nice on oblong face. Hairstyles that shortens the chin and forehead, add broadness to the sides of the cheekbones.
- Another hairstyle that may look good too is the one at neckline with both volume and width, especially at cheekbone level.
- A side part will help break up a long face.
- One-length haircut shortens an oblong face
- Layers add more body around the midsection
- Too much height on top and super long hair length should be avoided Long hair which is voluminous on the sides of the cheekbones will look very nice.
- Get an eye wear that does not go beyond the widest part of the face as this will make the face look narrower.
- One shoulder straps, square and boat neck bring out the beauty of the face.
- Avoid putting a head scarf of headband as this will make the face appear shorter.
- While contouring shade the top of your forehead along the hairline, and the bottom of your chin. Highlight the hollows of the cheeks.

Chapter 30

Diamond face

Characteristics of a diamond face

- Cheekbones are often high and pointed being the widest part of this face.
- Forehead is narrower than cheekbones and is almost of the same width as the jaw line and chin.
- Forehead may be wide and tapers at the hairline.
- The chin is usually narrow and pointy.
- The jaw line is wide and slightly fleshy, but it is still narrower than your cheek area.
- The face appears slightly longer than it is wide.

Try and get a chin length bob cut as it adds a bit of width to the chin area. Tuck the hair behind the ears to show off the beautiful cheekbone and chin structure. Side swept bangs will help hide the narrow forehead as well as show off the great cheekbones

Avoid very short hairstyles. Also, stay away from hairstyles that add fullness at the cheeks as that make your mid face wider and out of balance.

Get the sun glasses that are no wider than the cheekbones and frames with soft curves such as round, oval and rounded rectangle.

Get the jewelry pieces which are narrower on top and wider at the bottom such as tear, pear and triangle. Long chandelier earrings look nice on you because they add fullness to your chin.

The necklaces should have rounded beads and designs. Medium length necklace will look better than long ones as the long necklace will elongate your chin and make your jaw line narrower.

Contour by shading your chin and the edges of your face along the hairline. Highlight the four corners of your face.

Chapter 31

Heart face

A heart-shaped face appears like closed fist having wide cheekbones and a narrow and pointy chin. The shape looks like a normal heart, hence the name.

Characteristics of a heart shape

- Forehead and hairline are wider than your lower face.
- You may have wide cheekbones and angular jaw line.
- Chin is pointy and somewhat prominent.
- You may have a dip on the your hairline.

Features and styling for heart shape

- Try to create an illusion of a slimmer forehead to balance out with your lower part.
- To draw attention away from your wide forehead, the top layers should be soft and long
- Long, wavy layers that sweep across cheekbones will tone down the chin as well.
- Hair cuts till jaw length give the appearance of a fuller chin.
- Long hair with bangs will show off the cheekbones and keep the forehead looking narrow.
- Avoid too-clingy hairstyles.
- The eye frames should be angular and square. Oversized sunglasses will also look very nice.
- Best jewelry pieces are the ones that add width to your jaw line—such as chandelier, tear, pear and triangle.
- Rounded necklines look best with your narrow jaw line.
- V-neck emphasizes your chin.
- The heart-shaped is like an inverted triangle needing contour at the temples and cheeks. Highlight the forehead, under the eyes and chin to draw attention to the center of the face.

Chapter 32

Triangular face

The triangular face shape has a jaw line that appears wide or full and appears prominent.

Characteristics of a triangular face

- Jaw line is wider and fuller than the forehead and cheekbones.
- Face shape may sometimes appear round or squarish.
- Facial structure is narrow at your cheekbones and temple.
- Jaw line is very prominent, so to balance the shape, fullness has to be added at the temples to trim down the jaw line.

Features and styles for triangles

- You can hide your forehead with bangs or mid-part hairstyles.
- Add width to your forehead by having a voluminous hair style.
- A lot of textured and layered hairstyle on top of the crown and sides will look very flattering.
- Zig-zag part or off center parts will look nicer than the center part.
- Asymmetrical bob starting below the chin in front gradually getting shorter on the back looks nice on these faces.
- Try and avoid sleek and tight hairstyles because they'll only highlight the wide jaw line.
- Get the eye frames that are heavy at the top. Cat eye and oval glasses will look very nice.
- Wear earrings that are long rather than wide.
- Wear a mid length or necklace to draw the attention downwards.
- Low necklines will help slim your jaw line and chin area.
- Stay away from chokers.
- Contour the corners of your jaw. Apply high lighter along your hairline at the top of your forehead.

Chapter 33
Square face

The square face shows a lot of strength & power with a sculptured look.

Characteristics of a square face shape

- The jaw line is square and angular
- The width of cheekbones and forehead is almost similar
- The width of jaw line and forehead is also similar

Square faces are of two types: 1. Rectangular that looks like an elongated square, and 2. Square that appears kind of roundish. Even if these are two different sizes and proportions, they both share the square jaw line. Also the styling of both these faces is same.

How to style your square face

- Deflect the angle of the jaw by wearing oval or rounded jewelry shapes.
- Try to get layered hairstyles and soft waves to draw the eyes to the chin. Layers and asymmetric styles help soften your face.
- Avoid blunt haircuts, straight bangs and chin-length bob cuts as they make your face look harsh and emphasize your strong jaw line.
- Side-swept bangs will look very nice.
- Get sun glasses which have a catty shape and high on forehead. The main purpose is to keep the focus on the lovely chin.
- To contour, shade the four corners of your face, along the top outer edges of your forehead and corners of your jaw.

Chapter 34
Know your body shape

It's important for each participant to identify their body shape. Just because a garment looks cool on a mannequin or on your favorite star, it does not mean it will look same on you. Their body is certainly different than you. You need to know your body type before you pick up a dress. Your outfit should flatter your body!

To understand your body shape, the first thing you will need to do is to measure yourself. Grab a measuring tape and note down the following measurements: 1) across the middle of the chest; 2) your waist 1 inch above the belly button; and 3) your hips around the widest part. The main focus while measuring should be on body proportions and nor the height or weight.

There are basically 5 prominent body shapes. They being: 1: Apple; 2) Ruler or "H" shaped; 3) Hour Glass or "figure of Eight"; 4) Inverted triangles; and 5) Pear or Triangles.

- If your waist size is much larger compared to your hips and bust you have an Apple shaped body.
- If your body does not have a defined waist and is almost same proportions to shoulders and hips you are a ruler of "H" shaped body.
- If you're shoulders and hips are in balance with a well defined waist than you are a "figure of eight" or an hour glass.
- If you have broad chest and wide shoulders compared to waist and hips, you are an inverted triangle.
- If your lower half is much broader compared to waist and shoulders, you are a Pear or Triangle.

Wardrobe styling basically depends on body proportions. Once you are aware of which body shape category you belong, than it becomes easy for you to pick up your dresses, accessories and neck lines. Your clothes will fit better and flatter your body.

Keep the following in mind after you have identified your body shape:

Triangle or pear body shape

- Pear shapes have wider hips than shoulders.
- The waist is well-defined.
- Shoulders and torso is sharp and stomach is almost flat.
- Pear shape should highlight waist as that's their asset, add a

bit of volume to shoulders by using shoulder pads etc. and upper body and try to minimize the hips.

Dos and don'ts for pears

- Avoid wearing clothes that draw attention to hips and thighs, such as baggy pants, cargo pants or flared skirts.
- "A' Line skirts will camouflage wider hips.
- Hems of pants, skirts etc should be kept wide to balance the hips.
- Light-colored tops and dark-colored bottoms will hide the hips
- Boat neck, square neck and cowl necklines will compliment this shape.
- Try styles with shoulder pads, pleated shoulders and ruffles.
- Jackets should end right above the waist.
- Go for pointy-toed shoes to elongate your legs.

Inverted Triangles

Dos and don'ts

- Avoid bright colors on bottom.
- Wide-leg pants will look nice on you.
- Full skirts, flared skirts will make your body look balanced.
- Never wear spaghetti-strap tops or very deep cut sleeves.
- Avoid boat neckline tops.
- Wear tops that draw attention to your waistline.
- Experiment with high-waited styles.
- Wear clothes that create the illusion of a waist.

Ruler or "H "shaped body

Dos and don'ts

- Wear scoop neck and sweetheart tops to look curvier.
- Long jackets will create a lean look.
- Wear tops with collars, ruffles and details so that the focus is on the torso.
- Wear a good bra that will break the ruler shape.
- Add layer preferably of different colors to add more dimensions and draw attention away from body.

Apple shaped body

Dos and don'ts

- Always go for monochromatic looks.
- Wear v-neck tops to create the illusion of a longer torso.
- Wear a bra that offers good lift and support.
- Wear low waisted belts or at the smallest part of your waist.
- Conceal tummy bulge by wearing loose tops
- Boot cut and flared jeans will create an even line from the shoulders down.
- Wear short skirts to draw attention away from your tummy.

Hourglass or "figure of eight body"

Dos and don'ts

- Never wear baggy clothes, wear fitted clothes to show those curves.
- Wear a nice belt at the waist to enhance your hourglass shape.
- Try clingy wrap dresses.
- Spaghetti straps and cuts sleeves are just right for you
- Wear high-waisted skirts to show off your hips.
- In fact you will be able to carry all dresses very well.

Chapter 35

Clothing and personality

Have you ever bothered to check your wardrobe personality? It can tell so much about you.

Some people get totally confused when they go shopping. They might be fashion victims who are slaves to the latest fashion trends, but, even if they follow that...they may be feeling uncomfortable from within because somehow the dress is not projecting their true self.

They are mere copies of someone else. Knowing about your wardrobe personality is very helpful and helps one feel confident while choosing their dress.

Basically there are four clothing personalities, but sometimes people's persona may shift from one to a mixed, keeping the circumstances in mind.

- Dramatic: Very loud with their clothing, these kinds of personalities opt for clothes which get them noticed. They love to make bold statements. They get drawn to bold colors and striking combinations. They love to look funky and love to draw attention. They can go to extremes—one day they may be dressed to kill and the next day may go totally sober. Their main aim is to turn heads. Even though they may wear designer wear on and off they love to pick up stuff from streets as they have a knack of mixing and matching. They hate to fade out in the background. Their wardrobe is generally filled with tons of clothing often mismatched which they use to style themselves differently. They get very upset if they don't get noticed.
- Classic: Conservative and sophisticated, they tend to be much more self confident then their dramatic counterparts. Their choice of clothes is very conservative to reflect their personalities. They use their classic demeanor to reflect precision and strength. They are very sensible while buying their clothes and often look for quality over quantity. Their clothes would be expensive and also long lasting. Their look is timeless with sober colors, clean lines, and well cut clothes. Their jewelry, makeup, grooming...all are understated. You would find them well groomed all the time and they often get noticed for their flawless appearance. For classics, dignity is everything and they reflect it very well with their dressing sense. They will never do anything to draw unnecessary attention and like to merge in quietly.
- Romantics: Their clothes express their thoughts. They simply adore expressing their feminity. They are obsessed with soft flowery fabrics like silks, satin, lace, beading etc. Aesthetics are everything to them and they get attracted to anything that communicated luxury and expense. They have a fixed expenditure for their shopping and grooming and love to look pretty all the time. Their appearance is quite artistic with a lot of romance thrown in.
- Naturals: They are attached to nature. For a natural, comfortable and practical clothing is most important. Their personality is easy going, down to earth, friendly and open. They are not materialistic and find formal and designer clothing very restrict-

ed and fussy. They tend to be adventurous and lead an active life style. Some of them love to stay so natural that may not even own a makeup or a jewelry bag. They have easy maintenance and non fussy hair styles. Sometimes, their image gets projected very poorly due to their casual attitude towards their clothing.

Once you identify your clothing personality, it will help you to know what kind of impression people may carry of you. Accept your personality and express yourself. Don't ever be afraid to flow with your natural desire and with being who you are!

Chapter 36

The colors you wear

Colors have their own language. They influence our emotions and our reactions to various situations, people and ideas, and play a very powerful role in our lives.

Some of the major colors people like to wear are: red, pink, brown, orange, gold, yellow, green, blue, purple, white, black and grey. Below, you will find the significance and meaning of each color. Knowing so will help you to pick the right colors as per occasion and your mood.

Red

It's the warmest of all colors. It's the most favorite one of extroverts. On the negative side, it can mean dominance, anger and temper. Red can help you if you want to: develop leadership qualities; increase enthusiasm and interest; generate more energy, action and confidence to go after your dreams.

Grey

Grey is often a very dull and gloomy color. Hence the saying, "I am feeling Grey" "It's a grey day". Grey is actually the color of security, maturity and dependability. It's also the color of dependability. You will see most of the security guards in grey uniform. Use grey to develop: empathy and willingness; natural feelings; to feel detached and isolated; to relax your body of tension; for forgiveness.

Pink

Pink is the color of universal love. It's one of the softest colors of the universe. It's a combination of red and white and the energy of pink can be determined by how much of red has been mixed into it. Basic pink neutralizes aggressive behavior and is associated with feelings of caring, tenderness, self worth and acceptance. Pink can be used for: to stabilize situations and neutralize disorder; mental relaxation; acceptance and contentment; empathy; to project soft nature.

Black

Though favorite of plenty, it's the most misunderstood color. It's actually not a color but absence of all colors. It projects power and mystery. It's also a color of non intrusion and aloofness. It's also a sign of maturity and stability. Use black for: restful emptiness; to project stability; becoming inconspicuous; to create mystery; to prepare for unknown.

Brown

People who prefer brown are often conventional and orderly. The negative side of brown color is that it can project a laid back attitude and a repressed personality. Brown color is a mixture of red, blue and yellow. These colors gives one a feeling of solidarity and allows one to go unnoticed in background. Use brown if you want to: show organized and orderly nature; a solid wholesome feeling; want to blend and merge into the crowd; stability and connection with earth; someone who does not believe in taking risks.

White

It's the color of purity, kindness and innocence. It's again not a color, but a combination of all colors and merges well with any color hence help build relationships. You can wear white to project: diplomacy; to clear clutter and obstacles; for fresh beginnings; mental clarity; purification of thoughts and actions.

Orange

It's a very powerful color and has healing effect. It's also a color which shows a very emotional and affectionate nature. It helps balance extreme in emotions. It stimulates enthusiasm and creativity. Thoughtfulness and sincere curiosity and exploration are the main features representing Orange. Use orange to: express your emotions and affection; to spice up dull moments in life; to get involved deeply; to boost creativity; be fun loving

Indigo

Indigo is the color of deep midnight sky and can sometimes have a negative effect on someone who is already feeling low. This color works inwards and increases the speed of personal thoughts, insights and understandings. This is also the color seen in deep meditation. Use indigo to: think out of the box; to develop intuition; focusing on personal issues; solitude and inner communication; to get closer to divine.

Gold

It's a very powerful and rich color. It symbolizes health, wealth, wisdom and success. It's also a color of confidence and boldness. Wearing gold promotes courage, confidence, will power and health. Use gold for: good health; finding success; increase personal power; relaxation; confidence building; to stand out.

Purple

Purple or violet is the color of purpose, good judgment, royalty and spiritual fulfillment. It's the color of crown *chakra* and hence the color of enlightenment. It generates the feeling of peace. Use violet to: for overall peace and calmness; to let go and forgiveness; to rebalance life; to remove obstacles; to visualize; to connect with inner soul.

Yellow

It's a beautiful color depicting creative and intelligent energy. If you forget things easily, try and use yellow note pads or yellow ink pens to enhance memory. Yellow is also the color of wisdom, joy and happiness. It clears out the clutter of thoughts making one alert. Use yellow for: mood uplifting; sharper memory; concentration; relief from stress; making clear decisions; for creativity like poetry, design making etc.

Blue

This is the coolest color. It represents sincerity, trustworthiness, inspiration, spirituality, calmness and roundedness. Put on blue if

you want to: to appear trustworthy; for peace and calmness; to sooth your anger; to learn better; to open flow of communication; to counteract chaos and agitation.

Green

Green is the color of nature, fertility, life and movement. It's a very relaxing color. It also symbolizes self respect, well being and balance, learning and growth. Use green to: uplift self from anxiety and fear; pursue new ideas; for moving on; change and growth; balance of thoughts; healing.

Chapter 37
Wardrobe management

Life is a series of events and every event calls for you to be in charge. Whether you are attending a formal dinner or a charity ball, are at polo ground or at a funeral, you need to be aware what to wear. Sometimes, you may have to get dressed more than once for different activities, but without a system in place, you will be all lost. Wardrobe management calls for organizing your clothes in such a way that you can mix and match things at various occasions. It has an added benefit too. Sometimes we lose track of our purchases and end up hunting for the same thing all over again. This will help us to keep track of what we have.

Your wardrobe must include: business formal wear; evening formal wear; casuals; smart casuals; pub wear; sports wear; swim wear; night wear; inner wear; travel wear.

The above mentioned are a must for everyone. Either you have them separate or you mix and match according to your budget.

Organizing your wardrobe: First thing you need to do is to empty out your cupboard and spread out the clothes on a flat surface like your bed. Pick up each garment and decide which pile it should go to. Basically you need to sort the clothes in 5 piles: 1) everyday use; 2) infrequent use; 3) seasonal; 4) give away; and 5) repair or wash.

The seasonal clothes are the ones which can be stored away separately like winter, rainy and summer. The wash, dry clean or repairs can go to laundry, that leaves you with three piles to sort. Now sort the clothes according to the occasion mentioned on top and place them accordingly back in the cupboard.

If you have large space in your wardrobe, you can subdivide the clothes as per the category like shirts, trousers, dresses, saris, formal wear and mix-and-match options.

You can use the similar method for your shoes and accessories.

Chapter 38

Picking the right gown

Evening gown round is one of the most important rounds at a contest. Mistakes with your gown can cost you the crown. Choose your gown wisely thinking about the image your gown will convey: your height, your body type and any figure flaws, eye color skin tone, hair color. Use the lines, fabric, color and detailing of the gown to draw judges' attention to pretty features and away from flaws. Remember, you are painting your self-portrait for the panel. The moment a contestant steps on stage, her gown style and color reveal volumes about her personality, attitude and image. The objective is not to just go for a pretty gown, but to see that the gown fits well especially around the bust and waist. There should be no wrinkles or puckers evident as you walk.

Color white has remained the favorite color in all contests over many decades. The unpopular colors have been brown, grey, camel, rust, mustard, olive green, orange, checks and stripes.

A lot of contestants feel that they've got to buy an expensive designer gown to win. You don't have to do that. You need to wear what looks good on you Even if it's a homemade gown. If you do not want to buy, you can even rent or borrow a gown and get it altered to suit you. Judges do not consider the value of the gown. They will notice whether the gown compliments you, brings out your beauty and contributes to an overall picture. How you appear, and how you carry the gown is of upmost importance.

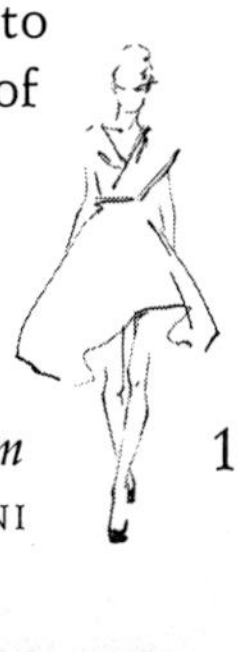

You might have to try on a hundred different gowns—gowns with sleeves, without sleeves, halters, strapless, backless etc., before you find the right one.

When you know that you have chosen your gown keeping all important guidelines in mind, you automatically walk with confidence, head held higher, shoulders back, and more gracefully. Gown is not officially judged, the image a contestant creates in that gown is judged keeping in mind the personal style she would bring to the title, and can set her apart as the winner.

As you shop for your perfect pageant dress or evening gown. The following guide will help you to choose your gown wisely:

- If your Figure is too Short, then create one long vertical line to look taller. All lines and seams should be going vertically. Don't "cut" the body with belts, waistlines, peplums and avoid contrasting solids, and full skirts.
- If you have heavy hips and thighs, then balance your body by concealing hips and widening shoulders. Draw eyes up off lower body with detailing on the bodice, shoulder ruffles, puff sleeves. Black velvet with an eye-catching bodice is the best bet. Avoid fish-tale gown styles that over-emphasize the hips.
- For narrow shoulders, draw the eye to outer shoulders to broaden the look. Wear padded shoulders and puffed or gathered sleeves to widen shoulders. Lace, ruffles, etc. help conceal shoulders. Avoid halters. Draw the eye inward toward the neck and face. Try halters, turtlenecks, and stand-up collars. Widen hips with a peplum or tulip skirt for balance.
- In case you are too thin then choose white, bright, or neon colors, or metallic color. Draped styles, graceful flowing fabrics with full sleeves and fitted waist will look great. Try fish-tale gown styles that may add the appearance of curves to your figure.
- In case you have a small bust or are flat-chested, wear padding on the bustling. Draped, wrapped, or heavily beaded bodices add fullness. Wear a gown with sewn-in bust cups.
- For a heavier or large bust, remember not to conceal, but to tone down necklines. Wide necklines are flattering. Make sure any cleavage show is reasonable. Wide skirt base, flared hems balance a large bust. Make sure you have full support for the breasts.

- If you have a thick waistline, wear a straight gown and don't emphasize the waist. Avoid belts. bust-to-hip busters will help trim waist.
- In case you have a short waist, avoid wide waistbands and belts and avoid color changes at waist. Straight gown lines can lengthen the torso.
- For long waist, remember not to wear dropped waistlines or gowns with a sash around the hips. Try a wide waistband or sash up to ribs.

Not only the gown, you must also take care on choosing your inner wear wisely. Undergarments like backless bras, bust-to-hip bustiers, silicone bust cups, waist cinchers, invisible panties; built-in panties etc., are very popular amongst contestants. Many contestants wear long-line bras cross front bra or bust-to-hip bustiers, which provide support and create a sleek line, especially with strapless gowns. If you have a real clingy fabric like Lycra, the lines will show and any extra flesh on the hips can bulge out where the garment ends giving a tacky look. To simplify this issue, sew brassiere cups or bustiers right into the gown. Wear panty hose with a cotton panty to avoid panty line. You can tell a party line in almost any straight dress. If you have a tummy, wear a body shape or a tummy tucker. If you are not wearing a bra, you can use heavy duty fabric stickers to stick the garments at right places.

The gown should not overpower its wearer, and should be well fitted. Avoid plunging neckline or excessive cleavage show. The gown should not be skin tight on an imperfect figure and should not be cluttered with detailing. Avoid gaudy colors and distracting shoes and jewelry. The gown should be flattering to your figure with necklines that compliment your face. It should have a gorgeous back view, fit correctly and should be beautifully accessorized.

Remember, if even one judge reacts negatively to your gown, the points that he or she deducts can mean the difference between your making the top ten or not, or your being the winner

Never keep your brand new shoes for this last day. Wear and practice walking in them as much as you can or else the new shoes might pinch or alter your ramp walk into the most uncomfortable walk ever. Most of the contestants like to wear transparent heeled shoes with their gowns, with a lot of sparkling rhinestones. I suggest not to go overboard with bling. The idea is not to look like a sparkling

Christmas tree. Grace shows when you keep your shoes plain if you have too much of detailing on your gown, and if your gown is very simple, you can afford to have a lot of work on shoes.

Open toed heels are much worn as it shows off your toes in a sexy way. Match the color of your shoe to your dress rather than going contrast. The right pageant shoes also finish the image the contestant is creating for judges. Wear high heels to create a taller, slimmer, more elegant body line with heels ranging from one to four inches. Nude color is always the safest choice.

The right jewelry add the winning touches that complete the look. If it overpowers you and people look at the jewelry rather than look at your face, then it's wrong. The earrings which you wear should be picked up according to your face shape, your neckline and your weight, hair style and eyes. You can also opt for a nice hair accessory or may be an elegant brooch. But wearing necklace, bracelets, rings etc., can create a cluttered look and will take the attention away. So, one loud piece....take your pick and period!!

Chapter 39

Pageant shoes

You just can't pick up any shoe or heels just because they are tall and pretty. When selecting pageant shoes, it's important to make sure that they create a long and lean look for you. Your shoes should look as graceful and nice as the dress you choose. Pageant footwear can be a total game-changer for any contestant. Get it right and you look like a queen, get it wrong, and you will look clumsy. Avoid huge clunky platforms. Not only do they look tacky, but also take away all the attention from you straight to your shoes. Shoes should not be noticeable on stage but should allow you to move comfortably on the stage.

Most of the contestants like to wear three to three-and-a-half-inch heels, however. Short girls who need to add height opt for four-inch heels. As a rule, the taller the shoe heel, the nicer the look, but it's difficult to walk properly in them.

The most important thing to consider is that whichever shoe you choose, it should fit you well. You can't afford to land up with shoe bites and injuries before your final walk. Aside from the fit, make sure you can comfortably walk in them

Comfort is crucial since the fit of a shoe directly affects how one walks while on stage. Wear your shoe often and break into them few months before. If you have bought new shoes for a pageant, get them months before and walk in them, work in them, do your housework in them.

Allow foot to recover from the abuse, so try and slowly ease out of your heels on and off and don't keep them on for too long during rehearsals.

Picking a pageant shoe also depends on your gown. If you've got a plain well cut dress, you probably won't want a shoe to take away from the impact of the dress.

For a pageant, as a coach, I always prefer closed pumps over open-toe shoes. The clear toed shoes look very tacky, because when you stand on stage your toes are hanging out. Closed pump is safe, comfortable, neutral shoe and it completes the look.

If you're wearing an outfit that is black or has black and another color combination, then a black shoe would look great. Metallic silver or gold shoes usually draw too much attention. Another choice is a delicate, open-toe, sling-back formal shoe in the gown's color. But sometimes sling-backs can get caught in hemlines as the contestant walks and can be dangerous.

When shoe shopping for a gown, consider the length of your gown. It should not be more than an inch and a half off the ground when walking so that you don't trip

For swimwear round, you need something understated so as to keep the attention on your body. Most swimsuit shoes are open ones or peep-toe, but closed toe can work too. Nudes are your best bet here. For the interview round, shoes are as what you would wear on a job interview–nothing strappy.

A beaded shoe should not overpower the dress. Some contestants also go for satin shoes that can be dyed to match the dress

The goal is to wear shoes that are not only beautiful but also allow you to walk comfortably, and with confidence. So, choose your shoes wisely.

Chapter 40

Basic make up tips

Just like any other skill, make up is also a skill which can be easily learnt. Understanding and applying perfect make up is a must for a contestant. Makeup is an art to enhance your face and draw attention to the best features.

Apply foundation with the help of a brush or your finger all over your face. Blend it well leaving a very thin layer on the cheeks, this helps to layer your blush well. Not doing so gives a artificial look. Take care that the foundation matches your skin tone. Not only on face, apply it on the neck and ears too so that the whole look is natural. If you are wearing cut sleeves, it makes sense to match your arms to face by applying thin layer of foundation.

To get a beautiful curl on your lashes, make sure your mascara is no more than a month old—fresh mascara is easier to apply and won't cake on the lashes. Wiggle mascara stick in at the base of the lash and sweep outward and upward in a zig-zag motion. The trick is to get the thickness into the base of the lashes and taper them naturally to the ends for the natural look. Nowadays 3D mascara is available in the market which gives you temporary eye extension. Do not pump up the mascara wand as it may introduce a lot of bacteria that can cause eye infection.

Make up should not stand out during the day. It's ok to go a little bolder in the evening. Wear nice nude peachish color during the day so that it can pop on the cheeks. Peach nude works on everyone. Creamy blush can be mixed with some moisturizer and blended on your cheeks. Powder blush works better during summer and creamy in winter. Cheek tints are also very popular nowadays.

Beautiful eyes lose their charm due to dark circles. Always hydrate the under eyes with a fast absorbing cream. This will allow products to go on smoothly. Apply a concealer or a corrector to cover the purple or green spots on the skin, cover it with a thin layer of foundation and finally, set the under eye area with a translucent pale yellow powder. Apply vitamin E oil regularly under the eyes to lighten the circles before you sleep. Sparkling shiny eye shadow around eye duct area opens up the eye.

Start with a sharp lip liner, of the same color as your chosen lipstick. Smile a little so the lips get tight and the liner goes on easier. Now take a lip brush and apply the lipstick within the line. Take a little concealer on a small brush to correct if you go out of the line by mistake. You can dot a shimmery shadow right on the center of the lips giving a pout effect or cover the lipstick with gloss. You will find long wear lipsticks in the market which last between 8-12 hours.

Liquid liner or eye gel is little tough to master, the trick is to keep your hand steady. If you are not very good at it, than first use an eyeliner pencil to trace a line just above the upper lash line. Next apply the liquid liner or gel directly on top of this line taking care to remain neat. Non-smudge liners are now available in market which will stay on even in the water. They need special lotion to remove.

Very few lucky ones are born with great cheekbones and sharp nose. You can fake it with contouring or sculpting: pucker up to find the hollows of your cheeks. Dab a deep brown blush in the sunken area just under the cheekbone, on the corners of your nose, sides of the face and under the jaw to hide any double chin. Blend well. Smile and apply a peachy blush at the apple of the cheek and slowly make larger circles with the brush to get instant cheek bones. A light reflecting powder on the bridge of the nose will sharpen the nose.

Kohl comes in many colors. Line the inner rim of the lower lash line, working the eyeliner into the lashes. Open your eye wide and line the upper lash lines. Make sure there's no gap between your lashes and the line. Use your fingertip to smudge it in. Next sweep an eye shadow across your lids and up into your eye creases, blending outwards and upwards elongating your eye shape.

Do not forget to comb your brows with a brush or with a clean mascara wand to see how they lay naturally. You will find brow make up kit easily in the market. Using a soft, slightly waxy touch, shape the brow whichever way you want. Then, take the flatter angled brush and fill in the brow using short strokes that look like hair.

A healthy bronze shine makes you look healthy, no matter what the season. Sweep bronzer on your temples, along the sides of the face,

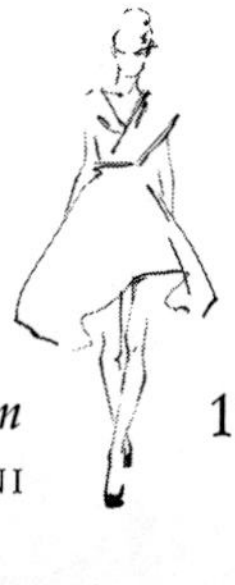

and right under the cheekbones. Keep the bronze color away from the center of your face—too much bronzer on the center can make you look older. Do not apply bronzer during the day.

Chapter 41

How to make down

No one is born perfect. People may look wow in pictures because they have learnt the tricks of make up. Make down is the term usually used to conceal or hide flaws on the facial skin and also to make the flaws unnoticeable. In other words, it's also called contouring.

The normal formula for the make down is just the same as the lighting. When you want to hide something, you keep it in the dark, so that the eyes don't fall on it. And if you want people to notice something, we display it in light. Similarly, everyone is not born with perfect face. Everyone may have a unique problem e.g., double chin, broad nose, heavy jaw line etc. Make down technique involves applying darker shades on the areas which need to be hidden and lighter on areas which need to be highlighted. Before you start contouring, you need to know what face shape you have.

What will you need for a make down?

- A matte bronzer or a powder a few shades darker than your normal skin. Always take matte powder only as it will not glitter or shimmer and hence will look natural.
- A white or peach colored powder eye shadow for highlighting.

Remember, anything which is contoured with dark shade will appear smaller or sunken, and anything which is highlighted with light shade will appear more obvious and raised.

Method

- You basically need two shades of base. Apply foundation that's one shade lighter than your skin on the center of your face, and another that's one shade darker around the perimeter of the face.

- Use a blending brush and mix the two shades well to create the subtle illusion of depth and dimension.
- Mark the areas you want to contour which can be the hollows under the cheekbones, temples, hairline, jawline, sides and tip of the nose and the crease of the eyes. Now take a lighter color powder and apply it on the top of the cheekbones, under the eye area, down the bridge of the nose, and in an upside-down triangle on your forehead. Gently blend the edges with a flat foundation brush.
- Once the highlighter is done, apply the darker color on the hollow of the cheekbones, down the sides of the nose, underneath the chin, temples, and along the hairline. Gently blend the edges, working section by section with a blending brush. Now, take a clean, wet sponge, and gently press over your foundation to give a nice finish.
- Set your work with a translucent powder. Boom. Your face will now look like a super model

Chapter 42

Image builders and image destroyers

An Image is the imprint of a person which gets registered in the psyche of people.

Image dusts

Image dusts are little mistakes in your overall appearance which will spoil your impression when you meet people. The saying goes "elephants don't bite…but mosquito's do!" The statement means that even if you have taken care of your major stuff like dress, makeup, hair style etc., little things can make eyes zoom on the mistakes and spoil your image. Image builders are little things, which when taken care can enhance your overall image. Few examples of image dusts and builders are listed below:

- Image dusts: Wrong foundation; too much makeup; lipstick on teeth; chipped nail polish; cracked heals; leaking lipstick; dirty neck, underarms and elbows; dirty back; unpressed dress; broken buttons; visible pins; ear wax; ungroomed hair in ears and nose; uneven stubble; visible dandruff; mouth odor; body odor; eye scum; dry and scaly skin; nicotine stained nails and teeth; visible inner wear and dirty inner wear; chipped shoes; shopping labels on clothes; rip in clothes; peak a boo in blouses; extremely bold necklines; ill fitted clothes; too much perfume; lady with a moustache; too much visible hair on arms and legs for ladies; unruly eyebrows.
- Image builders: Right makeup; well applied unleaking lipstick; no *kajal/kohl* scum in eyes; well polished nails; well groomed heels, elbows, neck, back, and underarms; waxed arms and legs; well groomed eyebrows for both man and woman; well pressed and fitted clothes; fresh and clean breath; perfect personal hygiene; clean and shiny hair; bleached or waxed moustache in ladies; no visible pins.

Section 2

During the Contest

Chapter 43
History of beauty pageants*

The first beauty contest was held on 19th September 1888, in the small Belgian municipality of spa. The final was attended by 21 (candidates for the title of "Beauty Queen". The girls for the finale were selected from the photographs sent to the jury; the participants were not known to general public and lived in a separate building. Audience came dressed very formally in tuxedos and long dresses. The winner was 18 year old Creole from Guadeloupe Bertha Sukkar, who got a prize of 5,000 Francs.

The first truly modern beauty contest involving the display of novatis faces and figures before judges can be traced to one of the Americas greatest showmen, Phineas T. Barnum. In the 1850s Barnum who owned a "Dime museum" in New York, started accepting entries in the form of photographic likeness which he exhibited at his museum. Public came to view these snaps and voted on them and the winners would receive specially commissioned oil portraits of themselves.

By the early decades of 20th century attitudes towards beauty contests begun to change. People became more open to display of woman's beauty in public. These contests slowly started spreading. In Germany first such contest was held in 1909 and the first Miss America was held in 1921.

By 1950 many little girls grew up dreaming that they one day would wear the crown and the popularity of contests started growing more and more.

The inaugural Miss India pageant was held in 1959, 10 years after India gained independence as a way to promote a new image of India internationally. Beautiful young women showcased Indian textiles etc. It wasn't until 1994, when two pageant winners went on to become Miss World and Miss Universe that this contest was elevated to prominence.

There are so many states in India and every state has beautiful women, but India being a country which believes in unity in diversity started looking for the perfect Indian woman and the answers came for the first

---

*: Source: Wikipedia.

time through Femina Miss India. Over the years the industry has really grown and loads of Directors are organizing various pageants at various levels where the winners go internationally to represent India.

Chapter 44

Types of beauty pageants

Before I describe to you what the different types of beauty pageants are, let's look at the dictionary meaning of a "Beauty Pageant". "A pageant is a public entertainment consisting of a procession of people in elaborate colorful costumes or an outdoor performance of a historical scene."

There are several types of pageants, each with a different set of goals. Some pageants offer winners scholarships for furthering their education while some pageants help teach people skills. Some contests have a cause attached with it and the winners work hand in hand with the organizers to promote it. Of course all this comes with various perks and award. Keeping in view the definition, the various types of pageants one can enter include:

Natural Pageants: Prize is based on natural beauty. No makeup is allowed for contestants under the legal age. A person has to be his/ her natural best and showcase ones natural inborn skills. Most judges do not like to see, too much pomp, and performances. Personality plays a big part, so that is why the interview section of the contest will be the most important part of the pageant. Natural pageants are basically confidence building pageants and helps improve one's skills. Sometimes judges are instructed to cut points when a dress is too blingy or isn't right length or is too showy. In natural pageants, the less, the better; however, sometimes depending on the age group or the particular pageant system, girls can use a little make-up and add hair pieces. Heavy makeup, elaborate costumes, wigs etc. are not allowed in such pageants, hence the name natural.

Scholastic Pageants: Scholastic pageants often have much elaborate and longer interview section, and the prizes are scholarships for higher education, be it college, private school or vocational skills. According to Wikipedia, judging criteria consists:

- 15% academics and school awards/excellence.
- 15% activities (leadership, extra-curricular activities and community service).
- 30% interview
- 15% evening gown
- 15% personal expression (trademarked category, decorate a pair of blue jeans and model them!)
- 10% on-stage question.

Hobby Pageants: Hobby pageants are for people who want to experiment with pageants and build self confidence. Contestants sometimes use hobby pageants for practicing before entering a glitz competition or working on their ramp walk, pose and presentation. Hobby pageants are usually small weekend events, with a nominal fee. It's basically the feel factor of the bigger pageant.

Glitz pageants: These are the most popular, glamorous, expensive pageants with big money in prizes. It involves tough competition and requires a lot of time. Professional coaching staff is recommended for anyone entering this type of pageant. Each dress worn in the competition is custom-made and a make up and glamorous styles are encouraged. Contestants are also allowed to wear false hair, teeth, eye lashes etc.

Chapter 45

Major international pageants*

The 'Big Four' pageants

The world's four largest and most famous female international beauty pageants that have proven their importance and advocacies to the society through the years are: Miss World (founded in 1951); Miss Universe (founded in 1952); Miss International (founded in 1960) and Miss Earth (founded in 20011).

These pageants have been recognized and acknowledged around the globe by different government agencies and institutions for their unparalleled contributions and clear advocacies to the society.

*: Source: Wikipedia.

Miss Universe

Miss Universe is an annual international beauty contest that is run by the Miss Universe Organization. Founded in 1952 by California clothing company, Pacific Mills, the pageant became part of Kayser-Roth and then Gulf+Western Industries, before being acquired by Donald Trump in 1996. Traditionally, Miss Universe lives in New York City during her reign.

Main pageant: The main Miss Universe Pageant is held over a two-week period in May and July. In the 1970s through the 1990s, the pageant was month long. Currently, the final placement of the finalists is determined by a ranked vote, where each judge ranks each of the final three/five candidates, with the contestant posting the lowest cumulative score (thus often, but not necessarily always, the contestant with the most number one votes) becoming the winner. If there is a tie, the higher semifinal scores become decisive. The winner is assigned a one-year contract with the Miss Universe Organization, going overseas to spread messages about the control of diseases, peace, and public awareness of AIDS. Special awards are also given to the winners of the best National Costume, Miss Photogenic, and Miss Congeniality. The Miss Congeniality award is chosen by the delegates themselves. In recent years, Miss Photogenic has been chosen by popular internet vote.

Final judgment: All the contestants compete in a preliminary round of judging (nowadays called the "Presentation Show") where the field is narrowed to a select number of semifinalists. There are 16 semifinalists, 15 chosen by judges and one chosen by most popular by Internet votes.

In the early years, the contestants were judged in swimsuit and evening gown only. In later years, the contestants also competed in a preliminary interview round in a one-on-one meeting with each individual judge.

> *Interview [33%]*: Pageant judges spend time with each delegate to learn about her successes, talents, goals and ambitions. Attention is focused on her poise, charm, self-confidence and her ability to communicate, as well as the substance of her answers.
>
> *Swimsuit competition [33%]:* Attention is focused on the beauty—face, figure, physical fitness, and the confidence with which each contestant carries herself. Numerical measurements are not considered in the judging.

Evening gown competition [33%]: Each delegate wears a gown she has chosen for herself. Attention is focused on each contestant's overall appearance, self-confidence, sense of style and the beauty she brings to the gown of her choice.

Miss World

The Miss World pageant is the oldest surviving major international beauty pageant. It was created in the United Kingdom by Eric Morley in 1951. Since his death in 2000, Morley's wife, Julia Morley, co-chairs the pageant. The winner spends a year travelling to represent the Miss World Organization and its various causes. Traditionally, Miss World lives in London during her reign.

The elimination system in Miss World pageant is done in 3 rounds: the Preliminary, the Semifinal, and the Final; each with its own scoring format. In addition, there are also 5 special mini competitions known as Fast Tracks under which the contestants earn bonus points during the Preliminary.

The Preliminary: In this round, each contestant will have a personal with the judges. The judges will score them in 3 categories: the first being beauty, grace and charm; the second being intelligence, poise and personality; and the third being figure and deportment. Each judge would score them from 6 to 10 points in each category and, unlike in Miss Universe which uses decimal numbers, the scores are given in whole numbers. Therefore, the minimum score that a contestant could earn from a judge is 18 points (if she was scored 6 in all 3 categories) and the maximum score is 30 points (if she was scored 10 in all 3 categories). The scores from all the judges would then be tabulated into a single Preliminary score.

The Fast Tracks: Prior to 2011 edition, winner of each Fast Track event automatically qualified for the Semifinal. But from 2011, the winner is no longer guaranteed a spot in Semifinal. Instead, the winner and all other contestants short listed as finalists for a particular Fast Track earn bonus points towards their Preliminary score. For each Fast Track, the points are distributed as follows: 20 points for the winner, 18 points for second, 17 for third, 16 for fourth, 15 for fifth, 14 for sixth, 13 for seventh, 12 for eighth, 11 for ninth, 10 for tenth, and 5 points for the rest of the finalists. This point distribution is applied for 4 out of 5 Fast Track events, which are sports, talent, beach beauty, and top model.

The only deviation for this distribution is 'Beauty with a Purpose', which carries higher points. For this particular event, the points are distributed as the follows: 30 points for the winner, 28 points for second, 27 for third, 26 for fourth, 25 for fifth, 24 for sixth, 23 for seventh, 22 for eighth, 21 for ninth, 20 for tenth, 10 points for the rest of the finalists, and 5 points for any contestants who did not make it as Beauty with a Purpose finalist but had a project/presentation submitted for the Fast Track.

The Semifinal : Once the Preliminary and all Fast Tracks scores are revealed, a selected number of contestants with the highest combined scores will advance to the Semifinal. Unlike Miss Universe, the scores that a contestant has accumulated in the previous round would not be reset to zero. It would be carried over to the Final. For this round, the judges would rank the semifinalists from the best to the last and their rank would be translated into points as: 50 points for first place, 40 points for second, 30 points for third, 20 points for fourth, 15 points for fifth, 10 points for sixth and seventh, 5 points for eighth to tenth, and 2 points for eleventh to fifteenth. Out of all rounds in Miss World elimination system, the judging criteria in this round is the vaguest one. No one (aside Miss World Organization themselves of course) actually knows what is the base used by the judges to rank these semifinalists from first to fifteenth. But the most speculated criterion is the overall visual stage impression of these contestants during the Grand Final.

The Final: After the semifinal scores are revealed, elimination occur and the contest is left with an even smaller group of contenders. At this point, the judging is down to the final question where each contestant would have one final chance to convince the judges that she is the one. Just like the Semifinal, once again the judges would rank the finalists from the best to the last and their rank would be translated into points: 50 points for first place, 40 points for second, 30 points for third, 20 points for fourth, 15 points for fifth, 10 points for sixth and 5 points for seventh. From there, all the scores will be combined and the one with the highest score is crowned as the Miss World.

Miss Earth

Miss Earth is one of the three largest beauty pageants. The reigning titleholders dedicate their year to promote specific projects and often address issues concerning the environment and other global issues through tours, tree planting activities, street campaigns, coastal clean ups, speaking engagements, shopping mall tours,

environmental fair, storytelling programs, eco-fashion shows, and other environmental activities.

The Miss Earth winner is the spokesperson for the Miss Earth Foundation, the United Nations Environment Programme (UNEP) and other environmental organizations. The Miss Earth Foundation also works with the environmental departments and ministries of participating countries, various private sectors and corporations, as well as Greenpeace and the World Wildlife Foundation (WWF).

Selection: Since the Miss Earth pageant has an environmental cause, it is primarily looking for young women who will stand for the protection and preservation of the planet. These women are pageant winners or chosen by national Miss Earth directors from different nations.

On national level competitions, the Miss Earth's cause is carried out to assure that each of the participating candidates is not just physically beautiful, but environmentally knowledgeable. As soon as the national winners are chosen, they will be subject to evaluation by the pageant organizer.

During the pre-finals weeks, the candidates are evaluated on each activity and event they have. Preliminary swimsuit and evening gown competitions also take place. In the pre-judging session, the delegates face the panel of judges for an interview in their simplest look (without make-up), where they speak of their environmental platform and personal thoughts. As soon as the preliminary activities and interview are completed, the judges and the executive staff will select sixteen candidates who will comprise the group of semi-finalists.

During the live finals, the sixteen semi-finalists will be announced. All previous scores will be disregarded and thereafter compete in the swimsuit round. The top eight scorers in swimsuit will move on the next level of competition—interview and evening gown competition. The scores from these two events will be averaged and the four highest scorers will continue with the last competition—the final interview.

In the final interview, all four finalists will answer one environmental question. The candidates will be assessed based on the judge's over-all impression about the candidate thus determining the final ranking. For the 9th edition of Miss Earth, no single final question was asked. Instead, images were flashed on screen and each of the eight finalists were tasked to tell something about it within 30 seconds

If in case the Miss Earth winner can no longer fulfill her duties and obligations as titleholder, the 1st runner-up will be the one who will take over the title. The Four Titles to be won are: Miss Earth, Miss Earth Air, Miss Earth Water, Miss Earth Fire. The four winners also receive a medallion necklace as part of their prizes. These medallions stand for the four elements that the winners represent.

Miss International

Miss International, also called "Miss International Beauty", is not based on looks alone. Contestants are expected to serve as "Ambassadors of Peace and Beauty", showing tenderness, benevolence, friendship, beauty, intelligence, ability to take action, and great international sensibility. The ultimate goal of the Miss International beauty pageant is to promote world peace, goodwill, and understanding. The judging criteria for this pageant comprises: Interview—40%; Fitness—20%; Evening Gown—20%; and Fun Fashion—20%

2nd Tier Pageants

These are the emerging beauty contests which have been able to stage their pageants well. However, they need to prove their "advocacies", as what the big four pageants have proven through the years. Miss Supranational; Miss Intercontinental; Miss Grand International are few examples of the such pageants.

3rd Tier Pageants

Miss Tourism International; Miss Tourism Queen International; Miss Tourism World; Miss Asia Pacific World; Miss United Continent; Miss Heritage

Minor international pageants

Other minor international pageants are: Miss Globe International; Miss Multiverse; Miss Progress International; Miss North America; Miss Chinese International Pageant; Miss Chinese Cosmos Pageant; Miss Model of the World; Top Model of the World; Queen of the Universe; Mrs. Universe; Mrs. World; World Miss University; World Muslimah; Phenomenal Bald Beauty® Pageant.

Continental and regional pageants

Arab League; Miss Arab World; European Union; Miss Europe; Hispanic America; Miss América Latina; Reina Hispanoamericana; Miss Continente Americano; Nuestra Belleza Latina; India; Indian Princess International; Miss Himalaya Pageant; Miss Tibet; Miss India Worldwide.

Women's prison beauty pageants

Some international jails are trying to inject a little sexiness into the penal system by throwing inmate beauty pageants, where female felons compete—bikini, evening gown, and talent portions included—for titles like Miss Prison, Miss Jail, and Miss Captivity.

Chapter 46

Major men's international and Indian pageants

Indian Pageants

*Ru-Ba-Ru Mr India Global**

Ru-Ba-Ru Mr India Global is organized by Ru-Ba-Ru group with pageant directors Sandeep Kumar and Pankaj Kharbanda. The aim of the contest is to raise awareness towards violence against woman. Contestants are trained by various international experts before the contest on various aspects of pageantry. Winners are sent abroad to various international pageants like: Mister Global; Mister Model; Mr Universal Ambassador; M-Mister United Continental; Mr Real Universe; Man of the Year; Mr Tourism World; Top International Model of the Year; Mr Pan Continental; Mr Global Teen; Mister International.

Eligibility Criteria: Applicants should be born to parents of Himalayan cultural background; between 17 and 25 years of age; minimum 165 cm in height; and unmarried.

---

*: Source: Wikipedia.

Mr India#

Mr India, a biennial event started in 2014, is a national beauty pageant that selects its winner to compete in Mister World pageant. Earlier Grasim Industries held the franchise for Mister World in India. In 2007, Haywards 5000 took the franchise for Mister World and organized Haywards 5000 Mr. India World 2007 Pageant to select India's representative at Mister World 2007. Since 2014, Bennett, Coleman & Co. Ltd owns this franchise. It also holds the franchise for Miss World India in India.

Eligibility Criteria: Between 17 and 27 years of age; Height 5.7" & above; Unmarried/single/not engaged; Born Indian National holding valid Indian passport.

*Mr Gay India**

Mr Gay India represents India at Gay pageants globally. The primary purpose of Mr Gay India is to identify leaders who will take responsibility of being a spokesperson not only in his own community but on a global stage speaking out for equal and human rights. Mr Gay India is a positive role model and will work on humanizing being gay and/or LGBT (lesbian, gay, bisexual and transgender) in the media both local and mainstream. It was introduced in 2008.

*Mr India United Nations**

Mr United Nations India, a national beauty pageant in India, selects its winner to compete in Mister United Nations Pageant. It was introduced in 2012.

*Mister India International**

Mister India International is a male pageant founded by the Mister Singapore Organization in the year 2006. The main objective behind the pageant as propounded by the Organization is to support and advance today's men. It is also committed to increasing HIV/AIDS awareness and works towards this end by designating the winners of the pageant as ambassadors for the cause.

#: Source: *beautypageants.indiatimes.com/mr-india*

The ultimate objective is that by "forging relationships with organizations committed to research and education, such as Action for AIDS, the men who champion these causes during their term personify the combination of handsomeness and intelligence that defines the 21st Century." As such, the criteria for selection of the winners remains the same—handsomeness, intelligence, a pleasant personality and one with a deep social consciousness and concern at a global level.

*Men Universe Model India**

Men Universe Model India originally Mister Universe Model India is a national male beauty pageant that annually selects representatives to compete in Mister Universe Model. India has been participating in Mister Universe Model since its inception in 2008.

Other international pageants

*Mister World**

The Mister World competition is a male beauty pageant sponsored by the Miss World Organization. The competition is biennial and was founded in 1996. The entrants compete in various activities including waterskiing, mountain biking, and marathon running. Traditionally, Mister World lives in London during his reign.

Unlike conventional male beauty pageants, Mr World is a 2-3 week competition designed to test the candidates in a variety of ways through a series of challenge events, interviews and a final stage show. These challenges test every aspect deemed necessary to be "The World's Most Desirable Man." At the global event, each candidate represents a single nation, with no two contestants representing the same territory.

Five challenge events take place: Fashion & Style, the Extreme Challenge, the Multi-Media Award, the Sports Challenge & the Talent Competition. Each one of these challenges has a winner, who takes his place in the Final Top Ten of the competition. There are also collective points earned through the team based elements of the challenges, with the contestants split into four teams throughout the event.

Five places remain for the other contestants, whose performances over the challenges, their behavior during the competition as well as their interviews with the judges will determine who takes their place in the Top Ten.

The winner is then selected by the panel of judges who weigh up the performances of each candidate before hearing from them on stage as to why they want to win Mr World, and what it would mean to them.

*Mister International**

Mister International is an annual male beauty pageant founded in 2006. It is owned and organized by the Mister Singapore Organization which also organizes the annual Mister Singapore pageant. Since the first edition, 72 countries have sent their representative to this contest, with an annual average of 31 contestants.

*Men Universe Model**

Men Universe Model originally called "Mister Universe Model" is the fourth largest pageant for men in the world after the Manhunt International, Mister International and Mister World with headquarters at the Dominican Republic. However, from 2015, it moved to Japan due to Dominican Republic's progress.

*Mister Global**

Mister Global, is an annual male beauty pageant founded in 2014. Since the first edition, 16 countries have sent their representative to this contest. The first edition of the Mister Global pageant, was held at Pak Chong, Thailand on 27 March 27 2014.

*Manhunt International**

Manhunt International is an international male beauty pageant which began in 1993, though the roots of the pageant go back a few years more to when one single national preliminary was held in Singapore. The pageant is held by Metromedia Singapore and Procon Leisure International.

Eligibility Criteria: Sex: Male, Age range:18 to 30, Marital status: Single, Height: At least 1.8 metres/5'11", Skills: speak English (optional), modelling experience, Additional attributes: Photogenic, good physique (not bodybuilder's), wonderful personality, cool character, enthusiastic.

Competition: Manhunt competition is staged on two rounds, preliminary and final. During the preliminary round, the

contestants are judged in national costume, swim wear, evening wear, and fashion wear. The contestants with most scores are named as finalists, from which the judges determine the winner and the runners up. During the pageant final, several other awards are also given aside from the ultimate title of Manhunt International. These awards are Best in National Costume, Best Runway Model, Mister Photogenic, Mister Friendship, Mister Personality, Mister Physique, and Mister |Popularity (voted by people via internet). Since the 2005 edition, Manhunt International has also given five continental awards to the best representatives of each continent. In the 2007 edition, it was announced that the winner of Mister Popularity would automatically advance to final round.

*Mr Asia Contest**

Mr Asia Contest is an male beauty pageant contest run by Mr Asia contest Organization based in Hong Kong

*Mr Gay World**

Mr Gay World is an annual international competition for gay and human rights. It is the most publicized gay contest in the world and features prominently in news media across the globe.

Continental and regional pageants

- Hispanic America
- Mister Latin America

Chapter 47

Major women's international pageants and Indian pageants

Femina Miss India*

Miss India/Femina Miss India is a national beauty pageant held in India every year where participants are invited from all over the world, but

*: Source: *beautypageants.indiatimes.com*; Wikipedia.

participants have to be of Indian origin. The winners go to represent India internationally for various contests like Miss World, Miss Earth and Miss International. Femina Miss India is so named because the pageant is organized by the woman's magazine Femina which is published by Bennett, Coleman & Co. Ltd. and owned by Times of India group.

Young women enter Miss India pageant fully expecting to change not only their bodies but emerge as confident individual women under the gaze of experts at the training program.

Femina Miss India is one of the oldest and most glamorous beauty pageants where beauty along with other essential qualities such as brains, wit, personality and confidence are given prime importance.

One of the most important question most of the contestants have in mind is about the swimsuit round. As mentioned earlier, beauty and perfect body is one of the criteria for judgment. The judges would like to see that the contestants can carry the swimsuit with confidence, how comfortable she is in her own skin and her body and image. Knowledge of swimming is not a compulsion. One is just required to wear a swim suit. Swimming costume round is compulsory for regional and pageant rounds.

If one is unsuccessful in one attempt, one can apply again till the age of 25. The learning during the training sessions takes the contestant a long way in life. It's a good platform to build a network of contacts and acquaintances that will be a useful foundation for various career options like Bollywood, Media, and Modeling etc.

The process of becoming Miss India begins every year in August or September when Femina magazine prints entry forms in both the magazine and The Times of India.

Miss India training

For 30 days prior to the contest, contestant's are housed in a hotel where they undergo a strict grooming and training regime that includes: first impression; physical appearance; fitness levels; confidence level; style; initial communication; small talk; introductions; vocabulary; diction; public speaking; voice modulation; cracking the QA in 60 seconds; body language; ramp walk; ramp pose; still pose; posture; stilettos; picture perfect; skin care/hair care; makeup tricks; dental fitness; social graces; the wardrobe; comfort vs. stylish; essentials/ must have; swimwear in style; Indian attire; what not to wear; accessories; footwear; pageant attire; the personality; SWOT analysis; what's your USP; a for attitude; etiquette; confidence building; general awareness; time management; the breakdowns; sportsmanship; coping up with stress; balancing act; the last-minute tips

Contestants are monitored and are not allowed to go anywhere out without supervision.

Sub-contests titles

Contest	*Criteria*
Miss Congeniality	To choose the most popular girl among the participants
Miss Beautiful hair	Thickness, lustre, shine and quality of hair
Miss Lifestyle Miss	Knowledge of contemporary luxury brands
Healthy Skin Miss	Skin tone, radiance, derma check
Fashion Icon Miss	Personal style quotient and their creativity
Vivacious	Fun-loving, vibrant, spirited
Miss Beauty with a Purpose	Views about socially relevant topics
Miss Iron Maiden	Last girl standing (Individual exercises)
Miss Adventurous	Activity on a scooty
Miss Timeless Beauty	Pictures from childhood till now, to see which one has transformed really well

What after the crowning for Miss India?

Femina Miss India used to select three winners who were then sent to Miss World, Miss Universe, and Miss Asia Pacific International pageants, respectively. In 1994, after India's historic win at the

International pageants, the organization ended the practice of crowning a single winner and instead decided that the top three winners were designated as winners with equal visibility and prizes. In 2002, the third winner was designated to Miss Earth instead of Miss Asia Pacific. In 2010, Femina Miss India decided that they would no longer send a representative to Miss Universe, and relinquished the Miss Universe franchise, choosing instead to designate the third winner to represent India in Miss International pageant.

In 2013, Miss Universe organization awarded back the franchise to Bennett, Coleman & Co. Ltd. A separate pageant Miss Diva 2013 was conducted to send representative to Miss Universe.

So, now the winner of Miss India pageant is send to the Miss World Pageant. Like other crown holders, she also has some social and moral responsibilities besides preparing for the Miss World crown.

Indian Princess*

Indian Princess (IP) is an annual beauty pageant for young non-resident Indian girls. Introduced in 2012, the pageant is conceptualized by Shri Sunil Rane, Chairman, IP and organized by Atharva Group in association with Essel Vision. The pageant has not only created waves in the fashion and beauty industry in the country but has also made a global impact through its globally popular Indian Princess International (IPI).

Participation in IP is from 20 states of India and in IPI from more than 15 countries like South Africa, Netherlands, the UK, the US, Malaysia, Germany, New Zealand, Latavia, India, UAE, Middle East, Spain, and Singapore.

Contestants after auditions from the different regions are trained in the areas of diction, fitness, grooming, etiquette, ramp walk, make up, styling, photo shoots and international mannerism by eminent experts from all over the world who groom them to achieve perfection at Five Star Blue Ocean Resort & Spa—Hospitality Division of Atharva Group.

Eligibility criteria

- Should be a non-resident Indian or a person of India origin or must have Indian roots.

---

*: Source: Wikipedia.

- Must not be married, pregnant or a parent.
- Age group between 18-27 years on or before 1 January 2012.
- Minimum height of 5'7 (170 cm).
- You or your immediate family is not related to any person employed by the organizers or sponsors.
- You are a natural-born female and not had a sex change.
- You are not under any commercial contract with any modeling agency at the time of appearing for the auditions.
- Once you are short listed, you cannot be a part of any other commercial contract or pageant.

Miss Himalaya Pageant*

Miss Himalaya Pageant is an annual pageant having headquarters in India. The pageant is open to young women from Himalayan region in the states of Jammu and Kashmir, Himachal Pradesh, Uttarakhand, Sikkim, and Arunachal Pradesh including recent arrivals Meghalaya, Nagaland, Manipur, Mizoram, and Tripura, as well as the hilly regions of two states Assam and West Bengal in India and Nepal, Bhutan, and Tibet outside India.

The pageant is produced and directed by Lobsang Wangyal of Lobsang Wangyal Productions, which has also been producing the Miss Tibet Pageant since 2002. The purpose of the annual event is "to bring women from the entire Himalayan region onto one platform to celebrate the beautiful cultures, people, and nature of the Himalayan region".

Eligibility criteria

Applicants should be born to parents of Himalayan cultural background; between 17 and 25 years of age; minimum 165 cm in height; unmarried and not having given birth.

Ru-Ba-Ru Miss India*

The pageant is organized by RUBARU group by the pageant directors Sandeep Kumar and Pankaj Kharbanda.

The purpose of this event is to raise awareness towards female feticide and violence against woman. The title holders of this pageant go to represent at various international pageants.

---

*: Source: Wikipedia.

Contestants after auditions from the different regions are trained in the areas of diction, fitness, grooming, etiquette, ramp walk, make up, styling, photo shoots and international mannerism by eminent experts from all over the world who groom them to achieve perfection. Pageants attached to RUBARU group are: Supermodel International; Face of Beauty International; Eco Queens; Top International Model of the World; Ms Tourism International; World Beauty Queen.

Eligibility criteria

Applicants should be born to parents of Himalayan cultural background; between 17 and 25 years of age; minimum 165 cm in height; unmarried and not having given birth.

Femina Miss Diva*

Miss Diva is a part of Femina Miss India pageant that sends India 's representatives to Miss Universe and other pageants after Miss Universe organization awarded back the franchise to Bennett, Coleman & Co. Ltd.

Eligibility Criteria

The height of the contestant should be 5’5 & above; Age should be 18-under 27 (as of 1 February 2015); Single, Unmarried and Not Engaged; Indian Passport Holder/Overseas Indian Citizen/ Non-resident Indian.

Campus Princess#

Campus Princess is a college-level beauty pageant organized by the Times of India that “scouts potential beauty queens by engaging with the student community.” Campus Princess is a breeding ground for scouting young talent which helps them realizing their dream of becoming a beauty queen.

Scheduled twice in a calender year, the winners of Campus Princess get an auto-entry to the top 24 finalist of Miss India and Miss Diva pageants respectively.

---

*: Source: Wikipedia.

#: Source: *http://vivacity.lnmiit.ac.in/campusprincess/*

Eligibility criteria

1. Nationality: Indian Passport Holder.
2. Age: Between 18-25 years.
3. Marital Status: The applicant should be unmarried.
4. Height: 5'6" and above (without heels).
5. Student of any recognized educational institution.
6. Selected participants will have to follow the dress code of a Black Cocktail Dress and Stilettos while walking the ramp.

The Title Miss India*

- Femina Miss India, a national beauty pageant in India that selects India's representatives to Miss World, Miss Supranational, Miss Grand International and Miss United Continent. In past years Femina Miss India sent India's representatives to Miss Universe (1964-87, 1989-2009), Miss International (1991-2012, 2014), Miss Earth (2001-13), Miss Asia Pacific International (1968-2005), Miss Teenage Intercontinental (1975-78), International Teen Princess (1967-1974), Queen of Pacific (1969-72, 1974, 1975), Miss Tourism (2005, 2007), Miss Heritage (2013), Miss Universal Peace and Humanity (2014) and Miss Nations (1964).
- Miss Diva, sister beauty pageant of Femina Miss India that selects India's representatives to Miss Universe. In past years it also sent India's representatives to Miss Supranational (2014), Miss Earth (2014) and Miss Asia Pacific World (2013).
- Miss Earth India, a national beauty pageant, selects India's representatives to Miss Earth. During the Miss Earth India 2016 contest, apart from the winner, they also had runners up like Miss Earth India Air, Miss Earth India Water and Miss Earth India Fire.
- Glamanand Supermodel India, a former beauty pageant, selected India's representatives to Miss Earth and Miss International (2014).
- Ru-Ba-Ru Miss India Elite sends India's representatives to Supermodel International, World Beauty Queen, Miss Eco, Miss Globe, Miss Tourism World and Miss Pancontinental.
- Elite Model Look India, a model search contest in India, sends its winner to Elite Model Look Contest.

---

*: Source: Wikipedia.

- Miss India Worldwide India, a beauty pageant, selects India's representative for Miss India Worldwide pageant.
- Indian Princess, a beauty pageant in India started in 2010, selects India's representative for Miss Intercontinental, Miss Tourism International and Top Model of the World. Earlier it also sent India's representatives to Miss Grand International (2013, 2014) Miss Supranational (2011, 2012), Miss Globe (2011, 2012), Miss Tourism Queen of the Year International (2011, 2012), Miss Model of the World (2011, 2012), Miss International Golden Skin (2011), Miss Exclusive of the World (2011) and Supermodel International (2011).
- Miss Heritage India, a beauty pageant in India, sends its winner to Miss Heritage pageant.
- India World Miss University, a beauty pageant in India, sends its winner to World Miss University pageant.
- Femina Look of the Year, a model search contest, sent its winner to Elite Model Look contest (1994 to 1999).
- Eve's Weekly Miss India , a former pageant in India, sent its winner to Miss World (1959-1966) and to Miss International (1960-1962 and 1968-1988) and a runner up to Miss Maja International and Miss Charming International (1972). It also sent India's representatives to Queen of Pacific (1967) and Miss Nations (1963).
- Bharat Sundari a former pageant sent its winner to Miss World (1968-1975). It also sent India's representative to Queen of Pacific (1973).
- Miss India CT, local competition in Connecticut.
- Miss South India, a regional contest.
- I AM She–Miss Universe India, a former pageant in India, sent its winner to Miss Universe (2010 and 2012) and runners-up to Miss Globe International and Miss Asia Pacific World.

Chapter 48

Miss India auditions#

If you decide to fill the form and apply for Miss India contest, you should be aware of certain rules and regulations you will have to abide by.

For these auditions the entire country is divided into 5 zones: North, South, East, West and Central. Several thousand young women from all parts of the country and world submit the form. All the girls satisfying the following criteria can apply:

- Age between 18-25 years
- Height 5.6" & above
- Unmarried
- Born Indian National holding an Indian Passport.

Steps involved in applying to the contest

Step 1: Applicant will be notified with a registration number (e.g.: P123456789) upon successful submission of online application.

Step 2: Contestants must email the below mentioned details to *missindiaorganization@gmail.com*: Name; Age; Height; Vital Statistics; Contact Details; City of Residence; 3 Photographs: close up, mid-length and full-length

Step 3: Submission of the following documents:

1. Copy of passport.
2. Copy of birth certificate.
3. Fitness certificate: May be obtained by a local physician/family doctor stating the applicant is physically and mentally fit.
4. Unmarried affidavit should be made on ₹100 stamp paper and notarized.
5. Three photographs: Close up, mid-length and full-length.

#: Source: Info as given on *beautypageants.indiatimes.com*

Articles required to be taken for the auditions

There are some basic things which the contestants are asked to carry during the auditions, but some requirements vary according to the city of audition. For example:

Contestants auditioning at all city auditions

1) Hot pants (shots): Denims.
2) White singlet/Ganjee.
3) Cocktail Dress: 1-2 options of short, fitted, black sexy cocktail dresses. Please DO NOT wear long evening gowns for round two.
4) Inner wear: Appropriate inner wear for all above articles such as skin tone panty hose, g-strings, strapless bras, silicone's and cups for swimwear, panty liners etc.
5) Footwear: Pair of stiletto heels in black, silver, gold or skin. Please ensure that these are not platforms or wedges and are minimum of 4 inch heels.
6) Jewelry: Appropriate jewelry, accessories to go with your wardrobe and attire.
7) Makeup: Cannot be loud, has to be minimalist and natural.
8) Hair: Cannot be pinned up, must be open and have volume.

Some special requirements.

1) Black Bikini: Please carry some options of black swim wear—two-piece, well fitted and in good condition.
2) Sarong: Carry appropriate sarong to go with the same.
3) Bathrobe: A bathrobe to cover up in between sessions and in the green room.
4) Hot pants (shorts): Denims.
5) White singlet/Ganjee.
6) Cocktail Dress: 1-2 options of short, fitted, black sexy cocktail dresses. Please DO NOT wear long evening gowns for Round 2.
7) Inner wear: Appropriate inner wear for all above articles such as skin tone panty hose, g-strings, strapless bras, silicone's and cups for swimwear, panty liners etc.
8) Footwear: Pair of stiletto heels in black or white or silver or gold or skin. Please ensure that these are not platforms or wedges and are minimum of 4 inch heels.

9) Appropriate jewelry, accessories to go with your wardrobe and attire (No jewelry with bikini).
10) Makeup: Cannot be loud, has to be minimalist and natural.

Audition Rounds

The first round will be the swimsuit round where the contestants will wear bikinis with sarongs for judges to assess the overall physical criteria—height, proportionality etc. This will be the second elimination round.

The second round will be the cocktail dress round. Here the judges could ask you a couple of questions to get to know you better- about yourself, why Miss India, questions on your interests, career, future, family etc.

Short listed candidates from the city Auditions join the respective City Pageant. Winners of the City Pageants gets direct entry to the finalist of Femina Miss India, while the Runners up are invited to the final round of auditions held in Mumbai.

Chapter 49
Kids contests

Times have changed. In today's world kids are exposed to so many different fields that some of them start showing interest in beauty contests right from their early childhood. Most of the kid's beauty contests are open to both boys and girls between 3 to 18 years of age. The contest is of three types: Glitz contest; Natural Contest; Online contest.

Glitz contests

The main focus of this contest is on Creativity; the contestant is expected to use ones imagination. Contestants are seen wearing elaborate and outlandish evening gowns, elaborate jewelry, hair extension, crowns, fake lashes, hair, nails, formal suits/tuxedos, wigs, fake mustache etc. Many oppose this type of contest as the kid go through a lot of pressure to look pretty or handsome with different kinds of beauty aids, waxing, threading and by using hairstyle products.

This can be very harmful for the child's health. Focus on physical appearance at early age may affect the confidence and self esteem of the child. Families need to be a bit cautious before registering their child for a glitz kids contest.

Due to age divisions there are various names for such contests like: "Junior Miss/Mr Contest"; "Baby Miss/Mr Contest"; "Little Miss/Mr Contest"; "Prince and Princess Contest"; "Kiddy King and Kiddy Queen Contest"

Natural contests/pageant

Natural pageants have strict rules and guidelines regarding a lot of issues like clothing, makeup, hair etc. Children are judged on their natural abilities, speaking skills, talents and confidence. Kids are allowed to wear whatever they feel comfortable in, do a normal/everyday hair look, and stay as natural as possible.

These contests have various rounds for the participants to project their best like, talent, interview, sportswear, casual wear, swimwear, western wear, theme wear, fancy dress, creativity and outfit of personal choice.

Some pageants go out of their way to make every child feel like a winner. They are all awarded trophies, certificates, gift hampers and sometimes each child walks away with a subtitle like most talented, sparkling smile, most observant, most congenial, most humble, beautiful eyes, great speaker etc. Everyone is made to feel like a winner. This does not harm the child and adds to their confidence level.

Online contests

In a computer savvy world of today, a new trend has come up which is online contests. Sites like Facebook, keep having many photo contests and have various pageant pages for various age groups where participant's pictures are judged by how many likes they have received or by commenting on them. Unlike the normal stage contests, participants here submit an application along with a picture or video for judgement. Sometimes the contest holders may ask the participants to write a few lines on a particular topic. Contestants are awarded downloadable certificates and virtual prizes. Sometimes they may offer them a magazine cover too.

Some pageants are for profit building and are used by organizers for self promotion, and some are organized by nonprofit organizations. Entry fee to these contests range accordingly. Please do check before entering.

Chapter 50

Major kids contests#

Kids beauty pageant is a beauty contest featuring contestants under 16 years of age. Competition categories may include talent, interview, sportswear, casual wear, swim wear, western wear, theme wear, outfit of choice, decade wear, and evening wear. Depending on the type of pageant system (glitz/natural), contestants may be found wearing makeup to fake teeth, as well as elaborate hairstyles and custom, designed and fitted, outfits to present their routines on stage.

While most beauty pageants cater strictly to girls, there are a growing number that include boys as well. Due to age divisions, these contests often have names such as "Baby Miss", "Petite Miss", "Little Miss" and more. Age divisions of these contests are generally: 0-11 months, 12-23 months, 2-3 years, 4-6 years, 7-9 years, 10-12 years, 13-15 years, 16-18 years. For boys sometimes, two age divisions are merged such as 0-3 years, 4-6 years, etc.

Typically, pageants have a guideline of "no more than one and a half minutes on stage" per child for beauty/formal wear and other modeling-based events. Talent usually is limited to two minutes or less.

Children are judged on individuality, capability, poise, and confidence. They compete to win a variety of prizes, such as electronics, toys, scholarships and grants, cash, tiaras, sashes, robes, and trophies. Some pageants do their best to make every child feel like a winner. There is a Queen for every age division, and there are Ultimate Grand Supreme awards, and Mini Supreme Queens for certain blocks of age divisions (0-5, 6-11, 12-16, 17 and up). There are also side awards and overall side awards.

A rising trend in pageantry is the online, specialty or mail-in pageant. Social media sites like Facebook have many photo contest and pageant pages where contestant's photos are judged by how many "likes" they

---

#: Source: *https://en.wikipedia.org/wiki/Child_beauty_pageant*

receive. Contestants in an online pageant submit an application and photographs/videos for judging. Judging criteria can range from past pageant achievements, numeric scale ratings and essays. Winners may be awarded virtual prizes such as downloadable certificates and being featured on a pageant's website or physical prizes and gifts such as tiaras, sashes, medallions, toys and more.

Some sites to explore for kids pageants are: *www.universalroyalty.com; www.sunburstbeauty.com; www.babymissamericapageant.com; www.babydollbeauty.com; www.indiaparenting.com/contests/babyphotocontest*

Chapter 51

First time contestant

The first time contestant always feels a little lost. With so many competitions happening, one is bound to get confused. If you would like to enter a contest, do some research and decide what type of contest you would like to enter: local, district, state, national, seasonal, and at what level etc.

The second step is to use the net to search and study about the pageants in your area that match your need. After finding the contest you want to enter, reach out to the organizers and apply to be a contestant. You might have a phone interview with the director or will have to fill out a paper application along with submission of your full length, half body and close-up picture shots. Face book is a very popular medium used by pageant directors to look for contestants.

Filing the application and entering the pageant is the first stage of the competition. It is like creating the first impression on the organizers and judges. Pageant participants should not hurry to fill out the entry form, ensure that you have made enough background checks:

- Who are the organizers/company/credibility in market?
- What are the requirements/essentials to enter?
- What is the aim of the contest/Is there any cause attached to it?
- What kind of investment is involved and what all is included?

- Where will it be held?
- What are the different rounds they may have?
- Will they provide the dresses or you will have to carry your own?
- Will they have an in-house makeup artist and hair stylist?
- Will you get the training or you have to do self grooming?
- How long the training will be?
- Who are the experts involved?
- What are the rules and regulations?

Your entry form is very much like your resume. Keep it neat and clean and readable. Be honest, creative. Give something different to the judges to think about and add some punch lines they can relate to you. Aim to stand out in a positive way. Do not leave any blank columns.

For your pictures, work with a photographer to create the image you'll like to project. Do not go crazy with Photoshop. Keep in mind that it should look like you when you greet the panel in person,

Just like in an interview, aim to put the best foot forward, perform in the initial interview (from the very beginning to the end) like there is only one winner—YOU!!

It's important that before you fully commit yourself to entering a pageant, get support of your family and closest friends. There are many cases where contestant's chances are affected by negativity from their close family. What's the point of entering a contest when you are unable to move forward with your related assignments? One of the major concerns is swimwear round. Be sure you are comfortable with it before you fill the form. There is no point quitting halfway as changing your mind.

Chapter 52

Filling up the form

The first step when you apply for a contest is to fill out the entry form or pageant Biography sheet.

Do not take this lightly. What you write and how you write matters a lot. A lot of thought and planning is required before you fill the form.

Pageant form is your visual resume and your first impression of the judges.

I suggest that always make a rough draft before you fill up the final form. It's because a lot of things will keep popping up which you may want to add or remove from the form. Crossing, uncrossing lines, scratches etc. Leave your form untidy and does not appeal to the judges.

Remember not to submit a hand written form (unless specified). It should be well typed fill in all areas and answers questions correctly. Do not lie or over exaggerate. If you are confused, seek help or recheck with pageant director.

Avoid too may 'I' statements. Use proper sentences and language. Avoid using slang.

Know what you are writing e.g., if you say you love reading, than be prepared that your interview question may revolve around it – like what do you like to read? Who is your favourite author and why? Which is his/her latest book etc. Do your homework.

Mention all your accomplishments and what made you stand out.

Information like your height, weight, bust, hips etc. should be correct as these will be counter checked.

Be careful about grammar and spelling mistakes.

Your brief elevator speech should be short yet very very impressive. Some judges read just that.

Make sure you submit your application on time, or much before the deadline.

Keep rewriting on the rough draft fill you feel you have the perfect statement.

Keep a copy of the application and work around in forming questions which might be asked.

Remember truthfulness matters. Be careful of what you are writing.

Chapter 53

Pre-contest audition

The first step for any contest after filing the application is the audition. It's always better to start preparing beforehand. Audition is like a mini contest. Do not think that the preparation and grooming for beauty contest should be started only after the audition. It's true that the candidates who officially clear the audition get a lot of time for preparation before the finale night. Never take the auditions lightly. This calls for the first impression management. If you perform well, and manage to impress the jury, you are sure to land yourself into the finale. The more prepared you are, the more confident and better performance you will have. Beauty pageant is all about preparations. Never be late for audition.

When you walk up on the stage for the first time....first few seconds matter. You can impress anyone sitting out there by appealing to their visual sense. So dress right. Know what suits you, focus on colors and styles that are appropriate as per your body and personality. Do not wear too much facial and body make-up. The jury might think that you are hiding something. Never keep your dress checks for the last moment. Try on all your dresses and take a feedback from others at home before finally deciding your dress. In case a dress code is given, follow that strictly. Appear as natural as you can. Avoid elaborate hair do's, false lashes etc.

Manners matter!! Do wish the jury members as soon as you are center stage. Hold your mike appropriately and at the right distance.

Know yourself. Make sure that your answers do not vary from what you have written in your bio-data. Also, when they ask you about yourself, its better not to just repeat exactly the same thing you wrote in the bio-data as you are wasting an open question. Besides repeating your identity, add something unique. It's a wonderful opportunity to add anything that you missed out in mentioning in the bio-data. Be honest. If caught lying, admit. That's the reason why it is important to keep a copy of your form so that you can check and master your answers on your bio-data. Cultivate some fine hobbies and have ambitions to speak about. Share your beliefs and values about life. Under no circumstances should you be verbose and also avoid any negative statements.

If the contest is being organized to raise awareness for some cause, do your home work. Understand the issue and why awareness is necessary. Express your thoughts on the cause clearly. Know how you can help as an individual. Give the judges a concrete reason why you should qualify and leave them with a feeling that they should let you in. Don't forget your P's and Q's on the stage. Do not argue with the judges and yes, do not forget to thank them after the interview.

Chapter 54

Checklist of things

Be it an audition or the final contest you will require many things. When you are a participant at a beauty contest, you have to be well prepared for any kind of an emergency. You need to be super organized. An emergency kit is a must along with the other essentials you carry to the pageant. Don't forget to label everything and don't forget to carry the kit in a transparent box so that everything is clearly visible to you when you need it.

- Emergency kit contents:

  Medical kit: Any medicine or vitamins which you take; headache tablets/pain killer; band aids; anti-acids; bandages assorted; antiseptic cream; analgesic muscle rub; medical plaster; stretch bandage incase of sprains and swellings; disinfectants (dettol etc.); throat spray/tablets for singers (talent round); breathe spray/mouth wash (listerine etc.); sanitary napkins (if you are a lady).

  Sewing kit: Various sized needles; thread to match each outfit; thimble (if you use it); small scissors; extra buttons, hooks, beads, rhinestones matching with your outfits; safety pins of various sizes (multicolored if available to match with your outfits).

- Clothing checklist: Arrival outfit/shoes/jewelry/accessories; Formal outfit/shoes/jewelry/accessories; Interview outfit/shoes/jewelry/accessories; Optional competition outfits/shoes/jewelry/accessories; Talent/speech/sportswear/shoes/jewelry/accessories; Rehearsal/comfort outfits; Casual wear; Casual shoes;

Swimsuit/cover wrap and sandals; Night wear; Bathrobe and slippers; Stockings/nylons; Slips/petticoat; Under garments; Jackets, Sweater, Hoodie, Shawl; Evening clutch/Purse/Daily tote; Garment bags.

- Makeup check list: Complete makeup; Makeup remover; Makeup mirror; Cotton swabs; Cotton balls; Cosmetic brush kit; Cosmetic sponges; Facial cleanser/moisturizer; Manicure/pedicure items; Artificial lashes.
- Essential pageant requirement list: CD of music for talent round; Pageant fee; Admission pass; Paper work; Hotel information; Passport/ticket/visa; Personal money; Identity proof; Few passport photographs; Few full and half photographs; Pen; Specs if you need; Mobile phone/charger; I-pad and charger; Laptop and charger; Family pictures; Gods pictures; Few small gifts; Sunglasses; Camera+battery+charger.
- Miscellaneous: Water bottle; Snacks; Hangers; Baby wipes/tissue; Super glue.
- Girls should not forget to pack extra pack of sanitary napkins.

Also, do a check if you have packed the following listed items: body wash; razors and shaving cream; hand and body lotion; dental floss/brush/paste/tongue cleaner; perfumes; sunscreen; shower cap; hair accessories; hair net; hair clips; bobby pins; dry shampoo (in case of emergency); shampoo/conditioner/serum; hair heat protector; teasing comb; large toothed comb; hair brush and regular comb; hair mousse/gel/spray/wax; hair rollers/velcro rollers/sponge rollers or twisters (whatever you use); hair dryer; hair straightening/ curling iron if you use; universal converter plug; power extension cord; towels in various sizes; travel press or streamer; stain remover; double sided tape; nail polish remover; acrylic nails/tips if required; clear nail polish to stop runs in nylon stockings and to fix chipped nails; deodorants/antiperspirants; face freshening spray/wipes; tweezers; hand held mirror; hair spray; nail filer and clippers.

These items may appear small, but are very handy and useful, and saves you from stress and any last minute running around.

Chapter 55

Orientation before the contest

Practice and grooming sessions are fun and a great learning experience. Once you are selected, you will be called for the grooming sessions. They may be full day sessions, or you may have to stay at the practice hotel till the finale. Take these sessions seriously. You will learn the tricks of the trade from experts which may come handy not only during that contest but also in the future.

Remember, you are being observed and marked as soon as you join the orientation session. Listen well and give your full attention during the briefings. As a contestant, you should understand how you would be judged and what is needed to be a winner. Be focused and try to learn the most from these training sessions. You might also consider going to the training room earlier than the other candidates to build a good impression on the coaches or clear any doubts you had.

As you enter the orientation, the schedule of activities are also discussed and you must note down the timings carefully. Always be punctual for various activities. If there are lots of outdoor activities, then you might consider getting a hat, umbrella or a sun block lotion with a higher SPF to be safe. You need to look active and healthy for the cameras all the time as there will be lot of opportunities for photo sessions. You need to be noticed, but please don't overdo it!!

Always maintain discipline and decorum. If you are not permitted to use mobile phones, internet, meet anyone without prior permission, not allowed to smoke, eat or drink some particular things etc., then do not break the rules. Remember, each and every movement of yours is being monitored and even a small mistake can earn you negative marks. Sometimes a chaperone is allotted to be with contestant and guide them.

If you are asked to do an assignment, do it sincerely. Do your homework well. Do not copy. Remember, it's a competition. Copying will get both you and the one you copied noticed and will scale your marks down.

It's always better to circulate a copy of the schedule to your friends and family members along with the do's and dont's so that they do

not disturb you during the training and also help you maintain the discipline. If you need to skip a session for some reason, inform your coach your absence may distort the placement and affect the practice sessions.

Don't land up in the class without any note book. How do you expect to remember all the instructions? It's better to write them down. Not only will you remember things but these notes will be handy for future too. Every contest has a group of trainers and you learn something unique from each one. Remember, whether you win or lose these specialized trainings will groom your personality for good. So, be an active participant and gather as much knowledge as you can.

Be punctual for all the activities and for all the sub contests. Dozing off during the session, taking long breaks after meals, hanging around in lobbies and wasting time is not looked upon well.

Be optimistic by all means, even if you feel others are doing better than you. Remember, tables can turn anytime…it's a competition. Activities can be tiring and stressful and can lead to arguments and mini fights, without intention; be sociable, but be cautious.

Get to know your pageant director, choreographer, and trainers. Be friendly but not over friendly or ask special favors from them. Be careful of not being impolite to them, they may have the power to drag you down. Do not take criticism to your heart. Take all the feedback in positive way and try to improve your self.

Chapter 56
Practice sessions

The only thing which will take you to success is practice. Practice and grooming sessions for the contest can be very tiring. As the pageant night gets closer, the immense pressure among the candidates is exhausting, thus, making them very stressful. The pressure of being the best and putting ones best foot forward take a toll on them.

The most important experts involved during the practice sessions are the communication experts and the choreographer. Two important things which are actually noticed on the stage are your walk and your talk. Listen to these experts instructions carefully and follow and execute them properly. Some students come to drink the knowledge some come to sip the knowledge and some come to gargle! So be in the category of drinking knowledge.

Keeping an 'I know' attitude and being inattentive will not help you. If you do not perfect your communication, ramp walk, dance steps, etc., then how would you perform well? The place where the judges sit is the best view one can ever have. Remember visual aspect on stage is most important. All the movements you make, mistakes and being not confident would be noticed by the judges very clearly.

By the end of the grooming sessions, you must be able to walk the ramp and dance very well. Always take notes when you go for these sessions. Draw the stage forms, visualize and try to follow each and every instruction carefully. Look carefully and listen well. Just don't keep the instructions in the book....do them practically and become familiar with the movements. Knowing the ramp walk or dance steps is different from performing it.

Understand and familiarize the stage platform. Sometimes on the final day there are unexpected adjustments and you may find yourself in an unfamiliar place or stage. Many a times the music track may change due to technical glitch and sometimes the whole sequence is changed at the last moment according to the stage available. Know how to carry yourself and how to react when you have committed a mistake. Don't make too much of it if you forget - just move with the flow.

Walk the talk and find a chance to practice the steps choreographer has taught you during the rehearsal Find a partner who ramp walks and dances well and learn as you go. Don't take things for granted. Do not be afraid to ask the choreographer's help or assistance if you are not getting the movements right.

Practice, practice as much as you can; not only on the stage but also in front of the mirror checking your angles and poses. Do not forget to look up at the audience and never forget to smile. Also, remember to wear your heels during the practice sessions so that you are comfortable with them on the final day.

Chapter 57

Understand your audience

Half the battle is won when you connect with your audience. Understanding your audience has profound implications on your winning strategy and beyond. The audience may be face to face with you or they may be connected to you through computers or television. When you are on stage, you want the crowd to understand and respond favorably to what you are saying.

The crowd which comes to watch a beauty contest is no different than the crowd which comes to watch a theatre show or a movie. Keep in mind that every individual thinks differently and has different likes and dislikes. However, the key to impressing the audience is to understand how they perceive the world around them.

We all use five senses to understand the world: Sight (eyes); Sound (ears); Smell (nose); Taste (tongue or gut feelings); Touch (through skin). The important thing to understand is that out of these five primary senses, three senses are mostly used by people i.e., the sense of seeing, hearing and feeling. Among these three major senses, one sense is always dominant in everyone. Either the person is dominantly visual (sight), or auditory (sound) or Kinesthetic (feeling).

Everyone in the audience may not like you if you just focus on looking pretty, or you just focus on your communication skills. So, don't just look pretty, but also focus on what you will say and also how you will say. Your introduction should have words that appeal to people of all three dominant senses. A simple example: "I hope to SEE (visual) India as a superpower where each and every citizen of the world has something wonderful to SAY (auditory) about the achievements of our country making one FEEL (kinesthetic) proud to be born in such a wonderful land". Here I have used all three types of words in the paragraph thus touching everyone sitting in the audience.

To impress visuals its important to dress well and perfectly, to impress the auditory, one needs to use the right words, sentences and tone, and to impress the kinesthetic, one need to stir their emotions by your punch lines.

To deliver a personalized and relevant experience, you need to know what makes your audience tick.

Chapter 58

Body language

Remember, when we speak, we speak 120-140 words per minute, but when we think, its 800 words per minute. This does not mean that the thoughts which did not get converted into words get lost somewhere. Going by the book, we speak all 800 words we thought. How? Almost 140 verbally and the others by the body actions. These body actions are considered leakages of thoughts and are called body language. Body language and facial expressions are an important part of communication. While preparing for a pageant interview or stage presence, tell someone to video record your performance. You will be amazed by the things that you will see and that others see.

Let's work on some of the noticeable:

- Practice a perfect posture. Stand up straight and tall. Relax your body so that you don't appear stiff. Don't slouch forward or backward. Roll your shoulders back, tuck your tummy in and hold your head high as if you are already wearing a crown.
- Do not fidget. Keep your hand movements slow and limited (especially above waist movement) Gestures should be made with your palms open, flat and visible (it's a sign of honesty); upward palm gestures are more positive then downward gestures. When any hand movement is not required, rest your hands on the waist with fingers facing forward. Don't wring your hands, crack your knuckles or touch your face and hair. Avoid any pointing actions. If you are on stage, don't hold the mike with 'both hands creating an invisible closed door or a barrier in front of your chest. Hold the mike with one hand and rest the other against your body.
- In case you are in front of the interview panel, try and use steeple movement (joining finger tips of both hands); it's a sign of confidence and also helps to engage your hands. Do not play with your rings or try to rest your hands on the panels table. If you are sitting, you can place your hands with open palms on your thighs. Do not hold your hands or wrists at the back. This will expand your upper body sending the signal of dominance.

My experience as a panelist over the years has taught me not to sit facing the candidate squarely as unconsciously this movement of direct facing makes them nervous and they don't open up. So, if you are facing the panel for the interview, drag your chair slightly creating an angle of 60 or 45 degrees between them and you so that both the parties feel relaxed and not intimidated by each other.

- One of the most important aspects of communication is eye contact. One should have a good eye contact not only just while speaking, but also while listening. This does not mean staring, look and break contact on & off.
- Make a perfect eye contact with not only the judges, but with audience as well. When a jury member asks you a question, make a nice eye contact with him/her. Then move your eyes amongst jury members. As you prepare to answer the question, use a light house effect movement (scanning the audience with a look from one end of the room to other) and as you complete the answer, repeat the light house movement. Doing this will make each and every member of the audience feel involved. Complete the answer by resting your eyes back on the jury member who had asked the question. People who do not make eye contact portray signs of aloofness, dishonesty and someone who is trying to hide something.
- Smile. It not only relaxes your facial muscles, but also makes you appear open, honest and friendly. Smile is a universal language which everyone understands, and it thaws the hearts. As a winner, judges are looking for someone who is outgoing, happy and extrovert, rather than aloof and an introvert person who is closed off. Smile most of the time, unless it's inappropriate e.g., talking about something sad and traumatic. Try not to have a closed lipped smile. Smile with your lips open showing a few teeth and with the smile reaching your eyes.
- Don't shift your weight. This makes you look nervous and insecure. These extra movements can be very distracting for the judges. Plant your feet firmly on the ground with one foot forward and another at the back with your weight on it. Don't sway your body back and forth. The lesser and slower the movements, the more confident you will appear.
- Don't touch your face. According to body language experts, touching your face, mouth, eyes or ears indicate doubt or lying and may put your jury in suspicion about what you are saying.

Touching your nose, scratching your eyes and ears appears gross in public and covering your mouth also make one hard to hear. So avoid these gestures as much as you can.

- Do not close your body. Crossing your arms, folding your palms into a fist, crossing your legs—all these gestures makes a person appear aloof and closed. This may not go well with judges and you may loose points.
- Don't be too stiff. Tilt your head slightly when someone is speaking to you; tilting head is a sign of active listening.
- Take your space. Normally when one is nervous, one tends to shrink and fold the body for protection. Taking space, with open body, and standing in comfort shows you are in command and helps create your presence in the room.
- Focus on your emotions. In order to engage your audience, they need to be emotionally connected with you. Before you go on stage, concentrate on your feelings. Be mentally and emotionally connected to what you are about to say? How do you want your audience to feel? The more you focus on the emotions your message is trying to convey, the more congruent and convincing your body language will automatically become.
- While you are waiting backstage, notice the tension in your body. Realize that being nervous is also a good thing...as long as it's in limits. Stand and sit with your weight centered before you go on stage, so that your weight is distributed evenly on your sit bones. Look down and loosen your throat. Take several deep belly breaths. Increase the tension in your body by making a fist, then tensioning the muscles in your arms, torso and legs. As you exhale, relax your body like a wave starting either from the head or toes relaxing the body in slow motion.

Negative body language such as drooping or slumped posture, poor eye contact, not greeting properly, uncertain voice, nervous mannerisms like biting nails, breaking knuckles, drumming fingers or shaking feet and leg indicates a person who is not sure of him/herself. These gestures also reveal the temperament like timidity, introvert, high stung or placid.

Non-verbal communication or body language has the power to instantly tell judges, "I am the title holder". It can make or break a contestant's image in seconds.

Chapter 59

Practicing introductions

Introduction round

Prepare your brief introduction before the pageant. Remember this is your first direct communication with the audience and jury members. A good introduction emphasizes more than your name. The introduction should neither be too short, nor very verbose. It should be few confident sentences that state your name, where you are from, an interesting fact about yourself like hobby or interest, with a powerful closing of belief or motto of your life.

Sometimes, introductions are video recorded before hand to ease out the contestants. As they walk, the video plays in the background

Practice good posture. A straight spine and a head held high shows that you are confident and well prepared. Do not fidget or touch your hair, avoid unnecessary movements or holding the mike with both hands. Just relax your body, hold the mike with one hand whichever you prefer and take a nice pose resting your other hand. Right positioning is very important. Practice well during the rehearsals.

Stand closes enough to the judges. If you are away from them, take center stage so that the lights display your persona to your maximum benefit. Play attention to your number tag. Check that its not covered or flipped. Your tag should be clear and visible to the judges.

Do not be stiff lipped. Smile as you speak. It relaxes the facial muscles and helps one to look confident.

Speak slowly, clearly and with confidence. This is easy to do when you have properly prepared your introduction. Modulate your words properly and speak with assurance and authority. Remember, you are talking on a subject which is closest to your heart—"Yourself"

Tips on preparing your introductory speech

Your introduction should have a personal touch, relate to you and should flow easily like a story about who you are, what your life is about, what is your life's purpose, what you stand for, what are your values, what accomplishments are you working on that will help you fulfill your life's purpose in a manner consistent with your values.

- You can open or close with a famous quote, question, and joke. What I have gathered in my experience as jury since so many year is that if you make your audience feel emotional, make them laugh, touch a chord or make them think, you can win them hands down... Try and capture the attention of the jury and the audience with the unexpected. They have heard enough of run of the mill introductions.
- Expand on the opening sentence and connect it to self. Every sentence counts. Say something about yourself. Be impactful with each word making most of your limited time.
- Draw attention to your words by making small movements without overpowering the message. Highlight your presence by minor body movements.
- Stand tall in a "T" stance. Place your left foot sideways with the right foot in front of it, facing forward. Bend your knees slightly....but do not slump.
- Practice with a microphone if possible and if not available, grab a deodorant bottle or a spoon. Keep it 2 to 3 inches away and not too close as you speak to avoid microphone catching your breathing sound. The more you practice the holding and placement of mike the more confident you will feel on the final day.
- Time your speech to avoid disqualification. An ideal speech should have a greeting, name, place you come from, hobby and a powerful message.
- End with impact. Tie the middle to the end and end to the beginning like a story. Challenge the listeners, engage their thinking and leave them with a powerful impression.
- Stick to the topic and do not divert. Keep the jokes simple and friendly and do not risk offending the jury or audience with non-vegetarian jokes, rude or inappropriate language. Avoid exaggerated movements. Deliver your message, reveal your perspective, relay your personality and do it all in about a minute.
- Practice the entire introduction in front of a mirror, friends or a video camera using all the facial gestures that support the content. Have other critique how genuine and believable you appear. There needs to be continuity in what is being said, how it is being said and how you look when saying it.

- Generally all the introduction, question answer etc., are done in English. Sometimes a contestant may not be fluent in English or does not know the language altogether. In such cases an interpreter can be provided by the pageant organizers. If you feel so, ask for an interpreter right on the first day and practice with them so that they understand you well and can convey your message to the judges and audience exactly as you want to. Do not leave this important decision till the end.

An example of an introduction:

> *Good evening esteemed jury members, Ladies and gentleman. My name is ----- and I belong to the beautiful land of India. I am an Accountant by profession and love to travel. I love to bring out my thoughts and emotions in the form of poetry whenever I have some spare time. I believe, "It's nice to be important, but it's more important to be nice." Thank you.*

Chapter 60

Practicing ramp walks

Catwalk for girls and panther walk for boys as they say is very important part of being on stage. A ramp is a narrow platform, usually a kind of protrusion from a stage, on which contestants show their personality and clothing during a contest. Ramp or runway walk, is totally different from a normal person's walk. Walks on ramp are different as they need a lot of confidence and grace. Usually a walk on the ramp is also called Catwalk. Every contestant has to learn the Catwalk before entering the final contest. This walk is just a basic step to enter and walk the stage during various rounds.

The way you walk plays an important part in the overall development of physical movement and on presentation of yourself. If you become conscious while walking, it makes your body appear stiff and suggests that you are not really walking but enacting a part and it thus looks unnatural. Exaggerated jumpy leg movement also should be avoided

During the contest, every participant is supposed to walk with the music on the ramp in order to show the beautiful dresses that they wear and to reveal their grace. The importance of a ramp can be realized from the fact that every contestant should have some knowledge about it.

Special training is given to the contestants by the chorographers so that they can properly walk on the ramp, and one of the main criteria of a winner is his/her ability to walk on the ramp for the competition.

Contestants feel that ramp walk is the easiest part of competition but in reality walking on a ramp is considered the toughest challenge that any contestant can face. Some of the contestants are familiar with it. On the other hand, some contestants who have never done this before find it difficult to walk properly with the right technique. Walking on the ramp should never be consused with the normal style of walking. The two are very different in nature. Balancing your walk with the rhythm of music is tough.

While walking on the ramp, various factors should be taken into account by the contestant. The level of confidence that he/she shows through the walk, along with being able to handle the dress that she/he is wearing along with walking to the beat of music. All contestants are taught how to walk on the ramp before the final contest. Teaching about ramp walks is a necessary part of all beauty contests so there is no way that a contestant can ignore it.

The best way to learn ramp walk is to walk straight by putting a book on the head. This helps compose the posture required where the shoulders and the head remain straight. Look straight ahead and do not allow the arms and shoulders to move a lot. Practice the walk by wearing pencil heels of about four inches and do not sway the hips a lot while walking. Walk in front of the mirror to see the performance and identify mistakes. With continuous practice one is able to achieve desirable results.

Remember the walking style can change depending on the mood of the scene. When you are happy, your walk will be different from that when you are sad or disappointed. The personality of your character will also determine the way you walk. In addition to the grace and poise that ramp walking teaches you, it also teaches you to take charge of your emotions.

Practice is the key here!

Chapter 61

Practicing for the gown round

This round is something which can make or break your chances. Generally, the final round of the competition is the gown round and it should never be underestimated because this is the time when judges are ready to forget about their favorite contestant and become more observant, and finally decide who really is fitting to be the top finalist. The marks of the previous round will be added here and this is your final chance to make or break it!

Gown walk is not just wearing the best gown, posing and walking with poise but it is all about the ease and comfort while you carry your gown. Many a times, contestant use head gears to enhance their gown. It's important to walk balancing the two. Lifting the gown from corner if you feel you may trip, gracefully maneuvering your moves, all this is taught by the experts during the practice round.

Know your body type and structure and choose the best gown for yourself in terms of color, style and personality. Visualize what image you want to create. Gowns are meant to flow and not to be lifted. Never hold your gown or raise it high unless there is something that is really meant to be held or you feel you are about to fall. If you have to lift it, see to it that there is no leg display.

Gown walk may be slow or fast depending on the chosen music by the choreographer. It's advisable to practice walking with the gown during the rehearsals rather than keeping it for the last moment. This will help you to understand your garment better. You will be able to correct the length and get familiar with the gown tail if it has one. Not just the gown, even the shoes you well wear should be practiced well.

Oftentimes, at many contests, swimsuit walk is given priority than the gown walk. Swimsuit walk is more difficult to perfect because of the catwalk involved. However during the gown walk, one must concentrate not just on the walk but also how easily and comfortably one can handle the garment. The sound created by the contact of the high heels and the floor should be minimized if it cannot be totally avoided.

As you practice the gown walk, pretend that you are wearing the crown. If possible get a toy tiara and place it on your head. This will give you the perfect posture and grace.

Practice as much as you can!!

Chapter 62

Practicing pageant hair styles

Hairstyle can ruin the impact of your costume, work against you and keep you from winning. Your hair style requires careful thought and advance planning, as you cannot start experimenting with your hair at the last moment. It can be very upsetting to realize that your hair has let you down in spite of having the best mind and body amongst all the other participants. Remember, judges are analyzing every detail of your appearance, dress, skin, figure, accessories, shoes, hair and ofcourse your fitness They are sure to notice how you do up your hair and whether the hairstyle suits your face cut. Hence, it is important to wear the right hairstyle.

We all have different face shapes and cuts and so not all types of hair styles will suit every person. You need to look at your face and carefully choose what you want to highlight and what to hide. It's not necessary that what you see on celebs or in magazines will have the same result on you. While choosing a hair style, assure that it will show your best attributes. Do not pick a hair style, which will bring into focus your defects. The right hairstyle can bring out your charm in a beautiful way. The hairstyle you choose should not only be flattering to your image, but should be appropriate for the contest you are entering and compliment the dress.

Though most of the time there is an in-house hair dresser, but sometimes a hairstylist or hairdresser may not be available. Every contestant must know basic hairstyling and should perfect the art of managing their hair on their own. Some of the popular hairstyles that have been favored by winners in the past are: Streaming cascading curls; Long, or short full glamorous layered hair; Long or short with fewer layers curled softly at the ends; Chignon or French twist; Low neck bun; Hair worn down with the crown pinned back; Softly upswept styles; Long straight shiny hair; Straight, shoulder-length blunt cut; Long hair left loose on the shoulders; Blunt cut; High pony; Creative braids.

If you are not blessed with good hair, you can try using the following: Hair extensions; Clip on fringes; Fillers; Fall, cascade or wiglet hair; Bumpits; Full wig, now made with natural-looking hairlines, and made from human or synthetic hair.

Practice a few styles which you can manage on your own. Knowing that you are in full control of your hair without any help will give you a lot of confidence.

Don't forget to carry: bob pins; bun pins; hair bands; hair dryer; hot rollers; teasing comb; hair iron; hair brush round; hair brush paddle; normal tail comb; wide toothed comb; hair voluminizer; hair spray; working spray; serum; good quality shampoo and conditioner; styling mousse; funky and colorful hair accessories like clips, ribbons, bands and tiaras to decorate your up do.

It pays to plan ahead, and practice the various appearances you have in mind with your aides. Do not get carried away and overly dazzle your hair-do to distract attention from the rest of your body. When you practice various hair style, click your pictures to see how you look and take opinion from others. Just because you like a particular style does not mean that it actually suits you.

Chapter 63

Creating the first impression

> *All the world's a stage, and all the men and women merely players; they have their exits and their entrances, and one man in his time plays many parts...*
>
> —William Shakespeare, from Act II, Scene VII of As You Like It.

Your first appearance on stage sets in motion your first impression. You are a performer and audience is the judge. Unfortunately, audience and judges are wired to judge people on their first appearances. They even make decisions as to whether they even want to keep hearing those people who come on the stage.

First impression starts forming within a couple of seconds. The contestant should remember that human brain is like cement…whatever falls on it makes an impression. One never gets a second chance to create first impression, so it's important to keep in mind that the first few seconds matter a lot.

Imagine when you go to buy an unbranded soap from the market. You have no idea what quality or color soap it might be. We usually make our choice by looking at the outer packet. Similarly, if one is packed well, people will accept you else they may reject you.

When you meet people for the first time, this is how they analyze you: Visual: 55%; Vocal: 38%; Verbal: 7%. You would notice that the maximum percentage goes in the visual effect. Before you speak, your image speaks. So, what do people notice in this 55%? They notice your dress, grooming, styling, accessories and of course your body language.

Subtle behaviors by a contestant act as social communication, and a first impression literally "sets the stage" for the entire contest. Some of the most important things people notice on a contestants stage entrance (both good and bad) are: eye contact; head movement; body posture; posture; touching of clothes; unsteady gaze; deep bow; appropriate walking speed; tensed mouth muscles; visual elements such as: odd hairstyle, flashy shoes, unappropriate dress

The unconscious body language they observe is: Any signs of nervousness like fidgeting, hair touching; nodding and involving the audience; the direction of their gaze; eye contact with judges; blank stares; how often they touched her/his (clothes etc.); stance width used on stage; walking pace used for stage entrance; walk coordination with music; smile; confidence; resoluteness; likeability.

It's most important to present yourself as a visual treat. Dress right, accessorize right, walk right and of course ultimately speak right!!

Scoring is based on overall first impression, physical fitness and health, overall physique, height, weight and bone structure, walk, posture and grace, sense of confidence and presence on stage.

Chapter 64

Pre-final round

As the name suggests, this round happens before the finale to rate the candidates by panel interview or by face to face interview in a closed-door set-up. This helps the jury to understand each candidate closely and how deserving one is to be a winner. During this time itself, the jury also decides on the subtitles and sometimes even the semi-finalists to be announced during the finale night. This saves a lot of time and make the pageant night show shorter. Long shows with never ending rounds tire everyone—contestants, jury and also the audience. Based on the decision of the organizers, pre-judging can happen days or hours before the finale night, depending on the pageant committee's decision.

Some contest organizers combine the pre-final round with talent competition and swim wear competition. The candidates first introduce themselves as they face the jury, proceed with their talent presentation or swim wear/physical body round.

Swim wear and body round should not be taken lightly by the contestants. Boys must remember to pump up their body before they come on stage. Girls and boys, both are allowed to wear a bit of makeup like bronzer or baby oil to highlight their body. Avoid creating fake muscles with bronzer. These tricks may work in photographs but can be a disaster on live display.

For the talent round, don't forget to carry your costume, props and music. Remember to stick to the designated time during the round or else you may get disqualified. Its better to always have a backup if your CD does not work.

Mind your body language. Whatever you say and whatever your body says should be congruent or else judges will get confused. Avoid exaggerated movements. Less movements and slow ones will get you there.

Catch up on your beauty sleep before the pre-judging day to make sure that you look fresh since you may not be allowed to wear make-up.

Prepare well for your one to one interview. Have clear ambitions and goals to express. Be honest and practical with your answers. Read up

BELGIUM

GW
GW
GW
13
19

BELGIUM

CAUCASUS
KOREA
NEW ZE
CHINA

DENMARK
BELARUS

INDIA

20

and be up to date with current affairs. If the contest is for a cause, express your views clearly and ofcourse do mind your manners.

A show of interest and determination to win will convince the committee to take you ahead.

Chapter 65

Final day

One saves the best look for the final day. All your practice sessions, experiments with looks will finally be visible to people. Every contestant tries to look wow and glamorous on the finale day. Keep in mind the type of pageant you are contesting and use the makeup accordingly. You will have to adjust your makeup for each phase and occasion of the competition. Do not go overboard with your look as makeup should enhance but not create a false you. You must look like YOU but more glamorous!! Your make up should be as close to your natural self as can be.

Don't forget to moisturize. Begin any makeup application with moisturized skin and conditioned lips. Standing constantly under harsh lights will make your skin dry and lips crack. You can try applying a bit of a sunscreen mixed with the moisturizer

Conceal well. Normally, it's not necessary to conceal every day, but you need it most on this important day to show a chiseled face and to hide any flaws. There will be loads of photo opportunities on this special day. Again, it's most important to blend well. Do not let any harsh lines show.

Use foundation in the proper way. An important tip is that as you apply foundation on your face, Do not forget to put foundation over the eyelids; under the eyes, around the nostrils, ears and neck. Forgetting this will make your face look unusually lighter in the harsh stage light.

Eye liner enhances. When it comes to a contest, besides having nice pearly smile on stage, the eyes need to sparkle. Apply liner as per your eye shape. You can either keep it basic or try smokey eye, a cat eye look, and much more. Apply eyeliner to lids also. You can change the slope, making the eyes look bigger or smaller. Don't forget to add shimmer in the tear duct area for added sparkle! Don't forget eyes are the biggest medium of body language.

Pump up your lashes. You can either wear false lashes, or add false eye extensions with the help of 3D mascara. Another way is to add false lash clumps to fill in the gaps in your natural lash line. Some eyes look great with two strips of false lashes for creating oomph that would show up on stage. If your eyes look droopy with false lashes than avoid them. Stick to heavy duty mascara instead.

Go easy with eye shadow. Eye shadow melt out due to harsh lights and sweat, be sure to set the eye with an eye shadow primer. Don't forget to use the "drop cloth" trick of catching extra powder fallout, or else your whole make up will get ruined. Apply shadow in thin layers to get to the level of intensity you want. Don't forget to highlight your brow bone to open up the eye.

Use mascara properly. Curl your lashes with an eyelash curler slightly heated in your palms. Apply mascara by wiggling the wand from the roots of your lashes on through to the ends. You can apply 2 or 3 coats.

Don't forget the brows. Groom the brows into shape with a comb brush and fill out the thin areas with shadow using little feather-like strokes. A coat of brow gel keeps everything in place. Don't forget to brush away excess loose powder from under the eyes.

Follow the blush trick. Smile first and then use a blush to accentuate the apples of your cheeks and cheekbones. Cover the cheekbone areas with a bronze. Blend upward toward the temple. Apply blush on the apples of your cheeks. The reflection of the bronzer looks great under the lights.

For lipstick to stay, entire lips should be outlined and filled in with the pencil. Then go over the pencil with a lip brush to make sure the color is blended and evenly placed. Now add a dab of lipstick in a matching tone on top of the pencil—just on the surface and in the center of the mouth. Wear a shimmery lip gloss over it.

Chapter 66

Last minute beauty fixes

Running around in limited space, from makeup to hair stylist and so forth, beauty accidents are bound to happen! From lipstick on the teeth to running mascara, a contestant may have to face all kinds of situations. Here's how to handle them.

- When you have finished blow-drying your hair, switch to the cool setting, flip the head over, and aim the nozzle around for a few minutes. This creates pockets of air between your locks so they look extra full and add volume.
- Remove splotches on your face by taking a flat q-tip and dip it into your moisturizer then apply it to the spot, use the other side of the q-tip to smooth out the makeup—no need to add any more moisturizer.
- Since you're going to be shaking hands with lot of people, spray some fragrance on your palms so that your hand touch will release some nice scent with whoever you meet.
- If your mascara is clumpy, it's probably old and expired. Throw it away. Clamp your lashes with a baby wipe to remove any excess formula.
- Heat your eyelash curler with your dryer for a few seconds. Be careful not to overheat. The warm curler will help lock in the lash curl, and then swipe on your mascara.
- If you have put too much blush then go over your cheeks with a CLEAN brush, add a dab of moisturizer or tinted moisturizer to tone it down. You can even dust loose translucent powder over your cheeks to diffuse the color.
- Enhance your cleavage by contouring it and dusting a shimmery body powder over the tops of your breasts. You can even contour your cleavage.
- Is your nose shining too much? Tone down a glaring T-zone with a piece of toilet-seat covers found in the ladies' room. It'll act as a blotting paper.
- If you have too much makeup on your face, sprit it with water, lightly, and smooth out with a damp sponge and be sure to blend well.

- As soon as lipstick is applied, always press your lips onto a folded square of tissue to blot. You can even stick your forefinger in your mouth and slowly pull it out to remove any lipstick that may strain your teeth later. Try lining your lips after you apply your lipstick
- Angry bright pimple at the last minute is a big nightmare. Put a little apple cider vinegar on the spot then apply yellow-based concealer with a lip brush. When you feel the pimple coming, wrap an ice cube in a thin cloth, paper, or a towel and put it on and off the pimple for 10 minutes. Don't pop a pimple. Apply Neosporin to it before you go to bed.
- When applying shadow, fold a single square of tissue and hold it underneath each eye. It will always catch any loose pigment fallout while protecting your freshly done foundation.
- Try a cold gel eye mask or a ziploc bag full of frozen ice or even cupping two frozen spoons over the eye area for a few minutes to reduce puffiness of eyes.
- Put a dab of makeup remover on a q-tip and wipe off the running mascara. A thin layer of vaseline can be applied to eyelids before using makeup to help shadow stay put and attain a soft, dewy glow.
- Camouflage gray roots and hide regret with powder eye shadow that matches your natural hair color. Set with hairspray.
- Plump your pout by dotting shimmery gloss in the center of your lips for creating a 3-D effect.
- Use a light shade of eyeliner to make tired eyes look brighter. Try lining the inside of your lower lid with white eyeliner, but be careful this doesn't look to harsh or makes your eyes look pink. Also, make sure to put a lighter shade concealed on the inside corners of your eyes; this is the area that creates a dark shadow under your eyes.
- Flaky skin happens due to frequent temperature changes. If your moisturizer doesn't work, apply a thin layer of liquid vaseline to the spot! Leave on for 10 min, rinse, wash and moisturize.
- For bikini bumps, put some concealer on it. If they are breaking out, apply Neosporin antiseptic cream and powder at night. Those little bumps may be kurtosis pillarist—it looks like acne, but it isn't. You can get this from wearing too tight clothing.
- Take a transparent or nude lip gloss adds it to the apples of your cheeks. It will instantly illuminate the skin and give a healthy glow.

- Instead of ripping off a broken nail, use a dab of super glue over the tear, then buff gently with a nail file.
- Apply your perfume to your wrist, throat, behind your knee, and your hair. Mix a drop of your perfume with your hair shine serum and pat it through your hair.
- If you have dry scaly skin, use a scrub or a handful of finely ground cornmeal, oatmeal, or even baking soda and put it on a damp washcloth then massage into your skin, rinse, and then moisturize.
- If you drop makeup on your dress, don't rub it, put some club soda on a cloth and press it into your stain then sprinkle salt on top to soak it up and brush it off.
- To hide your tattoos you need to use two different colors of concealer. First use a strong lighter shade concealer as a base to cover the tattoo, then add a darker shade (the color of your skin tone), powder and then buff extra powder away.
- Put a small amount of hair gel on an old toothbrush and brush baby hairs back from your forehead. Also try to spray a flexible hold hair spray and brush them back.
- Beauty contestants over the years have a great tip to give. Don't wash your hair the morning of the pageant, dirty hair holds the style better. If you land up with helmet hair, you have overdone the hairspray, spray it lightly with water, blow dry, and start over. If your locks smell like a bar, rub a fabric-softener sheet along the length of your hair, starting at your roots. Sleep on a satin pillowcase, it helps keep your hair smooth while you sleep.
- To hide large pores, apply plain cold yogurt to your skin for 10 minutes then rinse with cool water. This absorbs bacteria and helps your pores decrease in size.
- Save money on those pore strips, spread a wide scotch tape on blackheads, let it dry, and then peel it off! If they're not too deep, they'll come right up.
- If you feel that your face turns red and sweaty when you face the audience, then avoid any hot spicy foods and/or alcohol as this can cause your skin to flush even more. Hold a cold washcloth to your face before applying your makeup. In the moment, inconspicuously use deep breathing exercises—in through your nose and out through your mouth. For anxiety, ask your doctor about taking herbal remedies to calm your nerves. Simultane-

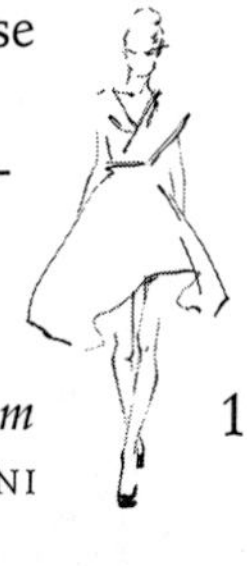

ously, to calm your nerves you can run your wrists under cold water, massage your shoulders and head in small circles (before you do your hair!) Sniff the scent of vanilla extract. Deep breathe for a minute.

- Deliberately recite positive statements and affirmations. Drink a glass of water, listen to some soothing music and pray.

Chapter 67
Talent round

This is another popular round of the contest. Every contestant gets about 2-3 minutes to showcase their talent on stage. The talent can be in form of dancing, singing, poetry recitation, monoacting, mimicry or playing a musical instrument. One can add an interesting twist to these acts by way of right props etc., and make them look unique.

- Poetry: Please remember that if you are reciting a poem, it should be original and written by you. In case you are reciting someone else's poem, then do give due credit to the writer. Simply reciting a poem is not enough. Do use expression and voice modulation to make it lively. Pick a poem which has a strong meaning and moral to it.
- Singing: I have personally seen a lot of contestants singing national anthem as talent. Remember, it's not a talent. Sing a proper song if you have to. Singing the national anthem in a unique way, with sign language sure can be a talent. A lot of contestants can sing, but singing in a foreign language will surely get noticed. Another way is to whistle an entire song, or may be sing a song backwards! Unique twist to singing can turn an ordinary vocal performance into an experience
- Unusual self-defense techniques: It's a great way to project your presence of mind, focus, strength—emotional, as well as physical; your ability to deal with challenging situations and how do you handle crisis.
- Monoacting and mimicry: These are the most sensitive and expressive talent and very few can pull it off. A well prepared mime has the power to make even the toughest of persons shed a few tears. These acts bring out your sensitive nature, ability to express emotions.

- Dancing: Pick up a unique form. It can even be a folk dance. You can act a story through dance. You can also promote your culture by showcasing dance forms specific to your state or country. Remember to match your costume and props perfectly. Avoid mixing and matching of other cultures and costumes.
- Stand-up Comedy: Such candidates project frankness, sportsmanship and a keen observation. It's a great way to release the tension in the audience and give everybody a good laugh! Stand-up comedy is not something many contestants attempt, so it is bound to be unique and make you stand out.
- Gymnast: A well choreographed gymnastic act or acrobatic performance could surprise everybody in the audience! You are sure to win everyone's envy—and hearts too.
- Art: Sketching, painting and drawing are very common. You need something different like making sand come to life and creating a painting by just throwing it around? How many can paint with the brush in the mouth? Creating something ordinary and making it extraordinary can surely get you a lot of attention.

It is very important to be unique and catch the judges eye. Talent round is the one chance where you get to be you, show your hobby or passion and get to project the best in you. It can completely change the outcome of the pageant and compel the judges to rethink about their decision!

Contestants during this round are judged on: 1. uniqueness of talent; 2. creativity; 3. costume; 4. props; 5. originality; 6. performance; 7. stage presence; 8. confidence.

Chapter 68

Swimming costume round

This is one of the most important rounds. Sometimes its conducted closed doors and sometimes contestants may have to appear on the stage wearing one. Decisions are based on over all physical fitness and the poise with which one carries oneself during the competition. The costume should always be in good taste.

Wearing pantyhose/see through stockings etc are not allowed but one can wear leg makeup. Pay special attention to swimsuit lining as the costume might appear transparent due to stage lighting. The swimsuit competition is only uncomfortable for those who are not prepared physically, mentally or may have some issues related to their family customs. It's fun for those who know they've worked hard on themselves and know that they look amazing.

A lot of contestants get confused about picking the right color. Whether to go for black, very bright or earthly colors. Keep in mind the background or backdrop of the stage. If the background is dark pick a color that will stand out, go bright, if the backdrop is white, go red and standout. Therefore always keep a choice of light & dark color with you. A colored swimsuit always projects confidence. Add some accessories. Be sure whatever color you pick, make sure it is not too close to your skin tone or color.

Next step is to pick up the right shoes. Swim wear will require a long leg look so don't pick a shoe that has a strap that will break up the illusion of the length of your leg. Judges are interested in looking at you, not your shoes, so don't pick a shoe that stands out more than you do. Huge clogged heels, too many blingy stones, outlandish colors are totally out. Keep it simple. Do not save your shoes for the last moment—be sure you practice walking in them well in advance so that the shoe is well broke-in. So practice, practice, practice! Walking in them will help you identify the sore areas and what to do so that when you walk for the finale you are able to walk in your shoes without pain

You will be judged on: overall fitness; body toning and balance; balanced vital statistics; body proportions; how gracefully you carry the costume; body language. Many contests world wide are now doing away with this round. However, some important contests still hold this round.

Chapter 69

Question-answer round

Every contestant dreads this round. It's because your performance in this round can turn the tables on you. Contestant have a lot more to do during this round, than just look nice on stage. A beauty pageant isn't just about looks and dazzling smile. It's about cracking the tough round of questions and answers with conviction. A competition is all about balancing beauty with brains. It can be an extremely nerve-wracking experience if you are not prepared well. As a winner one has to be fully aware of whats happening around the world, and should be well versed with general knowledge.

This is normally the second last round with the chosen semi-finalists before the common question round with the final five.

Each contestant will be given one unique question by the judges to answer. The jury intends to see your individual perspective on the issues addressed via these questions. The answers help gauge the strength of your character, knowledge, awareness and personality. These answers are your ultimate chance towards making an impression on the audience. Answering the questions with honesty and keeping your goals in mind will show them a confident side of you, and a wonderful balance of beauty and brains.

When the judge asks a question, repeat the question before you give your answer. Not only does it give a chance to those who missed hearing it but also sounds professional. It also gives you time to think and get the exact understanding of the question. Speak slowly so that your words are understood. Do not rush or get overly excited due to nervousness. Take a deep breath as the judges ask their questions. It will help calm your nerves.

Do not be too verbose. Be as concise as possible. Finish answering in the allotted time. Avoid unnecessary pause and hums.

Speak loud, but don't scream. Smile while you answer one judge's question, but make sure to have an eye contact with every judge, regardless of whether or not they were the one who posed the question.

If you did not understand the question, politely ask the judge to repeat the same and thank him or her when they do. If you are not comfortable with the language seek permission to answer in your comfortable language.

During the common question (final) round, you will have to write your answer on a sheet within a minute and then read it aloud. As you write your answer, a carbon copy will be made which will be compared to your reading to confirm that you are reading exactly what you wrote.

The judges evaluate the contestant on: presence of mind; knowledge;

ability to grasp the question; intelligence and common sense; conversational ability; sense of humor; confidence, high moral standards, sincerity and integrity; relevant answer to the question and not beating around the bush; body language.

Chapter 70

Final judgment

Judging beauty pageants is a serious task! Each candidate has worked so hard on themselves that it's difficult to choose a winner.

Contestants put a lot of time, money, and hard work into preparing for the contest, and they expect to be judged in a fair manner. However, in spite of the judges being fair and careful with their decisions, there will be some bitterness, hurt feelings and some disappointed contestants.

Areas of competition and judgement

Interview session

This is one of the most important parts. It helps the jury to interact and get to know each contest one on one. Each contestant will have a one-on-one interview with each judge where the contestant will be judged on his/her ability to fulfill the titleholder's responsibilities. Judges will assign marks based on the contestant's communication skills, personality, presence of mind, body language, and personal appearance, goals, knowledge and understanding of various issues. Contestants can freely express themselves as they will not be marked on their personal beliefs. The interview is marked keeping in mind the contestant's ability to articulate based on the age and maturity level. Sometimes there could be a group discussion for few minute with the panel of judges.

Swimsuit session

Contestants will be evaluated on her/his overall commitment to her/his physical health, fitness and lifestyle. Judges will assign marks based on the contestant's physical fitness, body proportions, sense of confidence and composure, carriage and display of drive, energy and charisma. Jury would also like to notice how comfortable one feels in their own skin and this will help in evaluating your self esteem and confidence.

Evening gown/formal wear session

Contestants will be assessed on her/his poise, body language, grace, and commanding stage presence in crisp formal garments. Each contestant will be judged on her/his total look. Judges will assign marks based on the contestant's walk, beauty, carriage and grace, personality, creativity, appropriate accessories, stage command as well as the sense of style.

Casual wear session

Contestants are judged on their personal style and how well they carry their everyday look. Does the contestant follows the fashion blindly as a fashion victim or creates an individual style by keeping one personality, body structure etc., in mind.

Sub-titles session

Sub-title competition allows a contestant to compete in a variety of categories. These competitions does not in any way impact contestants overall marks or the performance of the final day.

Overall main title

Depending on the pageant director's decision, three to five overall main titles are awarded to the contestants with the highest overall marks in the competition. Some contests name it as main title, first and second runner up, and sometimes it's a separate title altogether depending if the contestant is going to represent the country for the international title of the same category. Prizes for the main titles may include cash prize, gifts from sponsors which can even be a car, crowns, trophies and sashes.

Special titles

These titles have their own judging criteria and is completely separate from and has no bearing on the pageants' scoring or outcomes. Winners for these special title are mainly picked internally by the organizers, trainers and people involved with the event by observing the behavior of the contestants during their training and grooming sessions. All contestants are eligible for these awards.

- Congeniality: The recipient of the Congeniality Award is the most congenial, charismatic, and inspirational pageant participant.
- Photogenic: Contestants' headshots are judged by members of the media for their photogenic appeal, beauty, and warmth and personality projection.
- Dazzling Style: Contestant is judged on personal style, fashion sense and pageant modeling ability.
- Positive Spirit: The contestant who's best in sportsmanship, teamwork, time management, dedication, respect and compassion is the winner.
- People's Choice: This award is given to the contestant with the most votes from the general public. Voting takes place weeks before the pageant and contestants are encouraged to campaign for this honor.

In a nut shell, the judges are looking for:

- Facial beauty, complete make-up wear (if worn/applicable), personal hygiene and neatness.
- Originality of the outfit and how well it fits together and if it matches theme.
- Character on stage. The contestant should be happy, excited and want to perform for the judges. The personality/stage presence will also include body language and interaction with judges and audience and confidence.
- Confident ramp walk .
- Contestants introduction of himself/herself as well as how they handle the questions?
- Confidence in all kinds of clothing and how well does the contestant carry himself/herself.
- Overall look, how everything fits together, and the initial impression for the specific category.
- Communication skill.
- Presence of mind.
- Leadership qualities.

Chapter 71

On winning the title

Among the first final ceremonies of a contest is awarding of the sub-titles and sponser gifts/awards. Candidates are observed right from the day one of training by the pageant director and groomers, each giving their marks to pick the winners of various categories. These title also help the audience to guess on who would be the top 5 winners. Many a times this has no bearing on the actual scoring of the final candidates, but it is somewhat intimidating, depressing and scary not to have even a single sub-title. There are many contests nowadays where the Director likes to give a sub-title to each contestant so that they have something to carry home as motivation.

On the other hand, this is also true that the contestants who are awarded actually get highlighted and leave an influence on the judges. Therefore, its important to be on your best behavior throughout the training and the contest.

When called to receive a title, do not forget to clap for yourself, smile, wave at the crowd, use right greeting. You can also put your right hand on your heart and bow slightly. Clap for all the other contestants when they are called. When someone receives a title and you are nearby acknowledge them with a hand shake.

Do not hesitate to offer a hand shake to the official/celebrity/dignitary awarding you. If given a chance, do not forget to say a line of gratitude.

Help or guide the awarding figure on how to put your sash as some of them may not know which shoulder it should go; gracefully help them get through their dilemma.

Wait till the proper picture is clicked with your title and the dignitary. Do not rush back without a picture or you will miss out on a great memory.

Once back, stand in your own placement. Do not stand in front of other contestants by getting them ignored in pictures and hogging the lime light.

If you receive several titles/awards, do not hesitate to turn them over to the stage staff who is helping you.

Make it sure you tie up/fix the sash or sashes on you. It's a total disregard to what you have received if you walk around with them falling all over the floor.

Section 3

Post Contest

Chapter 72
Right conduct for a winner

Remember, it may be easy to find success, but its very difficult to maintain it. The right conduct and behavior would help you stay longer in the industry. Attitude matters. No one likes a winner who is egotistical, selfish and has an unkind heart. No one likes people who throw their weight around.

Winning a contest makes you a star in the eyes of the society, media and entertainment industry. Overnight your become a celebrity; you are the cynosure of all eyes, you lose your privacy. You may get unexpected number of followers and supporters who would be glad to see you. You will be surrounded by such supporters everywhere you go, asking for autographs and selfies. You will be treated like a VIP. Believe me, it takes you to a power trip.

Yes, there are many perks which come attached with the title, but along with that the expectations of the public go high. You would be expected to behave in a certain manner. If you do not fulfill the expectations of the public, they will write you off.

Remember to be nice to everyone all the time. Not only to the general public but also to your co-contestants and officials who are a part of the pageant industry. Make-up artists, pageant trainers, choreographers, stylists, and the directors etc., who have made you what you are and they deserve your respect. Be careful about accusing pageant organizers to be involved in some cheating or fraudulent activities.

Be willing to give your support to media. Be available for interviews and promoting the cause attached to the contest.

As a beauty ambassador, you might have to visit charity events orphanages, villages, hospitals etc. You will meet people from all cultures and all walks of society. So, do your homework. Read a bit about where you will be going and behave accordingly. Learn about various cultures, etiquette and customs.

A crown is a symbolic piece of majesty and royalty and comes with a package of roles and responsibilities. The right code of conduct would save you from harming your reputation and gaining respect and credibility.

Be like a tree loaded with fruits which is always bending so that others can enjoy the sweet fruits that grow on it rather than being a tall high tree where people can never reach out to taste the fruits. Be humble and never forget you roots.

Chapter 73

Responsibilities after winning[*]

Every pageant winner has certain responsibilities. The winner is going to be ambassador/ambassadress of goodwill. They assist encouraging friendship among nations. They share to the world the cultures of people. Everybody look up to them and thus they must be role models. They must maintain a good moral character, be prim and proper and avoid doing things that can dethrone them.

A titleholder becomes associated with many organizations, as a goodwill ambassador. The main purpose is to further an important social cause using the popularity factor. The fight against HIV, violence against woman, female foeticide, drug abuse, children's education and child labor are some of the causes addressed. The titleholder participates in events and operations organized for the cause thereby spreading awareness. A goodwill ambassador may also represent his/her country at an international event.

The magnetic personality of a title holder helps to attract people's attention and to sensitize the public about targeted social problems. This in turn helps raise funds for their eradication. The cause differs from country to country depending on the local problems. The title holder has to help raise funds to eradicate poverty and help the lesser privileged of her society.

As a title holder of a pageant, one of the skills you should possess is good communications skills. Most of your public appearances as a

*: Source: *beautypageants.indiatimes.com/;* Wikipedia.

goodwill ambassador or at a fundraiser event would require you to make a commendable speech about the cause you support. You would be expected to promote the event stating clearly why people should follow your example. Wendy Fitzwilliam, a Miss Universe from the Trinidad and Tobago, spread awareness about AIDS in the Caribbean and other parts of the world through her speeches.

A pageant title holder is not just an eminent person on special occasions. Apart from proving your intelligence, talent and pleasing personality as the winner, you are an advocate of social service. You has a huge moral responsibility and have to maintain a respectable character. You must also be appealing and approachable to people of all age groups, especially the young. Miss America 1998, Kate Shindle, was an active participant at the 12th World AIDS conference in Geneva, Switzerland. A title holder is an inspiration to hundreds of youngsters aspiring to be like them. You are an image of a well-educated and successful personality. With success, you play a big role in promoting your country.

Chapter 74

Dealing with media

Everyone wants to get noticed. There is no other powerful source than media which can make or break you. Media interviews make most people uncomfortable. You may have to give various interviews in print, radio, or television as a contestant or a winner. Given below are cetain points one should remember during media interaction.

- Keep your answers as short as you can. You may do a television interview for half an hour, but the average sound bite is just 10 to 20 seconds long. There is no point if your answers get chopped during edit and loose the meaning. So, be brief - as they say follow the principle of K-I-S-S keep it short and simple.
- Instead of quoting examples from outside, narrating personal experiences can be very powerful. Use them as often as possible.
- Use common language as used by the interviewer. Keep the audience in mind, and speak in terms familiar to them. Avoid any kind of derogatory language. Do not use any slang language.

- Pause before answering to consider your response. It's natural to pause when you are gathering your thoughts.
- Do not shy away from answering tough questions to build your credibility with people. On the other hand, you're not obligated to agree or disagree with whats being asked. Even if you refuse use a soft diplomatic language.
- Turn negative into positive statements. Respond by answering with positive statements and replacing objectionable words with more acceptable terms. Do not flow to negativity even if when someone provokes you.
- Use body language wisely and effectively. People believe in what they see rather in what they hear. Keeping your arms loose and gesturing in a natural way will make you appear calm and confident. Don't clasp your hands tightly together, or cross your arms and legs, never put your hands in your pockets. Use steepling gesture if you are unsure of what to do with your hands. Smile, and use natural expressions.
- Avoid going on and on in a verbose way. Interviewer often waits before asking their next question so that you keep talking. Answer in brief then stop talking.
- Avoid losing your temper. You can tell a reporter you prefer not to comment, but never get angry. Loosing control will go against you.
- Dishonesty, or the appearance of it, can severely damage your reputation. Be honest. Never lie or bluff. Do not beat around the bush. If you don't know an answer, say so.
- The print media like newspapers, magazines, etc., look for unique quotes, so be sure your messages are interesting and quotable.
- Keep few couplets, phrases, poems handy to use and to add power to your speech.

Telephone interview

- Echo can be your biggest enemy. Avoid speaker phone. The person on the other end may not be able to hear you clearly, which increases your chance of being misquoted.
- Hold the mouthpiece several centimeters away from your mouth to avoid breath sounds.

- Since an appointment is seeked by the reporter much before the actual telephonic interview, its best to collect your thoughts, or jot them down before answering. Don't leave this for the last moment.
- Emphasize key words, speak slowly and clearly modulate where required.
- Smile, sit up straight and animate your face; your tone will be warmer. Do not slouch.
- Don't get worried about the silence its ok.
- Avoid sounds like "chh" "hmm""ugh" or habitual filler sounds like I see, but, etc.
- Use certain punch lines and memorable words clearly and powerfully.

Television interview

- Television is a very strong visual medium. How you look, not what you say, will make the first and perhaps the most lasting impression on the television viewer. Your clothing and appearance should be least distractive. Properly used, they will reinforce what you say.
- To look your best, either do your own makeup or take advantage of television makeup artist. Style your hair properly. Keep your hair out of your face. T.V. makeup is a specialized art.
- Don't wear stripes, checks, big prints or colors as they causes vibrating lines on the camera and will distort the view.
- Wear green or a pale blue shirt. Ties of strong color will reflect color onto your face. Make sure your tie is straight. Avoid any reflecting things.
- Beards or moustaches should be well groomed and not cover the upper lip. If you are bald or have a receding hairline, ask for powder to avoid glare covered upper lip masks your words. You may have a viewer who is physically challenged and cannot hear you well. Such people rely on you lip movement to understand what you are saying.
- Keep jewelry to a minimum. Don't overload.
- Look towards the interviewer, not the camera. Maintain eye contact with the interviewer and smile.

- Exchange a few pleasantries with the interviewer when you are introduced. Its always nice to thank them for inviting you.
- Avoid look at yourself in the monitor
- Avoid too many gestures and fidgeting on your seat.

Stand-up interviews

- Stand with one foot at 12 and another at 2 pm position or with one foot slightly ahead of the other, toward the interviewer.

Radio interview

- Find out whether the interview will be live or taped. Most radio interviews are recorded in a studio. Remember, recording can still be edited but live interviews cannot. Be careful about what you're saying when you're on the air live.
- In case your interview is to be recorded, make some notes beforehand when you read from your notes, it should look natural. Be careful when you turn pages to avoid any shuffling sounds.

Checklist before agreeing for an interview

- Who will be interviewing you? And what is topic. Are you comfortable talking about it.
- Which media are they representing or are they freelancers?
- Who are the owners of their represented media?
- What is the interview about? Where would the focus be.
- What do they expect out of the interview?
- Will you be paid or it is complimentary?
- Is it an individual interview or are there others too? Will they be interviewed at the same time? Will they be live or recorded.
- When will the story be run?, Date, time and retelecast/or broadcast.
- Don't get upset with the reporter and view them as either an enemy or a friend. They are just doing their job and trying to add some spice to the interview.
- Always check first and don't automatically agree to the interview or refuse it.

- Keep track of what was said during the interview and watch closely for the story. Report and clarify immediately if you are misquoted to avoid any damages to your image. If by mistake you have said something objectionable admit. Your mistake and apologize soon as you can for damage control.

Chapter 75
How to be camera ready

Photographs are cherished memories and if preserved well can last for a long long time. Have you noticed, some people look wow in pictures but in reality they just seem ok. Remember, both pixels and film has a way of amplifying minuscule imperfections on even the most flawless face. How can some imperfect faces look so great on camera? It's because they are skilled, they have learnt the ways of being camera friendly. It's no rocket science...you can do it too. Here are a few things you must remember when you are being clicked.

Try to use light to your advantage. It's like a natural Photoshop. When you are indoors, always stand facing wherever the light is coming from as it will erase everything from your wrinkles to bags from under the eyes. Try not to be in direct sunlight as it will cast shadows. However, early morning and sunset has amazing soft lighting which makes everything and everyone look beautiful. If none of these apply, look for a place where light is little moderate. At night, it mostly depends on the type of camera and flash settings. Right amount of light at right angles is the trick.

Do not have a shiny nose. Powder your nose. If you have a shiny skin, grab a tissue and tap it on your T-zone. It's simple and it works great. Do not forget to apply a transparent lip gloss to add that glitter to your face. It comes out very well on camera. Smoky eyes too come out looking very interesting and with a touch of mystery. Moisturize arms, legs hands and feet. It looks great and gives a polished look. Keep wiping your sweat frequently, and keep retouching your makeup and hair in between shots.

Learn to pose well. Remember, a profile shot make you gain few kilos right away. If You pose right you can hide a lot of stuff you do not wish to be noticed. Figure out your best profile. We all have one!! And it's usually the left one. Know which one to flaunt, and it changes everything. You would need someone to take a few shots of you in various angels to decide which way you look the best as it's difficult to judge by just looking at the mirror. It happens most of the time with celebrities as they are well aware of which side is their best profile. They will always change place in a photograph, even if it's a group so that they always look their best whether posing for a picture, being on a TV or going live. This is your best tip to look great all the time.

You are human, not a robot. So, be animated. Don't just freeze in pose. Play a bit with the camera...move, laugh, make a sexy face, and touch your hair while photos are being taken. Try to find different emotions within you. Your picture should tell a story. Play the game. Blank poker face looks boring.

If you are standing and the camera is above you, you are going to get squashed and loose good 5 inches of your height. It's best to have camera at your chest level to avoid any deformations. If you are seated, however, a shot from above is going to look great. Lift your head and look towards wherever the light is coming from and the light hits you at the right angels defining your jaw and making you look thin. Similarly, if the camera is below chest level, you are sure to get a double chin.

Turn your head slightly away from camera. Elongate your neck and tilt your chin just a bit. Keep your shoulders back if you are standing. Turn slightly and rest your weight on your back leg. Standing with your one knee out makes you appear slim. You can cross your ankles to elongate your legs by positioning your shoulders on a different level; your body will give a geometric figure and make you look interesting.

Leave some space between your body and arms. Don't stick them to your body to avoid looking fat.

Even for selfies, look up and you will see a more chiseled yourself in the picture. Don't be afraid to go low to look a little taller. If the photographer is shorter than you, move to an area where he or she can stand on something or you can go below the lens. Look slightly above the lens while posing. You will be amazed at the results. Every movement cannot be a picture movement.

Sometimes you might have to say no to a picture. This could happen when conditions are not right. You may be sweating...your hair is in mess...you are caught in crushed clothes...you haven't slept well and your eyes are puffy. You are not well, have fever and red eyes. In such a situation, one can say no assertively. I know its tough, but sometimes it has to be done. However, if you still want the picture, put on the biggest sun glasses you can find! Yes, even at night. So what? At least you are still giving your best shot.

Pictures can be mindread. The best pictures come when someone is relaxed and themselves. So, just be yourself. Relax yourself and get rid of those stress emotions from your face. Close your eyes for a few seconds and then open them right before you take a photo. It gives an air of calmness. One tends to look more natural, less stiff and in control of oneself. Taking a few deep breaths before the shot can help.

Alcohol affects how you look. A picture under its influence spells disaster and can ruin your image. Why do you think paparazzi catches the rich and famous just outside the night club? In early hours of morning? Because if you want an unflattering picture of someone, then best is to catch them tired, and under the influence of drinks. Remember, being photogenic and drinking alcohol are not compatible. If you know you will be photographed and want to look your best, and then stick to mineral water or juices. Even a small amount of alcohol affects. Think of a camera as a sensitive breath analyzer. Alcohol is a muscle relaxant and reduces tone on the facial muscles making your facial features look less sharp with droopy appearance. It also affects the posture making one look stumped. Alcohol may make you sweat and ruin your makeup. If still a picture is to be clicked, use sunglass trick.

Wear camera friendly clothes. Wear the colors that flatter you. Don't wear clothes that have crazy patters. Stay away from stripes or checked clothes. Avoid horizontal lines to avoid looking very wide. Also, make sure your clothes are not wrinkled or bouncing up. You will look fat if your clothes are too baggy. Opt for a neutral color rather than bright ones. Feel comfortable in whatever you wear or you won't give a good shot. Avoid wearing pure white or black. Avoid flashy jewelry. Try to avoid wearing glasses as the lenses reflect light. Wear contacts instead. Soft blue is the best bet.

Make sure your hair is in place and not flying. Camera can catch even a single strand of unruly hair. Putting glitters and sparkles on the face are lightly to pick up a flash and won't look very nice this can ruin your picture. Cover any blemishes and skin redness with makeup.

You don't want your background to distract. Take a look at what is behind you. Aim for a clear background. Look for contrasts. Don't have black background if you are in black or white if you are wearing white. Great wall papers, painting, artifacts, fountains, plants, flowers, water bodies make a great back ground.

Chapter 76
Dressing to look slimmer

Nowadays, the world revolves around just one obsession: "I want to look slim". One of the most common question students ask me is how to look thin. Of course as you prepare for the contest you have to have a balanced proportion of your weight and height, but some garments make you appear a bit fat and so does the wrong make up. A healthy diet and a dedicated fitness routine are the keys to healthy weight. You may be spoiling your shape by wearing clothes that visually add weight to your frame. Here are a few tips to make you look thinner instantly. Ofcourse they are just temporary. To loose weight permanently you should look at your diet and fitness routine.

The first trick to make you look slimmer is to find out your body shape. Most women's bodies fall into one of these basic shapes—pear, inverted triangle, straight, or hourglass. Once you know which shape you are, aim to keep your upper and lower halves balanced by illusion dressing.

Get your hair highlighted. This helps to create vertical lines giving the effect of a slim figure. If you have a round face, don't go for a short bob cut hair style but grow your hair below chin level or long in one layer to elongate your face and body shape. Longer, curly, wavy hair gives the impression that your body is much smaller!

To look leaner, it's crucial that every item in your closet fits you properly. Always make sure the seams of your clothes, especially outer visible one sit perfectly on your shoulders, and that the sleeves end at your wrist. Fitting to body doesn't mean you let your fat tires show. If you have body fat you will have hide it with trick dressing.

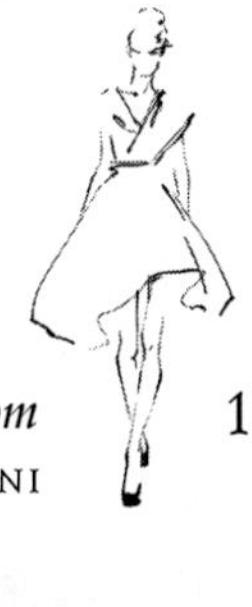

Be mindful of hemlines. Stay away from capri pants, pleated dresses, baggy shorts or shapeless calf-length skirts. Go for straight jeans in dark color that stretch and end exactly at your ankle. This will elongate the body, especially when wearing heels, ankle boots or pointy shoes. Choose dark colored trousers without pleats and slightly tapered leg. For the torso, try long shirts, dresses, blazers, or sweaters etc., that aren't oversized. Knee-length pencil skirt is the best, and so are fitted A-line skirts that end above the knee. For a great slimming look, pair your skirts with opaque black tights this will automatically make the legs appear longer and thinner.

Use just one color to enhance a slender effect as it helps create a long vertical line. Wearing head to toe black is the best option. Stay away from pale shades. If you don't want to wear all black, just try hiding your problem areas with the dark shade. The brighter the color, the more attention that body part will get and darker the color, the more it will hide.

Structured fabric conceals imperfections. Vertical stripes create long lines, thus making you look, well, longer and horizontal lines can make you look wider and fuller. Avoid checks, diagonal lines and large prints if you want your body to look balanced.

Contouring your face can make you look thin. Choose a deep blush that's a shade darker than your foundation. Sweep it upward from under your cheekbone to the top of your ears. Contour jaw-line, sides of your nose, temples and if you have a high forehead shade it too! Blend well. Dust loose powder over your entire face, neck and chest and do the normal make up over it. Apply dark concealing powder under jaw line to avoid double chin.

The most important thing to remember is that with these in a keep techniques you will appear thinner on film and video. These techniques are made for the camera. If you are slightly overweight then all the contouring and illusion dressing in the world is not going to help. I would suggest going to a fitness trainer for advice, start brisk walk or create your own workout routine.

Body shape issues get missed when someone is wearing unusual accessories like, dangling earrings, scarves, hair bands, pins, handbags, shoes as it distracts the attention of an on looker.

These techniques will surely help you to appear less full for your photo sessions. Even if you are not overweight these techniques will make you appear sharper, and more defined.

Chapter 77

Social introduction etiquette

Man is a social animal. We love to interact with people and make new friends. You meet tons of people every day in a variety of situations. The way we meet them creates lasting impressions. Proper introduction is a great way to build lasting relationships. Excessively cold hands, sweaty palms, forgetting a person's name, awkward silences or asking wrong questions can cause embarrassment and discomfort. Learning the way to introduce and being introduced is not tough. As far as those sweaty palms are concerned, try to carry a fresh napkin in your pocket. Before you shake someone's hand, discreetly wipe the moisture off your own. You can even sprinkle eau de cologne or talcum powder inside the napkin.

There is an order when you introduce people socially the name of the person being introduced is mentioned last, and the person to whom the introduction is made is mentioned first.

Introduction etiquette

- Try to stand when introduced. If you are stuck behind table at least make a gesture to stand Always smile and maintain eye contact.
- Never use an honorific such as Ms, Mr, or Dr to introduce yourself. Use your first name.
- Social introductions are made according to age, gender, and then social status.
- As you make the introduction, include a bit of a information about each person. This helps them to break the ice and start the conversation. Once the conversation has begun, you may excuse yourself.
- When introducing relatives, always clarify their relationship to you. Never introduce your own spouse as Mr or Mrs. Simply say "......, my husband," or "......, my wife" .
- It's not necessary to introduce a new face to everyone at a social event. Introduce that person to the closest group by saying his/her name first and then giving the names of the others.

- If people forget to introduce you, step ahead and introduce yourself. Extend your hand, smiling and saying something like, "Hi, I'm ………,."
- You can even walk up to a small group and say: "Hi, mind if I join in?" with a smile .Usually the response will be "Sure!" or "Welcome!" to this say "Awesome, thanks!"And extending your hand tell them your name.
- In response to an introduction, simply say "Hello". Add a phrase like, " "Pleased to meet you", and if someone says that to you, say, "Likewise".
- If someone says, "How are you?" say, I am very well, Thanks!" And ask back, "And how are you doing?".
- The key to winning people is to talk to them about themselves. Ask as many, or slightly more questions than you answer. Remember your questions should not look like an interrogation.
- Avoid using first names until the person indicates that familiarity is preferred.
- Repeating the person's name a couple of times during the conversation will help you to remember their name.

If you are nervous about meeting new people, learn and practice the proper way to make an introduction. The more you do it, the easier it is.

Chapter 78
Party etiquette

As a contestant, you will have plenty of opportunities to socialize, but it's important to mind your manners. Whether it's a formal party or a restaurant launch, there is always a set of etiquette one must follow

Remember to RSVP, in other words, reply and give them a clear answer if you're coming or not. RSVP helps the hosts to keep a head count. If you have to check your schedule and are not sure, just say so and make sure you give them an answer on time. It's very rude not to respond back and not land up as otherwise your host will presume you will be there. If this happens, you tend to lose face. If you are unable to make it at the last moment, still call up and inform so that no one waits for you.

Never take your hosts for granted. It's extremely rude to show up with uninvited guests. If you want to get someone along, do call and inform your host and take permission. This helps the host get an idea how to mix and match people and prepare things accordingly.

How will you like if someone lands up at your party in a track suit or flashily dressed, over the top! So dress appropriately for the occasion, whether it's a black tie event, white tie event, business formal, casual etc. If you are not sure of the dress code, check with your host. It's better to be a bit overdressed than underdressed. One can tone down after reaching the venue.

Its rude to go empty handed, take something along. It need not be too lavish or ostentatious. Etiquette says that if you're giving flowers, have them sent the day before with a hand-written card. You can carry a bottle of red/white wine or scotch, chocolates, pastries, confectionery or an assortment of fine cheeses.

Arriving too early or too late is not right. Your host may be in the process of last minute checks or may be dressing up and your arrival will inconvenience them. If you have not been able to make it sharp at time, no worries!! But do not be more than twenty minutes late. Call and inform if you are going to be really rate.

It's a fact that an extra hand is a great help, but do not force yourself on your host or insist on helping. Offer, but when refused, lie low. Don't park yourself in the kitchen and block the way. People like to do things their way, so once refused do not insist again and again.

Just don't sit in one corner and refuse to mingle. If no one has introduced you, go ahead and introduce yourself. No one like a silent spectator who prefers to stare blankly at the rest of the party.

Even if the drinks are flowing freely, avoid drinking too much and know your limit. Your behavior will label you as an obnoxious guest, particularly at more elegant affairs. Learn to hold your drinks. If you feel you are a bit too tipsy, find an excuse and leave before you damage your reputation or are about to get sick.

Avoid arguments and talking on controversial subjects like marriage, religion and serious politics. Conversations should be kept light and casual. You can safely talk about weather, fashion, films, travel etc. Avoid gossiping, especially about other party guests. Avoid cracking dirty jokes and also passing bad comments about food.

If you feel the music is too loud or AC is too cold, don't just grab the remote and adjust it. It's outright rude. Avoid using their internet unless necessary. If you want to use the internet, ask permission just because you were told to make yourself at home doesn't mean you take things for granted.

It's polite to wait patiently until everyone is served before eating rather than pouncing on the food the moment it's on your plate. If your hosts tell you not to wait—go ahead. Match your eating pace with others don't make everyone wait till you finish and on the other hand do not be in position where you finish fast and other are still eating.

Never smoke without taking permission from the others present in the room and certainly not indoors. If you must smoke, then go outside, and dispose the cigarette butt in a proper place. If possible gargle or use a mouth freshener before you return as everyone will smell it on you.

Hosts may politely ask you to stay on, but good etiquette says that leave at a decent time. Leave at the right time. If you notice that the host is yawning, looking at the watch Then, take the hint thank the host, and leave. Once you have said bye, leave rather than lingering on and on.

Next day, write a quick, hand-written thank you note, stating that you had a great evening. If you can't write, call! Avoid texting. Emails are too impersonal and posting on someone's wall on Facebook is an etiquette disaster.

Right etiquette at the right time will get you noticed and take you a long way.

Chapter 79
Meal time etiquette

Being a winner or a representative of a contest comes with a big responsibility of social mingling and networking. Going out for promotions, attending various events and having meals with fellow team members is a normal routine for a contestant. There are all kinds of opportunities to impress at the dining table. Your table manners can say a lot about your lifestyle background and your personality. A small dining mistake can cost your image a lot. Master the art of fine dining by paying attention to the nitty gritties.

- Etiquette says that you must respond to the RSVP. Accept or decline the invitation, but reply promptly, preferable the same day. This helps the host to plan well.
- If you've invited someone out for a meal at the restaurant, take care to book the table in advance. Restaurant reservations are like taking an appointment. Call if you're going to be late, and cancel at your earliest if your plans change to free the table. Nowadays you have to submit your credit card number to reserve the table. If you don't land up, you will still be charged "Not show up" fee.
- Hang your purse with a purse hanger, or place it in the nook of your back. Make sure it does not block any one's way.
- If you are a guest, mingle and make light conversation with everyone. Don't be too verbose. Give others equal opportunity for conversation. Talk about cheerful, everyday pleasant things. No one like people boasting about themselves. Stay in safe zone.
- Do not outright refuse a dish if you don't eat it. It's not right to say, "I don't like it". Take a bit on the side of your plate as courtesy. Avoid making any odd facial expressions.
- Don't touch the plate or play with cutlery
- Wait for the host or hostess to sit down before taking your seat. At a very formal dinner party, look for your name card and sit there. Sometimes at a very large gathering, a map is displayed outside the dining room indicating your table with a seat number. Do not try to change or exchange your seat. At a private party, the meal begins when the host or hostess unfolds his or her napkin.
- Never tuck your napkin in you belt or wear it like a bib.
- Try to pace your eating if you are a slow eater, don't hold everyone up. Avoid continuing to eat long after others have stopped.
- As soon as you are seated, open your napkin and place it on your lap. The napkin should remain on your lap until the end of the meal. If you need to leave the table for some reason, leave the napkin on your chair so that the waiter knows you will be coming back.

- At the place setting, the forks are on the left side and knives are always turned inward facing the plate and spoons on the right side. The butter knife is on the bread plate on left side. The glass is on the right side.
- The cutlery is placed in order of use. The rule is to begin at the outside and work in towards the plate! Dessert spoon and fork is normally placed above the dinner plate.
- Don't lean your elbows on the table or wave your arms wildly. Elbows on the table firstly is bad body language and secondly restricts the view of people sitting next to you. You can however rest your torearms on the table.
- At formal course meals, your tableware and used cutlery will be taken away and replaced during each course.
- When you eat your soup, dip your spoon from front to back swooping soup away from the body to avoid any spills on your dress.
- To show that your are done, rest your fork, tines up, and knife blade in, with the handles resting at five o'clock and tips pointing to ten o'clock on your plate.
- Never try to butter the whole bread or bun. They are broken off into bite-size pieces and butter is spread on each bite as you eat it. Never use a knife to cut the bread,
- Salt and pepper are always passed together, even if someone asks you only for one of them. They are a couple and not to be separated.
- Do not talk with food in your mouth. Loud eating noises such as slurping and burping are very impolite. Eat in small bites and slowly. Burping happens because you swallow a lot of air as you talk.
- Don't hold your glass with soiled hands.
- Never do any reading or texting at the table.
- Avoid making cutlery sounds as they clack on the plate drag your food instead.
- Do not blow your nose at the dinner table. Similarly, if your cough becomes unmanageable, excuse yourself to visit the restroom. Wash your hands before returning to the dining room.
- Turn off your cell phone or switch it to silent or vibrate mode before sitting down to eat, and leave it in your pocket or purse.
- Avoid grooming yourself on the table.

INDIA

HELP ME
REAL MEN
DON'T HIT
WOMEN
STOP
VIOLENCE
AGAINST
WOMEN

She
STOP FEMALE FOETICIDE
SAVE GIRL CHILD

- When you serve yourself multiple items, be sure not to pile them one on top of another. Place items separately on the plate. The plate should look near like a colored painting.
- Avoid sharing your plate.
- Always say please when asking for something. Don't reach over someone's plate for something; ask for the item to be passed
- Say "Excuse me," or "I'll be right back," before leaving the table. Do not say that you are going to the restroom.
- At the conclusion of the meal, place your napkin partly crumpled, at the left of your plate.
- Don't use a tooth pick without covering with your hands.
- Serving tea or coffee signifies that the guests are free to leave.

Meal time etiquette is a good opportunity to display your individual charm and imagination to make a dazzling impression. Meals should be eaten in a relaxed atmosphere, slowly and with ease. Thats why when you eat out, the place is called 'Restaurant' means rest-on-rent.

Chapter 80

Courtesy title etiquette

People love their names, but that doesn't mean you forget to be courteous. A courtesy title is a form of address that is used to address somebody out of politeness or at a social/professional do. In our everyday casual setup, we quickly revert to addressing someone by his or her first name. Many people, if they don't know you well, do not appreciate it. Addressing people incorrectly, whether orally or in writing, shows lack of respect and can potentially damage your relationship. Just because you know someone—you can't take them for granted.

Avoid addressing people on a first-name basis until you are invited to do so. It is always better to be a little more formal initially and wait until the other person invites you to use his/her first name. If someone uses your first name, you can assume that it is OK for you to do the same.

If you are unsure of what to call someone, it's best to simply ask one of these questions:

- May I know, what name should I call you?
- Can I call you by your [first name]?
- Is it okay if I call you [the nickname you've heard others use]?

Remember, you might not be the only person wondering about titles. Others may not know how to address you too. If they seem unsure about what you want them to call you, help them out. Listed below are a few forms of addresses used in daily life.

- Mr (mister): Till the time boys turn 6-7 they are addressed as Master. At approximately 18, they get the adult title of Mr.
- Mrs (misis or misiz): is used for a married, widowed/divorced woman before her own surname or full name of her husband.
- Miss (pronounced mis): is used to address young ladies from the day they are born until they get married.
- Ms (pronounced Miz): is used for women if one is not aware of their marital status. Many women prefer to use this title to Miss or Mrs.
- "Messrs": is only used when writing to unmarried brothers. It is not correct to address a father and son.
- Sir (pronounced sur): is used to address a man who is a title holder. Sir is also used for a man who is clearly older and/or more senior than oneself.
- Madam: is used as a form of address for a woman and is the equivalent of Mrs or Ms. It is also used before the name of a woman's official position.

Addressing within the family

- Parents: children address their parents as Mummy and Daddy, or Mum and Dad. Some prefer to use the formal Mother and Father.
- Grandparents: are usually addressed as Granny (sometimes Gran or Nanny) and Granddad.
- Aunts and uncles: are addressed as Auntie and Uncle usually with the first name. Aunt is also often used.

Addressing for professionals

- Doctor is used for medical practitioners or hen addressing a person with the degree of Doctororate of Philosophy.

- Professor – is used either with or without the surname (simply Professor is more formal.)
- Army: ranks such as General/Colonel/Captain, etc., are used before the name—they used with or without the surname.
- Audience. the common term in this situation is Ladies and Gentlemen.
- Chairman of a meeting: The chair person is addressed as Mr/Madam Chairman.
- Policeman is addressed as Officer—and second name, if one knows his rank, one may also address them Constable or Inspector.

Taking the time and making the effort to be sure about how you address someone formally or socially shows that you have respect for other person/s. In turn, this reflects the respect you have for yourself. When you respect others, they will make sure that you to give it back to you too.

Chapter 81

Gym etiquette

Fitness is an important aspect of a good personality and gym is like a second home for people who are into fitness. This is also a place which requires you to show utmost courtesy to others. Here are a few gym etiquette to keep in mind to enjoy your workout as well as not bothering others.

- Stick to the gym rules laid out by the management. Do not try to tweak them to your advantage.
- Keep the locker room neat and organized. If you've spread out all your belongings, you're taking up too much space. Its a eye sore to see wet towels etc. stewn all over.
- Stash your belongings in a locker while you work out. Taking your gym bag around the floor can be a safety risk to yourself and to those around you carry only very necessary things inside.

- In group fitness session, do not block anyone. Make sure you have a spot where you can clearly see yourself in the mirror, and do the same for those around you. That way, everyone can check out their form while they work out.
- Wipe down the equipment you used when you are done. Carry a towel or some paper towels with you. We shed skin flakes, hair and other parts of ourselves, so it is best to leave it clean. Similarly wipe things before you use them.
- Gym isn't about chats, it's about working out. In case you want to catch up with someone, find some other area or go out side.
- It's best to keep your cell phone in the locker. If you are expecting an urgent call, take it outside so as not to disturb others, and yes do not forget to switch off in case you keep it in locker.
- Try to keep the 'sound pollution' to a minimum. Grunting when tired is still acceptable, but shouting, yelling is unnecessary and can be quite irritating to others.
- Not returning weights to their rack is frustrating for other members especially if there's only one pair for each weight interval. Putting them away is just common courtesy. When you're done using the weights, put them back in the proper place and accordingly to weight size.
- Don't drop the exercise equipment. You are harming the machines, the floor, and the equipment is expensive.
- Avoid hogging machines. Keep moving. You do not need to be on any one machine forever. Be patient when waiting for others to finish. Wait for a break in the other person's exercising first, and then ask politely if they can indicate their finish time and leave it at that. Standing next to machine and staring at the user is uncourteous.
- Do not walk between others as they are exercising and in front of the mirror. Many gym exercisers are using the mirror to try to watch their body movements and they will not appreciate the distraction.
- If you notice a piece of equipment which is not right, or malfunctioning let a staff member know, as it could break for the next user and cause injury.
- Put on antiperspirant/deodorant before arriving at the gym. If you have a problem with body odour, it will make the environment more pleasant for everyone. Ensure that any clothes you

wear are not too scanty or allow glimpses of private areas when you move.

- Pay attention to where your personal space is. It is not very pleasant getting smacked with swinging arms. Backing into people, sticking sweaty armpits into others' faces and treading on feet are things you need to avoid.
- Leave the washrooms clean for other users. Don't throw tissue around. Close the taps and pick your hair if it's flown around after combing. Don't forget to flush!

Chapter 82
Networking etiquette

For many of us networking is something we hate. The saying goes, "if you are not networking, you are not working". In today's time, it's not what you know. It's whom you know and who knows you. To network, keep the following in mind:

- Networking is an opportunity, be vigilant to grab one. As people wait at the lunch area/buffet, you can strike up a conversation.
- Avoid walking around with food plate in hand. Juggling food & drink can be dicey when meeting people, shaking hands or while trying to carry on a conversation.
- When holding a drink, use your left hand. This will keep your right hand dry and available for shaking hands with others.
- Bring enough business cards, store a Cam card/mobile card with your detailing and profile picture on your mobile, which can be forwarded easily.
- Approach people standing on their own or may be in a group. Approaching people standing in two may be interrupting a private conversation.
- If you are sitting when someone approaches you, show respect by standing up, shaking their hand. Tell your name and in response to their name you can say, "nice meeting you".

- To meet and greet professionally, make eye contact, smile, shake hands & say hello. Introduce yourself with your first & last name.
- Listen to how people introduce themselves and follow their lead. Don't use first names or nick name if they havn't indicated so..
- Avoid taboo topics like politics, religion, violence, sex or money. In other words, stay away from anything personal or controversial. Instead show interest with small talk and light conversation. Current events, weather, movies, fashion make great conversation
- Give and receive business cards respectfully. Different cultures have different norms. Avoid giving your card with left hand.
- When a business card is given to you, receive it respectfully and look at it before storing. Always wait to be asked, before presenting your business card.
- Business card is YOU on print. Give it respect and do so for others too.
- My personal experience says that do not give your card to anyone and everyone. They may take it by courtesy, but eventually your card will land up in dust bin only give your card to those who you feel will respect it or when someone asks for it.

With a little effort and self control, business events can be a fast, fun way to build your network.

Chapter 83

Cultural etiquette*

As a pageant contestant, you will meet a lot of fellow contestants from different culture and backgrounds. People all over the world have different customs, etiquette, food habits etc. Cross-cultural awareness is an essential skill, regardless of whether you're working or traveling overseas, leading a cross-cultural or virtual team, or dealing with a global client. Knowing about the culture of the country where you're visiting will avoid cultural mistakes, and demonstrate respect

---

*: Source: *http://www.cyborlink.com/*

and understanding. Be humble. Whatever you learn about cultural differences, there will be local and regional variations that you won't know about. Admit that you're keen to learn, and encourage people to tell you about them.

Every culture is different, and has different styles of etiquette. Friendships and deals are lost through misunderstandings. A poor first impression could leave your prospective colleague or client with a bad feeling. Knowing the right etiquette can help you avoid this and save you a great deal of wasted time and money.

Greetings

One thing that as traveler to another country you will notice is that the rules for saying hello are very complicated, and can be quite different than the way it is at home. Over much of the planet, people shake hands when they meet. In many other cultures, they also kiss. Some kiss on one cheek, some on both, yet others kiss three times! There is nothing more off-putting than trying to kiss someone who is only expecting a handshake, or holding out your hand pointlessly while the other person bows.

Here is a guideline to few important countries and their greetings.

- Arab countries, close male friends or colleagues hug and kiss both cheeks. They shake hands with the right hand only, for longer but less firmly than in the West. Contact between the opposite genders in public is considered obscene. Do not offer to shake hands with the opposite sex.
- Albania, men shake hands when greeting one another. Depending on how close the men are with each other, a kiss on each cheek may be common as well. When a man meets a female relative, a kiss on each cheek, or two per cheek, is common. With friends or colleagues, normally a light handshake will do. Women may shake hands or kiss each other on both cheeks.
- Armenia, by tradition, and especially in the rural areas, a woman needs to wait for the man to offer his hand for the handshake. Between good friends and family members, a kiss on the cheek and a light hug are also common.
- Belgium, people kiss on one cheek when they meet, regardless of the gender or how well they know each other.

- Bangladesh, one makes a relaxed salute with the right hand.
- Bhutan, they ask, "Is your body well?"
- British, often simply say 'hello' when they meet friends. They usually shake hands only when they meet for the first time. Social kissing, often just a peck on the cheek, is common in an informal situation between men and women and also between women who know each other very well.
- Central African Republic: good friends slap rights hands, then grabs each other's middle finger using a thumb and middle finger, and then "snaps" the other person's finger. Sounds painful, but I'd love to have someone show me how it's done.
- Chinese: tend to be more conservative. When meeting someone for the first time, they would usually nod their heads and smile, or shake hands if in a formal situation.
- French nationals: including children, shake hands with their friends and often kiss them on both cheeks, both upon meeting and leaving.
- Greeks: back-slapping takes the place of shaking hands in many greetings.
- Hungarians, like to use the friendly greeting form of kissing each other on the cheeks. The most common way is to kiss from your right to your left. When men meet for the first time, the casual norm is a firm handshake.
- Iceland, their simple greeting means "Happy".
- Japan, the common greeting for men and women is to bow when they greet someone, as opposed to giving a casual handshake or a hug.
- Jamaica, "Waapun" one might say. It's a squished version of "What's happening?"
- Mauritius, they cut right to the chase in some villages here. Their hello literally means, "Speak!"
- Mongolia, Typical greetings are: "Hi How is you? How is the livestock? How is the living? How are the family members? People in the rural area exchange their snip bottle instead of pipes. Long time ago, people might have exchanged pipes. But nowadays, this gesture has been removed from the cultural greeting. People in Mongolia use the following gestures for their greetings: hand shake-smile-hug-patting on the back-kiss/mostly female friend's use this greeting. Usually they kiss the air.

- Oman, after a handshake, men might add a kiss on the nose (but THEY keep their eyes closed!).
- Russia, the typical greeting is a very firm handshake. Assume you're trying to crush each other's knuckles, all the while maintaining direct eye contact. When men shake hands with women, the handshake is less industrial. It is considered gallant to kiss women three times while alternating cheeks, and even to kiss hands.
- Singapore, greeters slide their palms together back toward their own chests, then end with the hand over heart. Smooth.
- South Africa, here another fun greeting shortened from English: "Howzit". Some Africans in South Africa have a complicated handshake; step one: interlock pinkies. Step two: clasp fists. Step three: back to the pinkies.
- Zambia, some greet each other by gently squeezing a thumb.
- Zimbabwe, the Shone people often show respect by doing a series of slow, rhythmic handclaps.
- USA, it is normal for men to shake hands when they meet, but it is quite unusual for men to kiss when they greet each other. Greetings are casual—a handshake, a smile and a 'hello' will do just fine.

Body language

Gestures can say more than words, and just as we are usually very careful when using foreign languages, we should consider carefully what hand gestures we should display whilst in different cultures. The world is indeed full of diversities. Body language can help you spot contradictions between what someone is saying and what they really mean. Finally, you can learn to be more sensitive to your own bodies, to see what messages you are sending and to see ourselves as others see us.

- Head: In most societies, a nodding head signifies agreement or approval. But in some cultures, like parts of Greece, Yugoslavia, Bulgaria and Turkey, a nodding head means 'no.' In most Asian cultures, head is where spirit resides and one should not touch another's head.
- Gaze: While good eye contact is praised and expected in the West, it is seen as a sign of disrespect and challenge in other cultures. The Japanese tend to consider even brief eye

contact uncomfortable. And, in some cultures, a woman should look down when talking to a man. In the US and Canada, intermittent eye contact is extremely important in conveying interest and attention. In many Middle Eastern cultures, intense eye contact between the same genders is often a symbol of trust and sincerity however, between opposite genders, especially in Muslim cultures, anything more than brief eye contact is considered inappropriate. Additionally, in Asian, African, and Latin American cultures, extended eye contact is considered a challenge.

- Face: Facial expressions reflect emotions, feelings, and attitudes. While expressing 'true' feeling and emotion is valued in the West, it is prohibited in the East. The Asians, who are taught to practice self-control, are often labeled as 'emotionless' and of possessing 'mixed-up emotions.' Smiling in the East is not necessarily a sign of happiness; rather it signifies 'yes,' 'I don't understand what you said,' can be a cover-up for embarrassment.
- Hands: While both right and left hands have equal status in the West, the right hand has special significance and the left hand is 'dirty' in the Middle Eastern and some Asian countries. It is best to accept or offer cards or gifts with the right hand or both. The 'O.K.' sign (the thumb and the forefinger form a circle) means 'fine' or 'O.K.' in most cultures. However, it means 'zero' or 'worthless' in France and many European countries. The same signal is an insult in Greece, Brazil, Italy, Turkey, and Russia. A 'thumb-up' sign indicates an 'O.K.' or 'good job' in most cultures but it is an insult in Australia, New Zealand, and in most African countries.
- Nose: Tapping the nose is more common in Europe than in the United States. It means 'confidential' in England but 'watch out!' in Italy. Blowing the nose on public streets, while seen as an impolite gesture in North America, is a common practice in most Asian countries. This rids the body of waste and; therefore, it is seen as healthy.
- Lips and mouth: Kissing is a sign of love or affection in the West. People kiss when they meet or when they say goodbye. But kissing is viewed as an intimate act in Asia and is not permissible in public. In some cultures, such as Filipino, Native American, Puerto Rican, and several Latin American, people use their lips to point, instead of a finger.
- Arms: Waving your full arm side to side in many countries is recognized as saying 'hello' or 'goodbye'. However, in East Asian countries it is considered overly demonstrative. Additionally in

some European countries, as well as Japan and Latin America, it can be confused for a 'no' or general negative response. In India, it means 'come here'. Some cultures, like the Italians, use their arms freely. Others, like the Japanese, are more reserved; in Japan it is considered impolite to gesture with broad movements of the arms.

- Hands: Of all the body parts, the hands probably are used most for communicating non-verbally. Hand waves are used for greeting, beckoning, or farewell. The American 'goodbye' wave can be interpreted in many parts of Europe and Latin America as the signal for 'no.' The Italian 'goodbye' wave can be interpreted by Americans as the gesture of 'come here.' The American 'come here' gesture can be seen as an insult in most Asian countries where they use it for calling an animal. Asians call others with a similar hand movement but with their palm downward.
- Legs and feet: Sitting cross-legged is common in North America and some European countries but it is viewed as disrespectful in Asia and the Middle East where a solid and balanced sitting posture is the prevailing custom. In Asia and the Middle East, resting the ankle over the other knee risks pointing the sole of your shoe at another person, which is considered a very rude gesture. One should never point or move an object with their feet in these cultures.
- One of the most well-known differences in body language across cultures involves the gesture known as the "peace sign" or "V for victory" in the United States, wherein the index and middle fingers are extended. Typically this gesture is made with the palm of the hand facing the viewer, and is recognized throughout much of the world as a positive sign. The orientation of the hand is very important, however; the same gesture made with the back of the hand facing the viewer is obscene and insulting, comparable to the extended middle finger throughout much of the English-speaking world outside of the United States.
- Another offending gesture for Americans is the "okay" gesture, wherein the index finger and thumb form a circle and the other three fingers are extended. People in many parts of the world will recognize the American meaning of the gesture, but it has a number of other implications as well, ranging from harmless to downright insulting. How the gesture is understood can often vary among regions of a country and among generations, but

there are some places where travelers should take care with it. In France, the gesture means "zero" or "nothing." In Japan, it traditionally signifies money, or a request for payment. But in Turkey, Venezuela, and some other parts of Europe, the gesture suggests that a person is homosexual. And in Brazil it is considered obscene and insulting, intending to evoke a particular unmentionable body part. Some parts of Germany will interpret it as a positive sign, but other areas will read it as a severe insult.

- The thumbs-up gesture is commonly used in many cultures to signify a job well done. However, if it is used in Australia, Greece, or the Middle East—especially if it is thrust up as a typical hitchhiking gesture would be—it means essentially "Up yours!" or "Sit on this!" The thumbs up gesture can also create some real problems for those who count on their fingers. In Germany and Hungary, the upright thumb is used to represent the number 1; however, it represents the number 5 in Japan.
- Counting with fingers starting with index finger toward the pinkie can make people confused in Germany and Austria as forefinger held up means two instead of one, especially when ordering a round of drinks. In Japan, the thumb alone means five. When Hungarians count on their hand, they start with the thumb being number one.
- Curling the index finger, or four fingers toward you as a gesture of inviting somebody to come closer, can be mistaken for 'good bye' in southern Europe. In Philippines and East Asia, curling the index finger is used only to beckon dogs.
- Pointing directly to someone or something using index finger in Europe is considered impolite. In China, Japan, Latin America and Indonesia it has very rude connotations. In many African countries, the index finger is used for pointing only at inanimate objects.

Touching

This is a big no-no. In some sects of Judaism, the only woman that a man will touch in his lifetime is the woman he is married to. In Japan, Scandinavia, and England, touching is less frequent. In Arab, Latino cultures, touching is encouraged. Urban India is touch friendly, but be careful in rural India. When you are out networking, just DON'T touch—except to shake hands. In Mediterranean and South American cultures, touching is an important part of conversation and connecting.

If you don't touch others, you'll be considered cold. However, in Eastern countries, touching is often considered taboo, and you'll offend your colleagues if you pat them on the back or touch their arm. If you are comfortable, let the other person guide what is appropriate to them.

Personal space

This is the distance that you keep between yourself and another person. It varies widely between cultures. In the United States, many people prefer to keep one to two meters' space between friends and family members, and up to three meters between strangers and business associates. These preferences are similar in the United Kingdom, Norway, Germany, and other European countries.

The personal space requirements of Saudi Arabians are much lower: they often stand very close to one another, even those they don't know well. Chinese and people from other Asian cultures are also typically used to less personal space than Westerners. It's important to understand the personal space requirements of a different culture, so that you're not perceived as rude (by standing too far away) or pushy (by standing too close).

Conversation

You'll usually find that most of the people you meet speak English, but you can score extra politeness points by learning some important key words and phrases in your destination country's language. You should also determine what makes for an appropriate topic of conversation. In the U.K., one's private life is just that. If you ask a British national personal questions about their lives outside of work, you may get a cold response. Better to keep the conversation light and airy—current events, weather, food...you get the idea.

Silence

Though it can feel like a void in communication, silence can be very meaningful in different cultures. In North America and the UK, silence is tended to be viewed as problematic. It is often perceived as a sign of inattentiveness or disinterest.

In other cultures, however, silence is not viewed as negative. In China, silence can be used to show agreement and receptiveness. In many cultures, a question will be answered only after a period of contemplative silence. In Japan, silence from women can be considered an expression of femininity. The North American/European cross-culturally perceives it as being pushy and arrogant.

Clothing

Dressing professionally and appropriately is an important aspect of your travels abroad. If you're not wearing appropriate clothing, you risk making a negative first impression, which could set the tone for how you'll be perceived through the duration of your trip. Muslim women often times wear a headscarf called a hijab, and Muslim men sometimes wear a small head covering called a kufi. Dubai tends to be quite formal, and women should dress modestly, covering shoulders, upper arms and knees. It's important to be well dressed in Italy and the United Arab Emirates, and sloppy or casual clothing is considered impolite. The color of your clothing could also cause offense. For example, never wear yellow in Malaysia; this color is reserved for royalty. In China, you'll make a better impression by wearing red, which is considered lucky, than by wearing white, which is associated with death.

Food and Dining

Good manners are prized, but if don't know your country's dining etiquette; it's easy to commit a dining faux pas. In Japan— when pouring a drink from the shared sake at the table, you should always serve others and never yourself? (Your host, or someone else at the table, will fill your glass for you.) Also, when dining in Japan don't assume you'll be seated at a table with chairs. Instead, expect to be seated on the tatami, a reed-like mat inset in the top part of the floor. Remember, people abstain from eating and drinking certain foods for many religious and cultural reasons. Manners and expectations at the table can also differ.

In Asian and Russian cultures, it's common not to talk during a meal because the food is the focus. Most conversation takes place after dinner. This isn't the case in, for example, Japan, where colleagues often discuss work after hours and while socializing over a meal. How much you eat can cause offense in some cultures. For example, your hosts in Russia, Greece, and Italy could be offended if you don't eat enough. Pay careful attention to how you use your chopsticks in Asian countries. Never use them in a gesture or for pointing, and never stick them upright in your rice bowl: this is an omen of death. Don't use them to spear a piece of food or to tap a glass or bowl, either. And never cross your chopsticks; they should always lie side by side. Try to avoid turning down vodka in Russia—when it's offered, it's a sign of trust and friendship. Vodka is served neat, and you should drink it all at once; Russians consider sipping vodka to be rude. Muslims, Mormons, and Seventh Day Adventists avoid alcohol. Hindus, India's largest religious population, consider it unholy to eat beef. Most are also vegetarian. Muslims and Jews are forbidden to eat pork (and, in addition, Jews do not eat shellfish), and Roman Catholics may choose fish rather than red meat on Fridays.

Gifts

Depending on where you're going, gifts in business may be expected in some countries (Japan), and could be considered a bribe in others (China). In many countries, it is also polite to give small gifts when meeting someone, but avoid giving overly expensive gifts that may make someone feel awkward if they don't reciprocate.

Punctuality

Rule of thumb: play it safe and be on time, no matter your destination. Maintaining punctuality is one of the easiest and most painless ways to make a good impression without a lot of effort. Yes, in some cultures, it's not expected to be on time, but wouldn't you rather not risk it? And if your meeting does get a late start, take a relaxed view, especially if you're someplace like Australia. While punctuality is considered a virtue in Australia, meetings often start five or ten minutes late.

Chapter 84

Small talk etiquette

While mingling with people, you may have to do a lot of "polite conversation"? .....it's known as "small talk".

Small talk is an art of discussing matters of little importance with strangers, its like everyday casual conversation that help in creating a

great first impression and building rapport. It's the conversation people use with one another to be social and breaks the ice. Knowing the art of small talk is an important part of communication.

One can say that small talk is unimportant conversation. It is used at parties, meals, conferences, networking events, tea and meal breaks etc., to begin or improve personal relationships. It is not a time for arguing or disagreement. Some suggestions: remember to stay away from any controversy if there is any associated to these topics: movies; fashion; weather; traffic; travel; books; food; sports; current events; art; hospitality; world news; hobby.

Topics to completely stay away from include: personal health issues; wealth (yours or theirs); gossip; politics; religion; personal matters; inappropriate jokes; sex; violence; crime.

Small talk requires combination of planning and plenty of practice! Keep the following points in mind during the small talk:

- While at a party, make proper introductions. In addition to exchanging names, offer a piece of information about each person, thereby facilitating a conversation.
- When meeting someone for the first time in any situation, be prepared to shake hands, stand up, have a great eye contact, smile and repeat the person's name a couple of times in the next few sentences to help remember it.

3. People enjoy talking about themselves, so keep the spotlight on others. Ask them about themselves. Do not let it look like an interrogation People will think you are fascinating if you get them to talk about themselves and their interests.

- Be a good listener. Careful listening helps you to ask good questions and keep the conversation going.
- Body language speaks before you do. Avoid folding your arms across your chest so you don't appear aloof or uninterested. Show an expressive face displaying interest. Have good eye contact and smile, making them feel they have your undivided attention.
- Limit the word "I" to the minimum. Tell your story in the short version and ask the other person to tell his or her story. Show interest in what he/she is saying asking questions about the subject.
- When joining a group, listen intently before contributing. Show interest, while respecting personal space. Use non-verbal com-

munication to gauge receptiveness of others and if you are not well-received, excuse yourself politely to join another group.

- When you are standing in a group, don't focus on just one person. Include everyone and take their opinion.
- Avoid whispering. It sends the message that you are gossiping or being secretive, which will affect your image.
- If you start a conversation and the other person seems distracted, do not insist. Let it go and wait for some other time.
- If you are talking to someone in a language that is not common to others and when some other people come along to join you, switch to a common language and include them in the conversation.
- Keep your conversations short. Don't be too verbose. Also, don't hold back if asked something forcing the other person to scramble for more questions.
- Disagreeing with someone doesn't mean to start a fight and generate resentment over the subject. Be polite all the time expressing your views and also listening to the views of others.
- Watch your vocabulary. Use words that are appropriate, and avoid, slang and trendy words. Always, think before you speak.
- Don't get too personal or touch subjects that are painful to others. Observing reactions, being aware of the tone of voice and being sensitive to other people's feelings helps to make it easier not to cross lines inappropriately.
- Learn when to exit a conversation. When you need to exit, try "Please excuse me".Your objective in all encounters should be to make a good impression and leave people wanting more. To do that, be bright. Be brief. Be gone.
- For every group of lovely people you meet at a party, there's bound to be a person who may spoil your mood...maybe someone who has met you on several occasions but acts as if he/she has never seen you before in his life or someone who invades your personal space. In such a situation make a clean getaway.
- Be you. Just be sincere, show empathy, enthusiasm, and a willingness to listen and this will certinly help you in becoming a master of small talk!

- Don't panic when there's a lull in the conversation. If you sense that the other person is dying to get away, give him/her the opportunity to do so.

As mentioned earlier, small talk is an art and needs practice. Feeling confident and at ease around strangers makes it easier not only to make friends but also in establishing meaningful relationships.

Chapter 85

Business card etiquette

One of the most important tools of networking is business card. These cards tell about whom you are and what you do. Whether you are making friends, looking for work or running a business, giving out business cards is an important skill you must have. Business card etiquette is an important tool of networking.

Here's a wonderful example of networking. A movie, entitled "6 Degrees of Separation" says we are 6 people away from knowing someone of influence. You could be 6 people away from knowing the President of India, your favorite sports star or someone who need your skills. Each of us knows someone, who knows someone, who knows someone etc. Developing this powerful networking will be a fundamental source of success.

Before leaving home, don't forget to carry your business card. Every meeting is an opportunity to give out a business card. It is considered courteous to provide a translation of the card on the reverse side in the local language e.g., Chinese, Urdu etc. Make sure that telephone numbers are arranged in the order appropriate for the country with country code mentioned.

Business card includes the name of the person, the company name, a company logo, and the relevant contact information (addresses, postal code, country, telephone and fax numbers, website and email addresses). Mostly black ink is used on white card stock. The typeface should be legible and professional. The international standard for card size is 85.60 x 53.98 mm (3.370 x 2.125 inches).

The basic etiquette rule is to present your card in the best manner, the same way you would present yourself. If traveling abroad and visiting a different culture, learn the custom of business card presentation accordingly. Business cards should be given out at the beginning of a meeting or towards the end.

Never carry your cards loose in your pockets or allow the ends to fold or get dirty. It is acceptable to write on your own card, but never write on someone else's business card unless directed to do so. It shows a lack of respect for the owner of the card. Invest in a small, discreet card case. Give the same respect to someone else's card as you will give to your own.

Use proper business card etiquette. Whenever you give a business card, expect back their card. If the other person does not give it, or forgets, ask discreetly, "How can I get in touch with you in future"? This would remind him/her to offer one, give you some other solution.

When given a business card, don't just take it and place it in your pocket. Make the person feel important by looking at their card for a few seconds. Use the opportunity to repeat the person's name, especially if it is in a language you're not familiar with. You will be corrected if your pronunciation is wrong. Then place it in your business card holder. It is impossible to convey respect if you simply toss your card at someone.

Here are some basic international guidelines.

- In Iran, only senior-level individuals exchange business cards.
- In Saudi Arabia, cards are given to everyone you meet.
- In Hungary, on the translated side, your surname should precede your given name.
- In Spain and Turkey the business card should be presented to the receptionist upon arrival.
- In an Islamic country, Africa and Asia, you should always offer a business card with your right hand. The left is considered unclean.
- In Japan, presenting a card with two hands by holding your card by the two upper corners.
- In Korea, nod your head as a gesture of respect and thank the person for the opportunity to meet with them while exchanging cards.

- In China, present your card with both hands with Chinese translation facing up before you ask for that of the other person. Bow and thank the person.
- In India, always use the right hand to give and receive business cards.
- In North America and in the United Kingdom business card etiquette is not very rigid. Do not feel obliged to hand out a business card to everyone you meet as it is not expected.

Business card etiquette acts as a key as it unlocks the doors to successful relationships.

Chapter 86
Greeting etiquette

Handshakes are the most common way of greeting all around the world. They are an important part of our personal life. Getting it wrong can a bad first impression. A handshake should be firm but should not be like a steel grip hurting the other. It should be a sign of sincere friendship, not dominating in any way.

Males and females shake hands the same way. On very formal occasion, men should wait for the woman to extend her hand first.

Always shake your hand with the right hand and not left. Of course there are some exceptions to this like scouts have a tradition of shaking hands with left hand. But, majority the world over, it's the right hand. While dealing with public, try to avoid left hand movement many cultures do not appreciate this as right hand is used for personal hygiene and hence shows disrespect to the other. If you are a lefty, use both hand. But handshake is a one hand movement Raise your right hand and extend it toward the person with whom you will be shaking hands. The hand should be extended straight out from the waist with the palm facing to the left and the thumb raised at a 45-degree angle. The hand should be always vertical to the ground. Allow the space between your thumb and index finger to fit into the space of the other person's hand while griping firmly. Grasp the whole hand, not just their fingers. The best handshake is to grasp hands fully so that the palms of both hands make contact. Give the person's hand a gentle squeeze and a solid, firm downward shake. The shake shouldn't really be noticeable by outsiders, just a quick dip of about an inch and then back up two to three times only. Look into the eyes of the person whose hands you are shaking, smile and say a few pleasant words. The interaction should only last a few seconds, so gently let go of their hand.

While meeting people from other countries and culture, respect the differences. The handshake mentioned above is appropriate for most of the Western World. However, in Asia, the Middle East, and China people prefer a weaker handshake. It is not appropriate for a man to shake hands with a woman in most Islamic countries, and that people in Thailand don't like shaking hands at all.

Chapter 87

Punctuality etiquette

The clock started ticking right from the time we were born—each moment is very precious. The nearest we can come to grasping the concept of time is to look upon it as a dimension like space where changes happen. Man is born, grows old and dies. Even though we know that each hour actually has 60 minutes and each minute 60 seconds, we experience time in different ways. Sometimes we are not aware of it at all. Sometimes it goes faster and sometimes slower. Time has its own psychology.

What is time management?

Time management is the ability to utilize it wisely by deciding what is important in life, to prioritize certain tasks so that we complete the task in given time without getting stressed. Good time management provides us with the ability to keep a balance in our lives, or to recognize where the imbalance is. Time management can be defined as carrying out the right tasks at the right time.

Steps towards better time management

Develop a personal sense of time; identify long term goals; plan the day; make best use of your best time; organize work; delegate

effect-ively; make use of committed time; manage your health; prioritize things; set target time; don't be trapped by surprises; learn how to say no.

Common time problems

Procrastination; taking on too much; failing to understand a problem; unorganized office and meetings; looking for things that are lost; laziness; interruptions; regretting and day dreaming; negative attitudes; wrong priorities; poor planning; just cant says no; the tyranny of urgency.

Life is comprised of limited time we have on this earth. We consider time precious but we often waste it. Why does this happen? There are several reasons.

- People do not realize that the way they spend their time is something they can control.
- They do not consider how little time we actually have to achieve success in life.
- They dont realize how much time they waste.
- They have neither system nor strategy for managing their time.

One of the most important strategies for using your time wisely is to drastically reduce the time you waste. One should take care of the minutes, for then the hours will take care of themselves.

Like any other new skill. Time management has to be practiced on a regular basis before it becomes a habit. How long does it take to develop a new habit? Try it….it can work for you!

Prioritize for effective time management

As the saying goes—the last thing one knows is what to put first. To prioritize, ask yourself these three questions: 1. What is required of me? 2. What gives me the highest return? 3. What gives me the greatest rewards?

So what do we need to do to achieve it.

1. Start everyday with a list of your priorities.
2. Write your priority out and give it a time schedule.
3. Beark down the tasks into: important and urgent; important, not urgent; urgent, not important; not important.

If you manage your daily timetable well, you will not only be able to live a stress free life, but also git plenty of self time.

Every one craves for quality time, your family, friends and you! work on your time management right now.

Chapter 88

Traveling etiquette

As a contestant or a winner you would be on the move. Its always nice to be safe and make you fellow travels feel safe too.

1. Do not constantly keep chatting to your fellow traveller. They may want to rest. Its rude.
2. Always request with an "excuse me" in case your have to pass their seat to reach to the other side.
3. Keep your music, laptop sound soft so as not to disturb others.
4. Do not try to read or peep at the fellow passenger's TV or laptop screen.
5. Do not hit the seats with your feet.

Remember what your mother told you about not putting all of your eggs in one basket. Well, never is that truer when you're traveling alone. I recommend that you carry credit cards, cash and personal ID in various places. Do not put them all together in one place. Scatter them out.

There is nothing worse than becoming ill or encountering safety problems when traveling away from home. Many women travelers are vulnerable to assaults, purse snatches, and sexual harassment, in addition to numerous travelers' ailments that can affect those who are unprepared.

Knowing how to plan for and travel with safety and health in mind could mean the difference between a rewarding travel experience and disaster.

Learning and practicing good health and safety habits can give you the confidence to experience the delights of travel without fear. Consider the following tips before taking your next trip.

Do your homework. Learn how to find out as much information as possible about your destination before traveling. Get brochures and maps of the surrounding area and know what to expect when you arrive. For example, avoid arriving at your destination late at night, especially if you have to find ground transportation to a hotel.

Take feedback from friends and family and use reputable transportation providers. Each time you board an airplane, get into a rickshaw/auto/taxi, or climb onto a train/bus, you are putting your trust in the person operating the controls. It is important that you choose transportation providers carefully.

When you are lady traveling alone and want to be safe then, when checking in, register under your last name and first initial. If possible ask the agent to give you your room number discreetly so that others cannot overhear. If you are traveling alone, ask the hotel agent for an escort to your room. Do not be afraid to ask about the safety of the room. For example, is there a deadbolt lock on the door? etc.

Practice safety habits such as locking your doors and keeping your hand on your purse at all times.

Many people become careless while shopping by leaving their purse gaping open unzipped or set aside. Keep an eye on your money, credit cards & passport at all times. Carry your valuables in various places such as a money belt, and an inside zippered pocket, with only few necessary items for the day in your purse.

Review your visiting spots for the day and dress accordingly and conservatively. Drawing little attention to yourself as possible will help you fit in with the local population thus reducing your risk of being targeted as a visitor.

Choose luggage with pull out handles and pack lightly! Bags with rotating four wheels are easy to drag.

Whether traveling by air, car, train, or bus, get up and move around frequently to increase circulation. Make sure you take a first aid kit and sun protection when traveling. If taking prescription medication, take extra in case of prolonged stays never eat from vendors from the road side.

If traveling to a foreign country, know how to get help if you need it. Carry important telephone numbers including numbers of your neighbors, so that you can be constantly in touch incase you can't get your residential line.

Avoid accepting any eatables or beverages from strangers, as these can be faced with sleeping drugs to put you to sleep so that you become careless. Also keep your luggage chained together and placed in such a way so that you can keep an eye on it.

Do not walk too far away from your bus/train as you may not be able to identify your bus or train. To prevent this do jot down bus number and roadways on paper and keep it safely with you.

Check your luggage. If you are traveling by bus, do check your luggage from time to time so that someone else on the way does not offload it from the boot. Sometimes similar bags get exchanged.

If you keep the mentioned tips in your mind while traveling, you will always have a safe and wonderful journey and would enjoy yourself.

Chapter 89

Social media etiquette

WhatsApp texting has become an integral part of our lives. It's convenient, easy and instant. Just like mobile texting, WhatsApp has its own do's and don'ts:

- You should know the person first before texting. If you have never actually met them, seek introduction first.
- Do identify yourself in text. It's difficult for people to identify you if they don't have your number stored.
- Put up your real picture if you are genuine. If you are worried about the close shot, put a long shot. At least let people identify you.
- Don't use WhatsApp while you are driving. If urgent, than park your car on the side of the road and take your time.

- Constant beeping sound of WhatsApp messages can be very annoying and distracts people. Reduce the volume or mute them.
- Avoid using WhatsApp when with people and engaging in a real, human conversation.
- Sending a message to a group during the late hours of the night is a BIG no. Save it for the following day.
- Adding someone to your group without asking whether they would like to be part of said group is unacceptable.
- Constantly sending pictures, videos and audio is bad etiquette. Non-stop posting to a group means you have no life and you will earn you disrespect. Go slow. Similarly, being part of a group and not contributing is also not acceptable.
- Replying with a single word is just as bad as not replying at all.
- Do not send people request for chat if their status is 'away' or 'busy'. You may be bothering them.
- WhatsApp has hundreds of emoticons to express you. Don't go overboard with them.
- Don't exit a group without informing and giving a reason.
- Don't use WhatsApp for important decisions like sending proposals, breaking up etc. Also, avoid text messaging when informing of sad news like death etc. Calling is always a better option.
- Don't expect instant answers even if the person seems Online. People could busy
- Do not chat with a Single Member of group unless it involves the whole group. If its personal send them a separate message on their Id.
- Texting during a face-to-face conversation is a big No.
- Giving one-word responses like, K for ok, Y for yes and N for no is a Big no.
- Blocking a person or deleting is a better option then pretending to be friends.
- It's really bad manners when you don't reply. Do reply even if it's taken sometime with an apology. Do not try to fool people with "my battery died" or "I didn't get any notification" or any number of feeble excuses as WhatsApp clearly shows when the message is delivered and read.
- 'Auto-correct' can really change the meaning of a sentence with one wrong word. Be careful while using it. Read once before you send it

- Make sure you're texting to the right phone number!
- Don't text-message anything confidential, private, or potentially embarrassing. You never know when your message might get sent to the wrong person.
- When group is made for specific purpose, copy paste of general jokes, videos, cartoons should be avoided.
- Except family or close friends group good morning/night messages are irrelevant. Don't send too many of these good morning posters. It blocks other's gallery.
- Verify authenticity of message when circulating messages for good cause.
- Last, but not the most important one—Put your phone on 'silent' in public places like cinemas, theatres, restaurants etc.

Chapter 90

Social etiquette

I remember a long time back when I was too shy to face people. If the social gathering has your known faces, you are sure to enjoy, but if you are caught in between strangers, it's stressful and can lead to anxiety and self-consciousness. Every time I had to attend a social get together with unknown faces around me, I would wish that I was somewhere else! It took me a long time to step forward from the background.

The good news is that you are not ALONE. Most of us go through this situation sometime or the other. The key to this is to find comfort in the truth that everyone has felt shy and awkward on occasion.

When we are shy and self conscious, not only our emotions get muddled, but we radiate the energy of anxiety and nervousness through our body language too. We may look for the remotest corner of the room to plant ourselves, wrap our body in a bundle and appear all unapproachable. Remember, our thoughts are energy...by radiating aloofness, you will never be able to attract anybody with positive energy towards you. So, what do we do in this situation?

- Before you leave for the event, take a deep breath and visualize yourself surrounded in a warm light that is protective yet accepting of others.
- Imagine people getting attracted to you as you radiate open and warm feelings.
- On arrival at the venue, take a moment to spread this same light of loving acceptance to everyone around you. Uncross your body and take a relaxed posture.
- Enter the room with a SMILE. Smile is a universal language. Firstly it relaxes your facial muscles and makes you look friendly, and secondly, a smile is always reciprocated with a smile by most of the people.
- Do not hesitate to introduce yourself.
- Look for someone who is standing alone or in a group. My suggestion...avoid people who are standing in a pair…chances are they are discussing something they may not want to share.
- Talk to people about themselves….they will love it! And yes, repeat their name often…there is nothing more sweeter to ears than hearing ones name.
- Focusing on how we can make other people at a social gathering feel at ease can help us forget about our own insecurities. Radiate the aura that no one can resist you.

You may think, it's easy to say, but difficult to do….I disagree….Everything needs practice. Take the first step from the backward zone to forward zone today! And see where it leads to. Most of all—BE you! Say and do what fits your style. Being the real you—and daring to let yourself be noticed—is what attracts friends.

Chapter 91 Gifting for all occasions

Gift giving etiquette

Who doesn't like gifts? We all do! But giving and receiving gifts is an art. Just like any other communication, it speaks volumes. Gifts not only tell about yourself but also what you think of the receiver. How important or unimportant the other person is in your life! A well thought of gift, packed in an innovative way and presented right can make anyone's day. Here are a few things you should keep in mind while giving and receiving gifts.

- Before you buy a gift, keep the occasion in mind. Also, keep in mind the kind of event—formal or informal.
- Clearly identify who you are buying a gift for: the family, friends or someone important? The higher the status the more exquisite the gift.
- Try to build the dots by understanding the personality of the person you are gifting to. What are their like/dislike, favorite color etc. It helps to keep these minute details in mind to pick the right gift.
- Always remove the price tag before you pack/get the gift packed.
- Avoid recycling your old gifts. It becomes very obvious to the receiver that you are passing on something!
- Always wrap your gift innovatively. You can use glittering paper, printed paper, wooden box etc.; there are endless possibilities. Be careful when you choose the paper. It will look very odd giving a gift to someone senior with teddy bears printed on it. If you can't find anything, try to use newspaper or magazine paper in an innovative way.
- Take note of cultural customs especially when giving a gift to someone from a different culture. Be safe and avoid wrapping gifts in stark black and pure white paper. Also, in some cultures giving clocks, knives, shoes, umbrellas and hanky's are frowned upon. So do your research.
- Do not give a very expensive gift. This will make the receiver feel obliged to return you something of the same value when their turn comes. It's better to be midway—neither too economical nor too expensive.
- How you give gift is important too. If you find your host is too busy, give the gift when you greet them and then ask where you can leave it.
- If you are saying bye to someone, avoid carrying bulky gifts and bouquets. They will never be able to carry them at the last minute.
- Do not expect your gift to me opened right in front of you. In some cultures they prefer to do it privately.

- If you are receiving a gift, receive it with a smile and a big Thank you. Look happy and surprised. If they ask you to open it, do so. Hold the gift and look at them and express the most sincere thanks. Also, if you are in a group and are asked to open the gift, check with the individual giver if its ok, to avoids any embarrassment.
- Do not brutally tear off the packing. Be gentle and open it with as much love and care as it might have taken the giver to pack.
- Never just grab the gift and chuck it aside.
- Avoid using, "why did you take the trouble". It embarrasses the other. Focus on the effort they took rather than anything else.
- If you did not get a chance to thank the giver, send out a thank you note.
- Even if you don't like the gift, never ever say that. Appreciate and thank the giver with sincerity.

Funeral etiquette

Funerals are extremely sad occasions where people grieve the passing of their loved ones. It's very important to do the right things in such a sensitive environment. Keep the following in mind when you hear the sad news of someone's death.

- The moment you hear the news, its best to call immediately to offer your condolence. Keep your call short as there will be many who would be trying to reach them or maybe the person is too busy making arrangements for the last rites.
- If the person wants to talk, let them do so...do not interrupt. Sometimes people want to vent out their emotions. Avoid asking too many questions like how and when. There's always time for that later.
- Its good etiquette to reach the home or the funeral site if it's a close family member, even if it makes you uncomfortable. However, if it's a private funeral, wait for the grieved family to ask you.
- If you decide to go for the funeral, dress appropriately. Wear light sober colors. Avoid flashy dresses and loud makeup. White and black colors are commonly used.
- Enter the place as quite as possible. Pay your respect in a calm way if the body is kept by the family for the visitors before funeral.

- To pay your respect, carry some white flowers. Acceding to Indian customs, you can carry a shawl or marigold flower garland to put on the body.
- Offer to help in whichever way possible. Normally, people are in too much of pain to think of food after they return from the last rites. So food would be more than welcome.
- Funerals are not social occasions. Avoid chatting, gossiping and giggling at such occasions
- Keep your mobile ringers low or on vibration mode.
- Be careful what you say. Avoid statements like, '"You must be relieved that this is over" or "It's for the best that he/she didn't survive", "This is a blessing in disguise", "Look on the bright side" or "Every cloud has a silver lining". Instead say, "I can feel your pain", "I understand what you are going through".
- Let them know how sad you are that they've lost a loved one. Lend a hand with the serving and clean up. Stand by their side. Just keep in mind that your presence is what's important.
- Some people have a phobia of looking at a dead body or attending funerals. In such case, visit them as soon as you can once the last rites are over.
- Good etiquette says to keep in touch with the family. Make a call often to check on them, let the bereaved family know you are thinking of them in the months after.

Wedding etiquette

If you are invited for a wedding, you must know the right etiquettes to follow as a guest.

- First and foremost, once you receive the invitation, do send your RSVP. This helps the host to do the head count and decide on approximate number of guests attending.
- Sometimes an RSVP card, in addition to listing meal options, will include a space for you to write in any allergies or food restrictions you might have. If the one you received doesn't, it is up to you to contact the host directly and let them know.
- You can even call acknowledging the receipt of the card, congratulating and telling them that you will be delighted to attend.

- If it's an out station wedding, it's always better to ask if there are any arrangements for guest or you make your own arrangements. Do not take your stay for granted.
- Sometimes the hosts want to have a very private affair with a few closed family friends present. Wait to publicly post your congratulations. You shouldn't spill the big news for them.
- If the card has only your name, you should be the only one attending, however if it says with family you can take the kids along with your spouse.
- Dress appropriately. Do not overdress and try to hog the lime light. Also, keep the customs in mind; some cultures do not appreciate white or black dresses on weddings.
- Wedding tend to start and run late because sometimes the most important people haven't landed up on time, but that doesn't mean you go that way. Arrive on time as indicated on the card.
- Greet the bride/groom and family on arrival, but do not expect them to tag along with you. They have other guests to attend too. Do not overstay with the couple too for the same reason.
- Resist the urge to pop in to the bride's dressing room for a quick hello. It's best to wait for her entry at the event.
- Avoid getting into every picture being clicked
- Think of a thoughtful gift which will be useful for the newlyweds or gift them cash which they can use later.
- Mingle around with other guest and make small talk. Avoid gossiping or making any comments about the couple, family or wedding arrangements.
- Wait patiently in a line to greet and bless the couple. Don't break the queue.
- Don't expect to be introduced instantly on the stage unless the bride or groom does it themselves. Just bless, smile, get your picture and leave the stage for others to follow.
- Don't jump on the food. Wait in a line for your turn. Just because the drinks are flowing freely, it does not mean you drink to ridiculous excess.
- It's ok to click pictures on your smart phone but don't outdo it. Don't get in the way of professional photographer... Often, a guest will post before the bride/groom has even had a chance to post him/herself, and that can be upsetting. Therefore, either asks permission if you can post or wait for them to post a few pictures first.

- Willingly participate in any traditions you are asked to. This is the day of the bride and groom. Do not get into any arguments about what is right and wrong. Do not pop up extra suggestions. Follow what they want to do.
- Most ceremonies reserve the first rows or special seating for the immediate family, grandparents, etc. So unless you're one of them, look for other seats.
- Don't overtake the dance floor. Let the immediate family and the couple have a few dances before you join in.
- It's rude to leave midway unless all the ceremonies are over. Yes, if the ceremonies are expected to last till midnight and beyond than the families will understand if you leave.

Overnight guest etiquette

Traveling is fun. Many a times when you are traveling and if the family and friends are at that port, they will insist on you staying with them rather than at hotel or motel. They will be thrilled to have you over and spend some quality time with you, but if you leave them upset instead of happy, then they will think twice before inviting you again. Therefore, if you are a house guest at somebody's place, follow the following:

- Send the host your arrival information so that they can track your bus/train/taxi or plane. If possible instead of asking them to pick you up at unearthly hours, arrange to reach their place on your own.
- Your hosts have gone out of their way to have you, made meals, done your room, so the least you can do is arrive with a gift to show your gratitude. The gift could be a general one or individual for all family members.
- It you are a picky eater or have dietary restrictions, best is to carry your own requirements. If possible, buy your own grocery or offer to pay when you all go grocery shopping.
- Offer to cook a special meal for them or take them out for a meal sometime. May be because they are working and due to their schedule you all have not been able to spend time together. This will surely be a good plan to be all together.

- Though the host will provide you with a towel, don't ask for more if you need more. Best is to pack one of your own. Hang them behind the bathroom door or outside on the clothes line to dry.
- Carry your own toiletries. Do not expect them to provide these for you. If you have forgotten to bring, it's best to buy rather than start using your host's personal supplies.
- Follow the house rules. Whats the lock up time? Can you operate the washing machine on your own? Where to dry the laundry? etc. Most people have certain ways they like and do things, so it's best to ask
- If you are expecting visitors to come and meet you, inform your hosts and take permission.
- If you need something or can't find something, it's best to ask than snoop around the house.
- Give them space. Don't expect to get included in every plan they make, and don't expect them to go with you everywhere. If they are working, they as it is cannot. Make your plans, inform them and wait for them to offer if they want to come. You can certainly take suggestions from them about various places you want to visit.
- It's nice to pick up something special for them when you go out shopping
- If you see your host struggling with various chores, let your host know that you're happy to help out where you can. They might say no the first few times out of politeness, but eventually they'll agree. Offer to do the dishes, fold and press the laundry etc.
- There is nothing more irritating than picking up after your guests. Be courteous enough to make your own bed, hang your wet towel, close the lights as you leave, keep the toilet clean and dry, wipe the bathroom counter and mirror, keep your stuff organized. They may not tell you on your face, but be sure you will never be invited again.
- Leave them with a nice parting gift
- Leave your used towels etc. in a neat pile in the corner of the bathroom before you leave.
- The hosts went out of their way to have you, so it's good manners to send them a thank you note and tell them how much did you enjoy the stay.

Monsoon etiquette

Everyone looks forward to Monsoons, but besides being an awesome weather, it sometimes causes a lot disgust on the roads. People forget their manners completely. Here are some points I wanted to share for all of us to follow and behave in a more civilized way.

- Be considerate to the pedestrians.... there are potholes full of dirty muddy rain water everywhere. Please slow down your vehicle as u approach a pothole with people standing or trying to cross the road. There can be nothing worse than splashing dirty water all over someone.
- Most of the red lights malfunction in rains; Please do not create chaos on roads. Let one side pass before you move. Just don't go and park yourself right in the center of the crossing and create problem for others.
- It's tough to drive in heavy rains, Pl keep your car dipper "on" to warn the approaching Vehicles.
- Umbrella is important in this weather. Please must make sure that it is just an anti-rain device not a weapon. Use it properly so that it doesn't hurt people around you and at the same time keep you dry. A little maneuvering will be necessary for a crowded city-walk. Raise or tilt your umbrella while approaching others.
- Before boarding metro or a bus, tap your umbrella and put it inside the umbrella cover or plastic bag to avoid dripping and wet others. Do not put your umbrella on a seat and wet the surroundings.
- Before entering indoors, step aside from the door and tap your umbrella a bit to avoid dripping to some extent. Leave your wet umbrella outside a shop and if you want to carry it inside, put the closed umbrella in a holder to stop dripping completely.
- Wipe your dirty wet shoes on a foot mat before you enter a shop or home.

Temple etiquette

We all visit temples/churches and mosques for praying, but instead of feeling happy and peaceful some of us get back home angry and agitated. I have been observing a lot of breach of etiquette at these places of worship. Few things I thought should be pointed out:

- Before entering please remove your shoes and neatly place them on racks or in the corner. It's sad to see people tripping over the sprawled out shoes.
- Please put your phone on silent mode. It's very distracting when your phone goes off full blast with the latest tone.
- Please...please... pray silently. God will listen to you anyway!! Chanting and singling loudly (unless its *kirtan* time) is not right. There are people who want to sit in meditation, pray silently, or may be in deep thoughts seeking solutions. It's very unjust to them.
- Stand in a queue for prasad, darshan or for bathing the deities with milk or water. Give preference to older people, pregnant women or ladies with kids
- Try not to interrupt any ceremonies by trying to distract the attention of the priest. Wait till the rituals are over.
- Some places of worship do not allow photography. Please do not break rules.
- Please dress comfortably and with decency so that you can sit on the carpeted floor. Some places of worship do not allow cut sleeves or shorts. Cover your head if the rule says so.
- No smoking in these premises.
- It appears a little odd to offer a higher denominator currency note and ask back for change. Go prepared with what you wish to offer.
- Offer the chair to elderly in case you are at a ceremony. It's difficult for them to squat down.
- Close the taps when you have washed your hands and please do not wipe your sticky dirty hands on the walls.

There are plenty more protocols, but we all are aware of them. These were the few I see almost every day. Please do follow the right etiquette as you visit these places of worship.

Chapter 92

Safety precaution for women

Keeping in view recent sexual attacks on women, it has become very important for women to be vigilant and to understand precautions to take to avoid such a situation.

First and foremost, learn to trust your INSTINCTS when you get uncomfortable about a person or situation.

Safety tips

- Be sure the doors of your residence are locked when you are there as well as when away. Install a strong chain on your door.
- Use peepholes to identify people before opening the door.
- Don't let anyone you don't know well inside your residence to use the phone; make the call for them.
- Never indicate to anyone that you are alone.
- Close windows and draw curtains at night.
- Keep entrances to your residence well lighted.
- Check the identification of any sales or service people before letting them in. Don't be embarrassed to phone for verification
- Have a telephone readily available near your bed for quick use at night.
- Think about the information you give out over the telephone and to people you don't know well.
- Tell servants, not to give information by phone about who is home, who is out, how long anyone is expected to be out.
- Never reveal your number to a wrong number callers.
- Hang up immediately on unwanted calls. If they continue to harass you, report the matter to someone responsible.
- Be wary of isolated spots—underground garages, parking lots, offices after working hours.
- Be alert when you go for a walk and avoid walking alone, particularly after dark. Wear clothes and shoes that give you freedom of movement in case of emergency. Stay in well-

lighted areas, away from tight lanes, bushes etc. Walk confidently, directly, and at a steady pace.

- Avoid talking to strangers.
- Walk on the side of the street facing traffic, this makes it harder for motorists to bother you. If a driver stops to ask directions, avoid getting too near the vehicle.
- Don't take lift and only accept lift from people you know well.
- Notice cars that pull up beside you or pass you more than once.
- If a someone appears to be following you, shout for help.
- If you are in trouble, attract attention in any way you can. Yell, shout, or break a window.
- Be aware of your surroundings and the people around you, even those you know.
- Never get on an elevator with someone who looks suspicious. If someone who looks suspicious gets on, get off immediately. Another elevator trick, if you are alone with someone then press the buttons for all the floors. Since the door will open at all floors, the other person cannot harm you.
- Avoid approaching your car with bundles that restrict use of your arms. Try and keep one hand free.
- Do not forget to lock your car while leaving it in the parking.
- Have your key ready when you approach your vehicle.
- Keep only those keys on the key chain that you use. This makes it easier to find the appropriate keys, quickly
- Check inside your vehicle before entering. Always keep your vehicle locked with windows up, even while driving.
- Carry a perfume or pepper spray which is now available in India to spray at the eyes of the assaulter so that you get time to escape if in trouble
- Avoid parking next to vans, as you can be pulled in through the sliding door.
- Park in well-lighted areas. Avoid isolated roads and short cuts.
- Never pick up hitchhikers or people you don't know well.
- Keep your vehicle in good condition . Make certain you have enough fuel.
- Remain inside your vehicle if you develop mechanical trouble in isolated places. Keep the doors locked and the windows up until identifiable help arrives. If someone stops to offer help, don't leave the vehicle.

- If you are being followed, drive to the nearest police picket.
- When dropping someone off, wait until passengers have safely entered their residence or destination.
- If involved in a minor accident at night or in an isolated area, do not come out to inspect damage or contact the other driver. Signal the other driver with your lights, and proceed to the nearest police station.
- Report suspicious or criminal activity to the police immediately
- Learn self-defense techniques by enrolling in a class.

Come what may, we must make safety our habit and instill the same vigilance in all the ladies of the family, and together we all can help reduce crime against women. Make safety a habit!!

Chapter 93

Garment care

Clothes are expensive and need good care. It really pains the person to see the favourite dress ruined due to negligence.

- While dry-cleaning is fine for basic silk pieces, it's even better to hand wash them in order to keep them in good shape. Always handwash silk in cold or lukewarm water using mild detergent or shampoo. Never wring out silk garments to dry! Instead roll the item up in a towel and gently press the water out by patting.
- Silk should be pressed while it's still damp. Press on a low setting and don't use steam, which can leave watermarks.
- Never store silk garments in plastic bags since the fabric is unable to breathe
- Swimsuit doesn't need to be washed everytime, but should be rinsed in cool tap water every time you take it off to remove most of the sunscreen lotion , dirt, sweat, and chlorine. To wash it, turn the swimsuit inside out. Gently squeeze—don't wring or twist—the water from the suit, and lay it flat to dry
- Silk, satin, and lace lingerie should be always hand-washed

and left out to dry Lightly wring out each item and lay it flat on a towel to dry.

- During a hot steamy shower, hang your wrinkled clothes in the bathroom so that the steam helps to release the wrinkles.
- Don't just carelessly stew away them expensive bras and silicone cups in a messy drawer—keep them organized and folded properly to maintain the cups. For padded or underwire bras, fold them in half with the straps tucked under the cups.
- Folding shirts and slacks with a piece of tissue paper or plastic bag in the middle can help to reduce wrinkles.
- Always hang sweaty clothes up if you can't wash them immediately, bunching them up creates mildew and fungus.
- Rolling your clothing can help minimize wrinkles since it keeps your clothing taut without hard creases.
- Staring your garments in flat layers can save you a lot of space.

Chapter 94
Sportsmanship

Pageants are like social gatherings. You will meet contestants from various parts of the country, at a national level, and various parts of the world, at the international level. Beauty is universally a common thing appreciated by everyone no matter where they belong.

Beauty contests play a significant role in promoting the philosophy of competition—"competition will be competed in the spirit of the competition". Rules of decency and decorum will on no account be violated and no favorites will be played by all those related to the contest.

Competition involves a combination of qualities such as fairness, honesty, integrity, politeness, equality, uniformity, discipline, courtesy, generosity, grace and decency or with one spirit called 'sportsmanship'.

Beauty pageant involves a whole lot of people like, contestants, spectators, pageant authorities, media, sponsors, etc. Each and every person is a fundamental part of that event and are expected to maintain a code of conduct and nurture the competitive spirit.

Sportsmanship is the core spirit or essence of competition. A mental altitude that arouses a sense of fair play. Unless this mental set-up is maintained, contest would become just a show of mere physical beauty and virility. Competition lacking sportsmanship is kind of a war where winning is the only goal encouraging outbursts of foul enmity and animal instincts laced with hatred, jealously, boastfulness, disregard of all rules, witnessing violence, in other words, it is war minus the physical killing.

For most contestants today, sportsmanship has secondary importance. People have turned from selfless to selfish. Fairness, generosity, courtesy and decorum have given way to violence, bitching and back stabbing, undignified behavior and abusive and condescending attitude towards fellow contestants. Some contestants feel that participants from other countries are not fellow participants but rivals.

Spectators who are part of the crowd too need to be supportive. A supportive audience can actually inspire and elevate the contestant to victory. However, the reverse is also true. Ruthless violent crowd can make the otherwise peaceful participant lose simply because they may not be to handle so much of negativity. A participant should be genuinely interested in contest, irrespective of who is contesting or cheering.

It has been said that it is only in defeat that a person reveals himself or herself. Unfortunately, the contestants and audience need to realize that lessons are to be learnt from defeat. After all, in any competition someone has to win and the other has to lose.

Obedience to the rules set by show Director, time management, discipline, team spirit, cooperation with one another is the key to sportsmanship. Sportsmanship consists in working in full harmony with others. Contestants must display their sportsmanship by working harmoniously, without friction or mutual jealousy.

Sportsmanship demands cheerfulness even in the face of a defeat. When a contestant wins a crown, the loser should not cherish any grudge or enmity against the winner. In fact the loser should congratulate the winner on the success and shake hands with him/her. Clap for them as they receive their dues and wish them well. Instead of grudging their win, one needs to take an internal feedback and check what made one loose. Improve on the weaknesses and try all over again.

Chapter 95

Stress management

A beauty contest is a competition like any other and leads to a lot of anxious moments, urgency, stress and pressure on the contestants. What separates the best contestant from mediocre ones is the ability to perform at their best despite the obstacles and adversity they may face. Stress cannot be avoided, but one has to learn to keep the calm and cope with it in an effective way. There are many strategies and techniques you can learn to cope with anxiety during competition.

Stress in not always harmful. Sometimes stress helps one to focus and perform better. The trick is not to buckle down under the pressure but to use the pressure to your advantage.

- The biggest stress a contestant faces is managing time. So much to do and so much to learn in a short period. Poor time management can cause a lot of stress. Planning ahead helps. Stick to the time table given to you rather than wasting time on unnecessary things. If you don't overextend yourself, you'll find it easier to stay calm and focused.
- Everyone is different. You may find yourself disagreeing with a fellow contestant or nor feeling comfortable in their company. This does not mean you withdraw yourself or be hostile. Learn to be flexible in nature. Adjust your thoughts to tune with others.
- If you are not comfortable about something, do not bottle up the emotions. Express yourself. Let others know how you feel. Be more assertive and communicate your concerns in an open and respectful way. Resentment will increase your stress level.
- Do not take little things to your heart. Learn to look at the bigger picture. If it's not a do or die situation, ignore. Focus your time and energy elsewhere.
- Stop being a perfectionist. Be willing to take risks and make mistakes. Mistakes are the mile stones to success and make you stronger.
- Many things may happen which are beyond our control—particularly the behavior of other people. Rather than stressing, focus on the things you can control. You can't control others but you can control yourself.

- Do not carry grudge in your heart. Learn to forgive and forget. There is no point going back and forth on the situations. Just let it go and move on.
- Learn to say NO. Taking on more than you can handle is a recipe for stress Understand your limits and stick to them
- Eat a healthy diet. Well-nourished bodies are better prepared to cope with stress. Do not skip your meals and go easy on extreme diet plans. Be watchful about what you eat. Exercise and get your beauty sleep.
- Learn ways to relax yourself. Go for a warm bath, listen to music or try meditation. Look for the humor in life.
- Avoid being in the company of people who stress you out and avoid stressful situations as much as you can. When you can, remove yourself and walk away from the source of stress.

In the end, it's all about you. Focus on yourself and your goal. You are at the competition to be a winner and that's all that matters.

Chapter 96

Giving and accepting compliments

Have you ever faced a situation when you give someone a gift, and the person outright rejects it? How do you feel? You made an effort to find something good for the other person, something he/she was worthy for, and the person did not acknowledge it. Same goes with compliments also. Sincere compliments are gifts of praise. Many of us find it difficult to accept compliments but easy to believe the slightest criticism. Compliments are a pat at the back for something nice someone has seen in you, like a wise choice or accomplishments or perhaps for your choice of clothes etc. There is no reason not to accept the gift of a kind word, but some of us argue against them, even giving reasons why they aren't true.

Compliments are like a positive energy being sent to you. When you receive it graciously, your gratitude then returns to the giver as warm, glowing energy, completing the circuit of good feelings. But if we reject a compliment, what could have been a beautiful exchange

becomes awkward and negative. How dignified it will be when you receive it with a smile and a thank you.

Not accepting compliments is an indication of low self esteem. If this is the case, then the first step would be to start believing good things about yourself. Try giving yourself compliments in the mirror and and smile. The second step will be to compliment others (genuinely) and see their face glow. Observe how the rippling makes you feel good and how the rejection makes you feel bad. Gratitude is the only acceptable way to acknowledge someone's kind remarks. Sincere thankfulness won't give off the appearance of pride or ego. It lets people know that you appreciate them for appreciating you.

Pleasant words are like honeycomb, sweet to the soul, and health to the bones (Bible). People always appreciate genuine words than gifts. Gifts have a life, but words remain with you forever. It's great to receive a compliment. I am referring to true and genuine compliments that come from the heart and are meant for the good, rather than random "compliments" that address objects that are materialistic in nature. A great compliment is about acknowledging the positives about another person.

Sometimes, giving a compliment becomes a challenge. Some people are just not cut out for it...some love themselves too much to see good in others, some may have low self esteem....and some may not be able to compliment beyond external materialistic things as they are unable to reach deep down to the core of the other person.

Did you know that the health and happiness benefits to the compliment giver are also well-documented? Compliments really are one of the easiest two-way street available for spreading happiness around you and increasing your own. The more you compliment, the better you feel.

A few weeks ago, I was spending some time with a good friend—someone I look up to in many ways. During a break in the conversation, I mentioned some things I admire about her. I didn't think much of it. In fact, her response surprised me. She lifted her head, looked me in the eye, and replied, "Thank you Rita. I really needed to hear that today."

Many people are fighting difficult battles. They put on smiling faces, but deep down, they hurt. Sometimes, a kind word is the only source of hope they find in their day.

Everyone craves praise, but to accept a compliment with grace is also a challenge. How many of us truly know how to receive a compliment? For whatever the reason, it's been my experience that instead of just simply saying "thank you", most of us do everything possible to deny or deflect the kind words.

Allowing ourselves to simply say thank you is a bigger deal than we may realize. First, we are allowing the other person to have their own opinion. Second, we are allowing ourselves to just receive (which is a lot harder for some than you may realize). Allowing yourself to receive these kind words with gratitude may very well open up the flow to many more beautiful things in your life.

Chapter 97

Writing thank you notes

There will be many occasions when you will have to thank people—receiving a gift, flowers, being a guest at party and so forth. It's very rude when you receive something and refuse to acknowledge it. Saying thank you in the right way and at the right time is very important.

- There can be nothing better than sending a hand written note. Electronic communication is very impersonal but a hand written note is full of warmth. Lot of people feel lazy to pick up a paper and pen to write and take the trouble to post the letter, but remember handwritten thank you note is the most sincere and appreciated form of gratitude. The extra effort you take goes a long way.
- Don't just pick up any paper. Invest in good stationery. If possible get one printed with your name on it. Try to match the paper to the envelope. Pick the paper sensibly, not everyone will appreciate pink paper with hearts printed on it. The paper should be plain, thin and sober in color.
- Always write a rough draft before writing it on final paper to avoid any scratches. The writing should be clear, readable. Use a nice, fine point pen, so the ink doesn't bleed or smudge. Never write a thank you note with red ink.
- Appreciate even the smallest gesture. You don't have to wait for big things. E.g., your neighbor collecting you courier in your absence etc.

- Do not over exaggerate. Avoid sentences like the gift you gave me is to die for, the soap you gave me are the most beautiful one I have ever seen. Stay in the limits of practicality with nice words of appreciation.
- Express your appreciation in present tense.
- While thanking for cash gift, do not mention the amount. Its right to say thank you for your generosity or maybe it's very thoughtful of you!
- Don't let the thank you note flow from one page to another. Be brief and sweet.
- If you have received a wedding gift, be sure to send a note for every gift received, no matter how small.
- Using personal names of friends helps, however, if its official one be crisp and use surname.
- Even if it's late, don't forget to send the thank you note.
- Some people prefer to send readymade thank you cards, but even if it has a printed text, write a hand written thank you and a personal note before sending.

In the age of insta-everything, a handwritten note is still something worth waiting for.

SECTION 4

Confidence Boosters

Chapter 98

Are you on a negative diet

Sadly, some people are so entrenched in seeing the negative side of things that they leave zero room for positivity. They love to stir up controversy and drama for no apparent reason. Don't buy into their propaganda. Stay out of other people's drama and don't needlessly create your own. It's unhealthy.

Arguing and fighting creates disease. Some people are impossible to please; you will not be able to get through to them no matter what you do. Negative people can only infest you with discouragements. Avoid such people and situations and save yourself!

Stay away from negative, selfish, energy-draining relationships that do not honor you, or even worse use you, abuse you and take advantage of your kindness. Don't buy into their negativity or the guilt trips.

Examine the goodness that is your life, and let your inner critic overhear those five-star reviews about you. Be cautious with what you feed your mind and soul. Please remember that sometimes the diet we need to be on is a spiritual and emotional one.

We all want to run away from the hustle bustle…constant noise, blaming, hurting, and shouting and away from the physiological suicide nombers who assassinate every positive step we take. Everyone goes through this. Why blame others, don't we all act exactly like this sometimes.

When things go beyond the line of control, we all want to escape. It's important to have some self time—appreciating and enjoying your own company. We look forward to meet our friends regularly, but have you ever taken an appointment to meet yourself? You are important too. Your needs are important too. If you ignore you as a person, you are slowly killing yourself.

People who are happy with themselves take care of the worldly affairs in a more efficient way. The way you treat yourself sets the standards for others. If you love yourself, you appear to be more confident and assertive. People will treat you exactly as you treat yourself. Remember the great quote, "No one can make you feel inferior without your consent".

Contentment with life is strongly based on contentment with who you are. Spending time alone gives you a feel for yourself, who you are and where you fit in this world. If escaping is a problem, designate an hour to yourself. Cultivate a hobby, step out in nature, sit in silence, or listen to your favorite track. Tune in to yourself.

Chapter 99

Happify yourself

Every human being is ultimately looking for happiness. Happiness means different things to different people. Many people believe that happiness is to afford everything, having fun at a party, delights of a fine meal, or making a name and achieving fame. What may be happiness in your eyes may not be so for anothers. In other words, we all are looking for happiness outside. If we don't find it, we feel depressed.

So, what exactly is happiness? Happiness means how much satisfaction you have in your life and how good you feel on the daily basis. In other words, happiness comes when you feel satisfied and fulfilled. Stop looking at the materialistic things for happiness. Of course you have to look after your daily needs....but try not to jump the line. What's the use if you are rich but an abusive person; you can afford to eat at the best of restaurants, but have bad health. What's the point of such happiness?

God has created a beautiful balance in nature. If there is a man, there is a woman, day and night, light and dark, happiness and sadness, seriousness and fun! We often ignore this balance of seriousness and happiness.

We talk of happiness as if it's a crime and talk about it in a dismissive way. We tend to value hard work and seriousness, but we forget to pay our respects to the equally important side of life—laughter and happiness. How light and uplifted we feel after a happy bubbly thought, burst of healthy laughter.

Laughter is contagious...it affects anyone and everyone around you. Fun and laughter is a powerful tool for changing the world and spreading happiness!

We all share our sad moments with friends...why not try sharing a funny moment, a happy moment. Laughter and happy thoughts heals the wounds and is a perfect balm for our pain. Think about it!!

Three things are the core of happiness...peace of mind, laughter and good health! Work on these and happify yourself!

Chapter 100

Swinging bridge

Have you ever seen a rope bridge on a river....it keeps shaking and swinging as one walks over it. Life is like a swinging rope bridge... it keeps swaying between sadness and happiness and sometimes remains stable and neutral if you cross it with caution. One has to be very careful while crossing this bridge...one wrong step and you may fall deep into the waters of misery and self doubt. Try to take stable and right steps on this unstable bridge of life and if you can't make it across this old creaky bridge, then build a positive, strong sturdy bridge with the experience you have acquired while swinging your way so far through this bridge of life. So sturdy a bridge that nothing can shake it. Pull out the rusty nails of self doubt, replace the worn out rope with the rope of hope, the wooden planks with planks of faith....balance the pillars of this bridge with wow's, hurray's and cheers rather than sighs, cries, and whys!

Let's take an example of fog! Haven't we all been caught in fog sometimes? It may just come suddenly and lift off on its own...or it may be seasonal. When we drive through it we mostly slow down..We know that if we move too fast we might bump into something hidden in the mist. We try and follow the tail lights of the vehicle in front of us and when nothing works, we pull over and wait for the murkiness to clear. We have a choice to keep driving or wait! Ultimately the fog will clear...and it does! But we just don't keep sitting and brooding. As we wait, we roll down the windows, the clouds breeze in and we enjoy the moment...it's kind of soothing and romantic. Fog is not always bad....it has a charm of its own.

When we feel emotionally muddled, lost and unfocused, unsure of which way to turn, we say we are in a fog. This fog is coming from within. It may pop up suddenly or may have been getting denser by the day. So, when you are caught in this inner fog, and are struggling to get out, slow down and park yourselves. The haze will lift! It's not going to last forever. Try to look at both sides of the coin. Don't just focus on the negative, focus on the positive also and learn what the situation is trying to teach you. I personally decode fog as: "Focus on Good".

A beautiful saying goes, "When things go wrong, don't go with them..." Pain helps us to grow. Sometimes life will put a road block on your way because it's time to move forward. And that's a good thing because we often won't move unless circumstances force us to. Moving forward requires some type of worthy struggle to get there. Life moves ahead in baby steps. It takes time for the seed to grow. Stay patient and stay positive. Everything is going to come together; maybe not immediately, but eventually...and that's the biggest truth of life.

Do not let the pain hurt you, but port you to look at the other side of the coin and anchor your thoughts on changing you. when Night falls, but it surely turns to day, seasons change, things always change! But still we often forget this universal truth, and instead choose to believe that the bad phase will last forever. It won't. Nothing lasts forever. Circumstances too change. Don't keep poking at your old scars. Don't allow your scars to hold you hostage to your past experiences. Don't look at life's scars as something to be ashamed of. A scar is tattoo of your triumph, be proud of. Look at them as a sign of strength....a reminder of your recovery, your healing. An affirmation of you incharge of yourself!

Chapter 101

The rolling pin of life

In the process of learning to make a round bread (roti), we keep pressing the rolling pin in all directions, the dough gets unevenly scattered, eventually thinning out the center and tearing it apart. Just like rolling out a bread, sometimes our life's crust becomes too uneven...

as we roll out our thoughts....the thoughts get scattered in uneven way and the life's crust becomes very thin from the centre (core). Once the person's core is weak, he/she is sure to break down. When the bread tears out, we gather it back in a bun to roll it out again. It may take umpteen times to learn to roll out a perfect even bread. Similarly, if our thoughts are scattered and our soul is weak, we need to gather the thoughts together and center ourselves to become whole again.

When we feel unfocused, stressed, and our actions are out of sync, it's time to gather our thoughts. How do we do that? We need to disconnect from the "five senses" and focus on inside into ourselves. The easiest way to center oneself is to concentrate on our breath with. Our breath flows into out from our center. The ebb and flow of breath is the energy we need to rejuvenate, to be in harmony with the universe.

It may appear to be difficult in the beginning, but just like practicing on rolling out perfect bread, you will sure master it someday. This will help you to face life challenges more calmly, be focused and respond from the center. Once your core is empowered, you will be able to handle your life and daily situations like a winner.

Do you know why its so quiet in a library? So that we can concentrate and read in peace. You should treat your mind like a library. Stop the constant "chatter" of the mind ...become silent, and you are able to identify your problems and solve them in peace. Allow your mind to reset and to receive the gentleness of that quiet environment. When you rest in quietness, your image of yourself and that of the world fades, and your ideas of others fade. And what you're left with is a brightness, a radiant emptiness that is simply what you are.

Chapter 102

From moments to minutes

You grow each day. You change each day with new experiences, learning's of life and how you deal with with them. We change not only emotionally, but physically too, Some people get so comfortable in being what they are that they resist change…a grey hair…a wrinkle on the face etc…they are unable to accept the change gracefully and become depressed to the core.

I have seen people change within second's because maybe they have learned a lot or they have been hurt a lot. Remember, there is no use looking back at what you were yesterday, you are no longer the person you were. Every morning when the sun rises, you are a changed person. Changed by age, the experiences you've had, the lessons you've learned, and the love you've received. To others you may seem to be exactly the same, and yet in each moment you're changing. All day, every day, you're moving towards change. This very day you are currently living will only ever happen once.

I know people who resist change out of their fear and stubbornness. Don't let this be you. Open up to your own life's experiences and learn to grow with them.

From the time you were born, the clock of your life has been ticking. This is something we all come to face eventually, but we usually ignore it for most of our lives until it's too late to do much of anything.

Move forward and embrace the life that's been given, be grateful for the many blessings that have been bestowed upon you, there will always be ups and downs, good times and bad, losses and gains. The fear of death is the most powerful fear known to the human race. We can either be in denial of it or emabrace this universal truth and strive to make our life proactive and fruitful. Don't let your fears hold you back.

Life is about learning lessons, and in the process, growing into the beautiful soul you are meant to become. Don't let yesterday rob you of your happiness today. Every time the sun rises, it's a new opportunity to make the best of your life. Enjoy every moment.

Chapter 103
Tearing down life

When we don't like something in a structure...we normally tear it down and replace it. This is exactly what we do with our life also.... if we don't like something happening in our lives...we try to replace it with something else.

When we feel uncomfortable, we start complaining! Complaining is a person's way of acknowledging that they are not happy with the way things are. In small doses, its tolerable, but if complaining becomes a huge part of our life, it's time to take a good look at how we are spending our precious thoughts.

When we complain or criticize, we are tearing down an undesirable part from our life in order to make room for something new. But if all we do is tear down, never bothering to replace it with something new...all we are collecting is rumbles which can lead to stress and sickness.

Quite a few people often get confused by the difference between "venting" and "complaining". Venting is a good thing. Venting is simply blowing off some steam. It's positive and healthy because you are expelling your negative feelings about the situation and once you're done, you are done. It's temporary. However, complaining unlike venting isn't a temporary state of blowing off steam. Complaining is also not good because we sometimes tend to focus on other people, whom we can't change, rather than focusing on someone we can change—ourselves.

The best thing to do instead to of constantly cribbing and complaining is to check within and ask your inner self—what you would like to build or replace. When we do this, we divert a negative habit into changing the world around us in a positive way. Your mental, emotional, and even physical health would eventually decline if you didn't make a decision to stop complaining and wallowing in negativity everyday.

This isn't about living a complaint-free life. It is about challenging yourself to do something that's potentially life-changing and will make you a peaceful soul. Think about it!

Chapter 104

Share to care

Life is like a tree in the garden of universe. We are all trees bearing different fruits....some fruits go bad and some are really juicy. The difference between being just a tree and the tree in the garden of universe is, that we are not just trees...we are gardeners too. We plant our own trees! The gardener always look after the tree, and similarly you need to look after you, your own self. Water your self (tree) with hope, faith, determination or else you will wither away in the wind of hate, jealousy, negativity. When winter comes and your tree doesn't give you fruits, keep in mind that this is temporary. The tree may not be giving fruits now, but its roots are getting stronger. Its storing all its strength to be in full bloom again. And when the summer will, and you will be able to enjoy the fruits again. Some of us feel that the tree is dying in winter as we don't see the growth. We give up on it and stop nurturing it. Never do that! Never give up on your tree...day turns to night, winter turns to spring! Nothing lasts forever and this too shall pass.

Life is unpredictable. Things can go wrong suddenly; sometimes it can turn upside down. It could be a health, finance, relationship issue or so on. Life is queer with its twists and turns. Some people crumble like a cookie and give up, while others face it head on! We often forget the bare truth that life is constantly changing. Night turns into a day.... seasons change...everything is a passing phase. Situations too will change. When we hit the lowest, we give up! Remember, the night is darkest before the dawn....It's when things seem worst that you must not quit.

Every time you are trying to break a rock, it gets weaker from inside. We look at it from outside thinking nothing is happening. Constant hits on the rock will ultimately break it. Its often before the last and final hit that we surrender. What we need is a focused mind, will power and determination to carry on. There a beautiful saying, "Every time you quit, someone else gets your prize!" So hang on....

The only predictable thing in life is that it changes. We all go through pain, shock and loss sometimes and feel as if universe has closed the door on our face! We feel lost and lonely. Grief is an integral part of the human life. Some of us go into denial...close our eyes like a dove who's seen the cat expecting it to go away. And some of us withdraw within our own world to keep ourselves protected.

If you swallow your grief, that lump in the throat will only surface later as illness. It's important during these times to reach out to those who care about us the most. You never know when someone else's experience can give you the courage and hope that you need. The universe speaks to us through many channels, and when we open ourselves up to receive its messages, we can understand all the

why's and how's. Sharing our vulnerability is what creates truly close bonds in our relationships.

When there is a crack in the outer shell of our life, we are all raw from within. This is the time when we discover who is truly willing to walk with us. The most trusted ones disappear and someone who you least expect extends a helping hand, gives you a shoulder to cry. Once you have found the trustworthy, do share and unwind your grief rather than keeping it stored inside.

Sharing our grief helps to process our inner thoughts and feelings through the filter of a trusted advice. Never ever forget that the other person is going through his/her own challenges. When you trust others, they trust you in return. It always helps to share with each other. We may be the messengers sent by the universe for each other's benefit, and it could be the mission of our life. By sharing our hopes and fears, joys and pains, we accept the universe's gifts of wisdom and trust. Time does not heal in itself. It is what you do with it, and it is important to remember that the length of the course of grief is not a sign of weakness. We are unique and deal with our emotions in our own way. So, do share and care. You sure will feel better.

Chapter 105

Geometrical shapes of life

What is life? Is life a line moving forward with many loops on the way! Or could it be true that what goes around comes around? Does good and bad times run in a circular motion? Does hate and love curve in on itself? Is life simply a line or any other shape? Could life just begin nowhere and end nowhere? Could this circle be made of many lifetimes? Could we be living, or even re-living, the circle we created? Does everything including life itself get recycled? Is life a circle joined by lines? Or is it a wave? Is life composed of the repeated circles of our daily lives like families, groups, peoples and humanity as a whole? Life....Uff...What a mystery!!

Sometimes I wonder if I am responsible for what I have started. In the current of my life have I started circular spirals of love or hate? Caring and help, hope and fulfillment? Can I escape my spirals of suffering and sorrow? Do I have the power to escape or choose? Do my choices make a difference? Can I re-create myself? Which circle of life am I attracting? Can I blame anyone but myself for my own circles?

What appears to the eye as life is definitely a circle. The sky is round, the earth is round and so are all the stars. The wind gushes in circular power whirls. Birds make their nests in circles; the sun comes forth and goes down in a circle. The moon does the same and both sun and moon are round. The seasons move in a circle by changing and always coming back. The life of a human is a circle, from childhood to childhood. And so it is with everything

Life is what is. It has no opposite and so it cannot have ends or beginnings. Some say that life is neither line nor circle but it is experienced either linearly or circumstantially by the limits of our mind. Life in reality is unbroken, unending bliss if we choose it. However, for some it may be straight lines of sorrow...or the zigzag waves of negatives and positives. How do you see your own life? What geometrical figure is it for you?

Chapter 106
Did you attend your life university

No one is alike on this earth...No one walks the same path as you... and no one has the same story as yours. Some people are born with golden spoon in their mouth, and some are born poor. Each person learns lessons, makes choices, and develops a unique perspective, which only they can claim and share. So, each person remains a treasure trove waiting to be explored. When we ask questions and listen, we find that every person has a fascinating story to tell and an utterly unique life journey.

Unfortunately we all are so caught up in our own world that we don't pay any attention to the stories around us. Of course except for the stories which get flashed on the news and Internet...and sometimes, we only get to know the distorted versions. Imagine the treasure we will be able to explore if we pay attention to everyone who crosses our path and get to hear their stories. Any random person...on the bus,

metro, in the shop...anywhere may have a fascinating story about where they came from and how they got to be who they are, variety of paths taken in this world, from a laborer to being a President, from rich to being homeless, is indicative of how much we can learn from each individual. Sometimes the introvert and quiet person at your work has the most amazing life story.

If you really want to experience life...approach the world around you in a new way. There is never any reason to be bored in a gathering, or on the metro, or in a conversation with a stranger. When we have spark of curiosity and the warmth required to open someone up, we always have in front of us the makings of a great story. All we have to do is ask. But never let it look like an interrogation...if they don't open up in one go, let them be. Slowly as they unwind, they will. Sometimes it helps sharing your story first for someone to trust you. Some people are up to their neck with things they want to share. Not only will you be able to relive them by giving them an ear, but learn from their experience. Life is the best University!

Chapter 107
Turning green

Don't feel bad when people talk about you behind your back... or when people are jealous of you. Infact, take it as an indirect compliment. People are jealous of you because you have something which they don't have! They talk about you because they are obsessed by you and find you very important to talk about. There is no rule in life that everybody has to like you. Life works on 80:20 formula.

There are admirers and there are haters. Haters watch you every day. Your downfall is their joy. No matter how many times you fall, rise up for the things you believe in. Giving up means you have given in. Haters love those that give in. On the other side you have admirers who look upto you, who take inspiration from you and feel proud of your achievements. Both haters and admirers follow you. So, value your importance in their eyes, feel proud of yourself and pledge to keep on doing better and make people more and more motivated or may be jealous!

Instead of feeling bad, nurture the feeling of gratitude. GRATITUDE... what does the word say? Break it into two = Grat + titude. The word means Grateful + Attitude. We must be grateful for what we receive from anyone...be it the universe or a fellow human being. Unfortunately, we take all the receiving for granted...claiming it's my right!

By gratitude we not only affirm and appreciate the gifts given to us, but also recognize that the sources of these gifts are outside of ourselves... Higher energies...fellow human beings and so forth have showered us with gifts big and small to help us make a better life. Sometimes, these gifts are in abundance. Do look around and find people who can benefit being a part of it. Just like you have received, give lavishly. The more generous you are, the more generous the universe will by appreciating your empathetic actions. Repay or pay forward whatever you get. The best source to happiness is attitude of gratitude.

Chapter 108

God's gift to you

Sometimes I wonder how innovative and creative god can be! He has presented all of us this gift called life. Superficially each of us is leading a different life, so uncommon. However, if we explore deeper, we will see that we all have the same common things happening in our lives. Our gift named LIFE is absolutely same from within wrapped in variety of boxes, wrapping paper, ribbons and bows. We all experience joy, bittern, love, grief, happenen, excitement, anger, fear and anxiety.

Our external gift packet appears different as each one of us has to learn a different lesson in a different way. Maybe one person needs to learn the value of relationships, while another may need to learn about money etc. We each learn with experiences that are tailored to our particular perspective. Superficially it appears that some people have it easy while others are suffering. The truth is that we are all learning our lessons, in different ways. Appearances never reveal, whats going on inside the life of other person. There are always two sides of a coin.

Judge tenderly, if you must. There is usually a side you have not heard, a story you know nothing about, and a battle waged that you do not have to fight. Look beyond the packaging by skin color, clothing cars, and financial status to the heart of a person, Respect the differences, in our packaging. Always remember, no matter how different the packaging, the gift inside is the same... his, hers, yours and mine!

Chapter 109

Be your own mentor

We all look for role models, mentors throughout our lives to guide us and lead us in right direction. But when happens when we can't find such a person? Do we ever turn to our own selves and be our own mentor?

We carry within us all the power of self realization. We all have great potential hidden side us and have magnetic force that will attract all the qualities we need from the external world.

The question is what do you want to attract? Good or bad – you can become whatever you want to be. We often underestimate our strength and fall pray to our weaknesses. The darkest part of ourselves trap us in and take pride in keeping us captive, and its upto us to borrow our way out.

Everyone is not lucky to meet their role model. Many such successful people have made it by believing in themselves. They try to develop all the qualities required for success. If you want to be looked upto, trusted, admired and turned to by others in work and in life – you first have to trust and admire yourself. Even if you have people helping you to grow and advance you're going to have to do it inside your head. When you see yourself as the hero of your own story, you instantly feel more confident. It makes you feel like you have control over your life. You know your successes are your own.

So, when you loose yourself on the road of life, not knowing which way to turn and wishing for a guide, you should turn to yourself. You may not know the right answer to what should you do! But if you wait patiently, an answer well come.

Being your own role model is no small task, but neither is being a role model to someone else. You will still make mistakes and maybe even disappoint yourself. To become our best selves, we first have to be our worst selves, So make your mistakes, and take them in stride, they are just part of the road map leading to the person you always wished you could be.

Chapter 110

There's no emergency stop button in life

Life has been compared with a roller coaster again & again... some curves and loops are very long and curvy and some very short. The ride is going to go its own way, regardless of how tightly you grip the bar. There is a thrill in simply surrendering to the ride and fully feeling the up's and down's of it, letting the loops and curves take you rather than fighting them. Your whole being becomes tense and anxious, but when you surrender and go with ride, accepting what you cannot control, freedom and joy will fill you up.

Similarly, the ride of life's roller coaster will go its own way. The divine sitting up there has designed the machine and he is in control. You can't just scream STOP midway and get off the ride. Its not always easy to let go even of the things we know we can't control. Most of us feel a great discomfort with the givins of this life, one of which is the fact that much of the time we have no control over what happens. We can either give in to our fear and anxiety, or we can surrender to this great mystery with courage. Anais Nin quotes, "life shrinks or expands in proportion to ones courage." When the curve is taking you down, always remember, it will soon be going up too. The only valid excuse you have to give up is if you are dead, and the divine hits the STOP button. As long as you are alive you have hope. The journey from start to stop will surely have many many curves and loops... get used to them... they happen!! When you have given your hundred per cent to a situation and its not happening... surrender... may be god has better plans for you! Grip the safety bar... scream you heart out and let the ride go!

Chapter 111

Misfits!

You are born unique... you will never see a xerox copy of yourself! We all boil at different temperatures. You can only have your head above waters if you stick your neck out a bit! The big question is should you stand out from the crowd? When a small fish stands out from the rest, it gets eaten by a big fish. When a deer stand out from the rest of the herd, it gets eaten by a lion. When a dove stands out from the rest of the flock, it gets eaten by and eagle. As social creatures, we often hear people say "Don't do anything too outrageous, don't look different, you will be judged". Like a little explanation mark, some of us feel that the standing out from the crowd is a bad thing or is just plain weird. The need to fit in exists because there is a lack of awareness about the things that make us unique. More often than not, we are the only ones that doubt our selves. You are born to be unique. We forget that being different also means being special. With so much 'moos' from the herd... how do you expect ever to be heard? The hardest part is not just standing out from the crowd, but to handle the pressure of standing out.

Being different is a choice. Just because every one is trying to be like every one else, it doesn't mean that you can't be your own self. Standing out from the crowd doesn't place you in mortal danger, when you stand out from the crowd you position yourself to change your world. The need to fit in exists because there is lack of awareness about the things that make us unique. More often than not we are the only ones that doubt our selves. Meredith west says, I f you want to stand out do be different, be outstanding!"

Inspirational quotes...

The only time you fail is when you fall down and stay down

—Stephen Richards, *Cosmic Ordering: You can be successful*

Every great dream begins with a dreamer. Always remember, you have within you the strength, the patience, and the passion to reach for the stars to change the world

—Harriet Tubman

Shoes transform your body language and attitude. They lift you physically and emotionally

—Christian Louboutin

Good manners will open doors that the best education cannot

—Clarence Thomas

A girl should be two things: classy and fabulous

—Coco Chanel

All our dreams can come true, if we have the courage to pursue them

—Walt Disney

A fit, healthy body-that is the best fashion statement

—Jess C. Scott

Beauty is about being comfortable in your own skin. It's about knowing and accepting who you are

—Ellen Degeneres, *Seriously... I'm kidding*

The voice of beauty speaks softly; it creeps only into the most fully awakened souls

—Friedrich Nietzsche

If you think you can then you can

—Stephen Richards

Style is a way to say who you are without having to speak

—Rachel Zoe

If you try, and you just believe, you can; you will

—Hayden Panettiere

Elegance is the only beauty that never fades

—Audrey Hepburn

Doing the tough things sets winners apart from losers

—Stephen Richards, *Cosmic ordering: You can be successful*

Don't let mental blocks control you. Set yourself free. Confront your fear and turn the mental blocks into building blocks

—Roopleen, *Words to inspire the winner in YOU*

Live your life, sing your song. Not full of expectations. Not for the ovations. But for the joy of it

—Rasheed Ogunlaru

Mind is a flexible mirror, adjust it, to see a better world

—Amit Ray, *Mindfulness : Living in the moment - Living in the breath*

You will never gain anyone's approval by begging for it. When you stand confident in your own worth, respect follows

—Mandy Hale, *The Single Woman: Life, Love, and a Dash of Sass*